175702

SOCIALIZATION AND SCHOOLING

Basics of Reform

B. Othanel Smith
Donald E. Orlosky
University of South Florida

Phi Delta Kappa
Bloomington, Indiana
1975

10705

GIFT

PREFACE

As the nation approaches its bicentennial celebration it faces a situation of increasing peril, a situation of which it is scarcely aware, and yet one that rivals in the gravity of its ultimate consequences the discrimination against minorities and the hazards of environmental disruption. It is the breakdown of the processes of socialization resulting in an increasing dissipation of the productive potential of youth and their moral fiber. The youth of all social classes, of the cultural majority no less than the minorities, are being squandered in idle dissipation, assigned to martydom by isolation and monotony. The way this situation is dealt with is the test of our national will to survive. The discourse set forth in the following chapters faces this problem from the standpoint of both the adult world and the school.

In ever increasing numbers the young are denied association with adults in the social functions by which society is sustained and advanced. Nowadays the home and the school almost alone bear the burden of preparing the young for the adult world. This abandonment of the young by the adult community is not only alienating the youth in increasing numbers but also placing an insuperable burden upon the school and the home. When the family is in an agonizing struggle as it is today to adjust itself to the impact of technology and the changing status of women, it can hardly socialize its young children, let alone occupy its youth in meaningful activities. By its nature the school isolates youth from the adult world. The advantage of such isolation is found in learning activities free from the distractions of other responsibilities. The isolation of youth by the school, their rejection by the adult community, and the waning influence of the home give rise to a problem of socialization seldom encountered in history.

A critical pedagogical consequence of the abandonment of children and youth is the plain fact that the school is forced to attempt the schooling of many individuals whose potential for acquiring systematized knowledge has been all but destroyed. This sets a problem whose solution will require a radical reconstruction of the socializing processes of the adult world and fundamental changes in schooling. Make no mistake about it, school reform alone will not suffice. Innovations such as adaptation of instruction to learning styles, introduction of new content, alternate forms of schooling, voucher plans, or whatever can have only meager effects so long as youth is denied the right to participate with adults in the productive activities of the social system.

The proposed approach to this overriding problem is empirical rather than prescriptive. Unlike many treatments of reform, no pat answers are proposed, no slate of ready-made, sure-fire solutions is urged. Instead, the importance of formulating clear-cut plans and studying them in operation is emphasized. The road to a better social as well as school environment for the development and socialization of children and youth is full of pitfalls. Those who tread it are about as likely to fall into them as to avoid them. The pitfalls are political and economic as well as pedagogical. The creation of such an environment is a task that may well extend over a generation. It will require a higher pedagogy, one that includes statecraft rather than politics, the commitment of adults in all forms of enterprise and the professions, the family, and the school.

At a less exalted, if no less important, level of pedagogy all available resources must be devoted to the systematic reform of the school program—its curriculum and its methods, its administration and its personnel. Despite the progressive improvement of the school and its teachers during recent decades, there is still room for the improvement of teacher education at both preservice and inservice levels. Changes in the curriculum are sorely needed even though far reaching improvements have been made since the beginning of the century. No less important is the need of criteria for determining the utility of schooling, criteria that call for data and that transcend the objectives of instruction and avoid the word-magic of educational goals. These needs are addressed as the major responsibility of the teaching profession.

As the manuscript developed it became evident that since the proposals set forth were to be developed in a research context, it seemed appropriate to consider the adequacy of educational research itself. Insightful consideration of this question is presented in Appendix A. Another question also plagued the authors: What is cultural pluralism and how is it to be recognized and preserved in the proposed approach to socialization? Since this topic received scant treatment, the authors sought critiques of the manuscript from persons who would be sensitive to the question. Appendix B contains the critical views of four individuals. The interested reader will find these two appendices both stimulating and instructive.

Since this book is the product of a joint effort, something should be said about how responsibilities were distributed. The preparation of the various chapters was shared, but each chapter was initiated by one of the authors who then assumed major responsibility for its completion. Professor Smith initiated chapters 1, 2, 3, 4, 6, 7, 8, and 10, and Professor Orlosky initiated chapters 5, 9, 11, 12, and 13. Discussion of each chapter took place to coordinate the work and establish acceptability of the content by both authors. The final product is the result of these discussions and provides a book whose content and continuity is agreeable to and the responsibility of both authors.

Assistance was provided by others who reviewed the manuscript in various stages of its development. It would be impossible to single out the critics who were most helpful, since many individuals contributed ideas and reactions. We acknowledge the help we received with gratitude, and trust that those who gave of their time and recommendations will derive some measure of satisfaction from the completion of this book, though the responsibility for the views expressed rests entirely with the authors.

If time and ability had permitted the authors to take advantage of the suggestions given to them, the book would have been much improved. But if the book serves to emphasize the harmful consequences of the practice of placing the total burden of bringing up the young upon the family and the school, if it succeeds in driving home the point that influences of an adult society mobilized for the benefit of the children and youth should be coordinated with those of the school and the family, if it helps to move the school toward a program rich in cognitive and ethical interests and to provide teaching personnel free to exploit for good the spirit of adventure and hope that is the endowment of all the young, the book will have satisfied the purpose for which it was written.

B. OTHANEL SMITH

DONALD E. ORLOSKY

Contents

CHAPTER I

Socialization and School Reform

A society replenishes and maintains itself by births and socialization. If either of these is seriously impaired, the society is threatened. If the birth rate continually falls significantly below the death rate, extensive economic and social adjustments become necessary. If the mores and folkways break down, the society will develop cleavages and severe conflicts, and may ultimately disintegrate. The birth rate in the United States presently is not a matter of concern. But socialization is a profound issue. The entire country is suffering because of the deterioration of the processes by which the young are prepared to assume the responsibilities and activities of adults. The development of new modes of socialization to cope with the conflicting stresses and strains of modern technological conditions is one of the most pressing matters facing every community and the nation as a whole. The problem is critical in metropolitan areas and barely less so in rural communities.

De-education of the Adult Community

Schooling and socialization are related as part to whole. Socialization is the total process by which a nation reproduces its societal type.[1] The individual perishes, but the society continues; it survives by shaping each new member to the type. Socialization, except for schooling, is automatic in the sense that it occurs without tuition. It requires no financial support, no trained personnel, and no particular institution to carry it on. To participate in the functions of a society is to be involved in the socializing process. In sharp contrast, schooling takes place in an institution established to teach the young and is designed to accomplish definite goals. Schooling is neither inescapable nor automatic but is deliberately provided. It is typically supported and controlled by the civil government or some other organized authority. Schooling, unlike informal socialization, is not an inherent feature of society; it emerges in its modern form when symbolic skills and abstract knowledge become significant in the view of those who are empowered to make political decisions. The school has a very limited function despite the fact that in recent decades it has taken on responsibility for the development of personality, the reconstruction of values and attitudes, and the solution of social problems. Since the school is not the whole of socialization, it is pointless to demand that it shoulder the entire burden of shaping the youth to the societal type. This the school has never been able to do. It can only reinforce the formative influences of selective aspects of the culture.

If socialization were perfect, there would be little change in either the societal type or the society. If it fails to reproduce the type in sufficient numbers, the life of the social system is threatened. When the process by which the individual is shaped to the type is critically impaired, the young will grow up confused, unstable, and adrift. In a deep and prolonged social and economic crisis they are likely to be attracted to those who promise them status and a share in the action. If recent history in other lands is any lesson, the leaders most likely to attract them are those who have a taste for tyranny.

The idea of societal type is likely to be anathema to some

individuals who believe in a pluralistic society. It need not be: A pluralistic society is possible only among a people of a particular character. They must have high tolerance for differing opinions, exercise patience with the use of power by those who hold minority views, be committed to constant negotiation among those in different centers of power, and be willing to engage in the search for evidence and to accept compromise.[2] Pluralism can exist only in a society whose members, like members of other societies, are committed to certain values and modes of behavior. The difference between a pluralistic and a monistic society is not that one breeds a societal type and the other does not, but that each breeds different types.

It is often pointed out that the culture of some minorities differs markedly from that of the Teutonic population; the language, norms, values, and experiences of these minorities are not the same as those of the Teutonic group. These claims are partially valid. The cultures of Afro-Americans, Mexican-Americans, American Indians, and other minorities differ from the dominant American culture just as they differ from each other. Cultural pluralism is the recognition of and respect for these diversities. The view that all groups share a common set of beliefs is not inconsistent with pluralism.* These beliefs legitimize power, rationalize institutions and social practice, define right and wrong, and give whatever sense of social direction the people recognize. A multiculture society is one in which the folkways and mores of various groups overlay basic and pervasive beliefs and social practices.

The youth is the nation's indispensable resource. Yet an ever larger proportion of the nation's youth is being squandered in idle dissipation while the adult community is engrossed by its own concerns and successes, leaving the care of youth largely to the street and the school.[3] The adult community senses that something is not right with its youth, but it does

---

*The question of socialization of minority children in a dominant culture is considered at some length in Appendix B.

not recognize that the technological, corporate society of today is progressively isolating an ever larger proportion of the younger members of society. They have few responsibilities and little opportunity to share in the life of adults. Consequently, they grow up having few experiences from which to learn the various roles adults are required to play. It is a great waste for the young to be kept waiting and dependent, assigned to a life of idleness, while they pursue learning in an institution that cannot perform alone the massive task of preparing them for adult life.

Although the school is in need of fundamental reform, the nation's primary educational problem today is not the school. The young do not grow up absurd, as some have claimed, because of the school, but because the adult society has shut them out. The waning influence of the home has long been acknowledged, but that is only part of the picture. The entire adult society—professions, services, trades, farms, commerce, corporations, mass media, press, industry, whatever—has made the young into a social class that approaches a caste in the rigidity of its barriers. No group is more isolated, more reduced to uselessness, and more denied the chance at profitable employment than the youth. They wield little political power, even though suffrage has been extended to 18-year-olds, and they have only minor economic value except as consumers.

The emptiness of youth's experiences not only denies them preparation for adult responsibilities, but also renders them incapable of taking full advantage of their years of schooling. The profession's interest in school achievement has been so battered by an ever growing number of pupils uninterested in learning that some theorists appear to be saying: It makes no difference whether a pupil learns anything or not so long as he likes school. There can be little doubt that many of the imperfections for which the school is being criticized stem from the unwitting isolation of youth by adults in every walk of life. School reform alone is thus unlikely to bring about an appreciable improvement in the socialization of children and youth, or for that matter, in the effectiveness of schooling.

The matter is more profound than the problem of schooling; it reaches into the purposes and programs of all institutions and agencies of the community, forcing adults to face a responsibility that they have evaded by delegating it to the school. The first duty of those concerned with the plight of children and youth should be to renew the processes by which the young are inducted into society as responsible members. The path to adulthood must again wind through the activities by which society maintains itself.

Reference to a few facts will serve to point up the isolation of youth. Today about 94 percent of the 14- to 17-year-olds are in school. In 1900, only 11.4 percent were enrolled. At that time, the school was not primarily a socializing instrument for youth of high school age. About 62 percent of the males and 27 percent of the females in the 14–19 age range were employed. Many of the remaining 38 percent of the males were involved in responsible family activities. A considerable proportion of the females not in the labor force were housewives. Today only 25 percent of youth 14 to 16 years of age and 33 percent of the 16- to 17-year-olds who are in school are also employed. These statistics hide important facts. In 1900, employed youth worked full-time. They worked in a great variety of jobs; many of these had little future, and the job experience itself often had little educational value. Nevertheless, the working youth assumed an adult role in the sense that he became responsible not only for himself but quite often for his family. In sharp contrast, the youth in the 14–17 age range who work today usually have part-time jobs. The socializing influences of the work are usually meager since associations with adults on the job are likely to be casual, uninstructive, and impersonal. The money a youth earns contributes little to his family income. It is typically used to satisfy his own wants. He has little opportunity to learn about responsibility to others or the meaning of personal sacrifice. In short, the adult community has become de-educating.

Optimum schooling is possible only when other social institutions nourish the development of the young. Since an increasing number of youth are denied experiences with adults that could make schooling meaningful and its importance evident, the youth of all social classes are increasingly turned off by the school. They cry out for something relevant, but what significant knowledge can be relevant to a life that is rooted primarily in an adolescent culture?

For young children, the school is frequently a source of enjoyable activities accompanied by a sense of achievement and pleasure. The school is a peaceful retreat from a world that offers them little to do. Their development has not reached the point where isolation from the adult world is dwarfing their interest in school activities, nor do they realize the predicament into which they are growing.

To deal successfully with the plight of youth is to attack the problem of socialization on a broad front. The attack must include both the community and the school. In order to renew the educative influences of the community, the adults in all occupations—government, trades, professional, service, or whatever—must assume responsibility for incorporating youth in their various enterprises. This cannot be accomplished by haphazard procedures, nor can it be realized by assigning socializing responsibilities to industry, the home, or any other single enterprise or agency. The renewal of socialization requires a comprehensive plan in which every occupational group participates and every youth is involved. This means that an operational structure must be evolved that makes socialization an inherent feature of community life.

The renewal of the socializing influences of the adult community is an undertaking for which there is little experience and practically no fund of knowledge upon which to draw. The way to a successful program is not over a secure path, cleared of pitfalls in advance of the journey. It is a path fraught with unknown obstacles, and it will require the most capable leadership and public support to negotiate.

Some Effects of Societal De-education

As society becomes more and more de-educating, the school assumes ever more responsibility for the life of children and youth, giving it a regulatory function in addition to its traditional instructional one. Almost fifty years ago Counts called attention to this flaw in thinking about education when he said:

> This exclusive emphasis on the school, however, constitutes a fundamental weakness in the American theory of education. Obviously the school is but one among many educational institutions, and its power can easily be exaggerated. Certainly the American people place too much confidence in what it can do. One need only recall the family, the church, the press, the theater, the cinema, the library, and the museum to realize that the school, if it works alone, can accomplish but little beyond the performance of certain rather definite tasks with which other institutions and the ordinary processes of living are not concerned. And a theory of education which is devoted altogether to what goes on in the school is sure to be lacking in reality and vitality.[4]

His warning has gone unheeded. The schools have been pressured to assume one social responsibility after another. As the home began to feel the impact of industrialization and urbanization, the school was called upon to bolster family life through courses in home economics, marriage, and sex education. The physical defects of young men enlisted for duty in the First World War led to compulsory physical education in the school. The breakdown of the apprentice system and the demand for competent labor created public pressure for vocational education that resulted in programs based on federal legislation. The teaching of patriotism, child rearing, citizenship, the evils of alcohol, tobacco, and drugs, driving of motor vehicles, responses to death, and a host of other causes are urged upon the school at one time or another.

Behind this conception of the school's function lurks the notion of the school as a regulatory agency. The school is not only supposed to teach the basic skills and elements of knowledge but is also to develop the kind of person who will utilize his learning to perform socially acceptable tasks. This means, in broad terms, that what the teacher does in the classroom should regulate the behavior of pupils outside of school and even through adulthood. To determine how the individual will use what he is taught is far beyond the pedagogical means and the political power of the teacher. A teacher of chemistry, for example, can hardly ensure that his pupils will not use their knowledge to construct bombs; nor can a teacher of the humanities guarantee that his pupils will not accept bribes on quiz shows. The profession of teaching has thus far developed no curriculum or method that reduces the divorce rate, although worthy home membership has been one of its major objectives for over fifty years.

Certain consequences of the tendency to increase the responsibility of the school are discernible. These new obligations are incorporated into the regular school program and are often absorbed by existing courses. This multiplies the burden of teachers already heavily loaded with instructional responsibilities in the fundamentals of learning and basic categories of knowledge. The assimilation of these added responsibilities often requires major changes in programs and courses, the collection and organization of new materials, and endless hours in workshops, courses, and conferences. Administrators, too, become involved. They must consider every aspect of each new responsibility. They must view the political and financial aspects of each demand as well as its program requirements, facilities, space, and personnel. These added burdens distract the school's administrative resources, thus reducing the time administrators can give to the primary functions of the school.

Any candid analysis of what is happening to the public school will show that it is well on the way to becoming the sole agency for the socialization of children and youth. The profession of teaching is staggering under the weight of this crushing responsibility; its energies are so scattered and exhausted as to make reform of the basic aspects of the school ever more difficult. Equally significant is the fact that the tendency to place more and more confidence in the school blinds the adult community to the fact that it is shirking its responsibility for the socialization of its children and youth.

The de-education of society has been accompanied by a succession of movements to change the school. Although these movements are usually justified by psychological, philosophical, and economic considerations, they are not unrelated to adjustments of the instructional program to the poverty of child and adolescent experience. In the last few decades these movements have followed each other in rapid succession: project method, problem method, experience units, inquiry method, nondirective method, and a number of instructional plans: Winnetka plan, contract plan, Dalton plan, open air plan, supervised study, socialized recitation, child-centered classroom, nongraded classroom, and open classroom. A number of curriculum patterns were evolved to accommodate some of these methods and plans: the correlated curriculum, the activity curriculum, core curriculum, integrated curriculum, experience curriculum, and broad-fields curriculum.

Many of these movements are *tours de force*—an amazing display of energy in pursuit of inordinate ends. They appear like comets and sweep through the schools periodically, sapping the energy of the personnel and leaving little residue to mark their path. The activity movement and child-centered movement of the 1920s are good examples. Today one sees the open classroom, behavioral objectives, performance contracting, alternative schools, alternatives to schooling itself, and neo-humanism as potential *tours de force*. These displays of energy exact a heavy penalty in the shape of bewildered school personnel, exhausted from activities extraneous to their daily problems and arrested in the development of their ability to cope with the problems of teaching. The university personnel responsible for the preparation of teachers become possessed by these pedagogical formulas, divide into camps, and substitute doctrinal disputes for a study of the problems of learning and teaching.

The theorists who propound these reform movements seldom

attempt to validate them empirically. Instead, they are developed from "ideologies" and are represented as the logical and necessary consequence of sound psychological, philosophical, and social principles. If the theorist is deeply imbued with the spirit of freedom, the formula will ordinarily stress the reduction of authority, a curriculum that encourages pupil choice and initiative, and instructional methods to release pupil activity. It will be irrefutably justified by an appeal to logic, liberal and humanistic doctrines, and theories of learning and development. Those who hold an authoritarian orientation will prescribe a curriculum, methods, and other elements of the process of schooling in keeping with their view of a stable society and their conceptions of the nature of learning, human development, and social reality. The philosophical, psychological, and social bases, or principles, on which a particular movement rests, is merely a pedagogical formula. The intoxication of such formulas is overwhelming, rendering the school personnel virtually incapable of assessing them and resulting in their ascendency as an approach to school reform.

In spite of the plausibility of these formulas and the meticulous application of them, many pupils do not learn to read, to do arithmetic, to grasp the conceptions and principles of science, or to appreciate the arts. Neither the teachers who follow these formulas, nor the university instructors who espouse them, can explain the failure of these pupils any better than teachers who follow the conventional patterns of classroom organization and ways of teaching. Yet these pupils are the very ones whom a professional should be able to help.

School Reform and the Need for Criteria
If all other agencies were assuming their socializing responsibilities, the influence of the school would be enhanced. Even were this so, however, the school would still need reforming. Some considerations that indicate this need are as follows:

—About 94 percent of the 14- to 17-year-olds are enrolled in school. The school now enrolls a large number of pupils who are not academically inclined.

—The school program—courses, policies, and personnel—continues to be academically oriented despite the fact that the character of the pupil population has radically changed.

—Knowledge previously ignored by the teaching profession and excluded from the school program has now become essential to satisfy the wide range of interests now represented by the pupil population.

—The profession has not been as successful in teaching the fundamentals of knowledge and communicative skills to the children of the lower classes as to those of middle America. The poor suffer most from this deficiency largely because instructional procedures and materials to alleviate their learning difficulties have not been used.

—The dropout rate among pupils of the poor is inordinate.

—The children of the poor fall behind year by year in the acquisition of basic skills and knowledge, a condition that undercuts their competitiveness in the labor market.

—Pupils with the greatest intellectual endowment are not being challenged in many schools.

—Teachers are locked into an operational structure that all too often renders it impossible for them to perform as professionals. It is imperative that conditions compatible with the exercise of professional competence be instituted.

While the road to school reform is rocky and at some points indistinct, the task can be analyzed into problems. These can then be approached theoretically and empirically. In time these problems can be solved, but reform, all can agree, cannot be accomplished overnight or wholesale.

One of the basic problems of school reform is the determination of criteria for deciding whether or not changes are improvements. Sometimes the school is held to be an independent variable, evaluated by reference to the quality of its products. On other occasions it is viewed as a dependent variable, reflecting society—its structure, social controls, purposes, and economic well-being. As a dependent variable, the school is often judged by the amount of its financial support, the preparation and spirit of its personnel, and its facilities. This mode of evaluation is frequently employed, for these presumptive indicators of an effective school are more accessible than the quality of the school's product. By implication, however, even as a dependent variable, the school is assessed by its product: The factors just mentioned are held to be important only because they are taken to be determiners of the outcomes of schooling.

As an independent variable, the quality of the school is judged by reference to pupils' achievement. The implications of this mode of evaluation have only recently become apparent. In the final analysis, the teaching profession is itself being weighed when the results of schooling are used as a criterion. The effects produced by the school personnel in individuals and society indicate the status of the field of knowledge they represent and their competence as professionals. If changes are made in variables that bear most directly on the interactions and associations of teachers and pupils, the criteria for determining their effect become crucial for the profession. It is precisely here that the profession is in trouble, for it is unwittingly using self-defeating criteria.

In determining the quality of the school program, the profession has constantly considered effects on pupils as measured by reference to the central tendency of a distribution of achievement test scores. Each pupil's success is determined by his standing in the distribution, the average typically being used as the norm and a pupil's rating being expressed in terms of deviation from the norm. For the purpose of comparing schools, grades, or classes, norms are generated from an extensive pupil population such as that of a city, state, or nation. This means that pupil learning, expressed as test scores, is used to develop its own standard of evaluation.

If the average of the pupils of a given class or grade, or of a school or entire system, falls below the norm, it is a matter of public as well as professional concern. But why should one average be considered less desirable than another? Why is the pupil performance of a school whose average achievement in reading is lower than the national norm be considered less desirable than that of a school that exceeds it? Viewed purely as learning, there is no reason to make such comparisons unless learning is conceived to be good in itself—that it is just good to have and the more of it the better. Of course, it can be countered that the higher norms are taken to be more desirable not in themselves but for what they portend. Pupils of a school whose grade averages compare favorably with national norms are likely to succeed in further studies. But this reasoning is basically no different from that of the position that learning is good in itself. It only concludes that learning is desirable because it leads to further learning.

It will be objected that the foregoing analysis is an attack on a straw man, that few have ever held that the purpose of learning is merely to enable one to learn more. Instead, as everyone knows, schools are established to teach the knowledge and skills that enable individuals to lead productive lives in their communities. Even if this counterstatement is admitted, the case for achievement norms is not strengthened. There is no measure of the knowledge and skills required for a responsible role in society against which to compare the levels of achievement in school. Hence no one knows what level of achievement in reading, arithmetic, and conceptual knowledge is required for the performance of one's role as an adult.

From the foregoing discussion it should be clear that the teaching profession has no defensible criteria by which to assess the benefits to be gained from changes in the school. This deficiency of professional knowledge is doubtless one of the most serious stumbling blocks to school reform. In the absence of established criteria, the profession will continue

to be harassed by a constant parade of pedagogical formulas
leading to one *tour de force* after another.

Reform Variables

Another problem of paramount importance is the determination of factors whose manipulation will result in the satisfaction of the criteria of reform. What variables are most closely
associated with school effectiveness measured by benefits
to the individual or society or both is a controversial question.
There is no consistent body of theory from which to derive
or justify such variables. Consequently, authorities consider
different variables to be relevant depending upon the particular standpoint from which they approach school reform. Some
hold the view that curriculum design and content are crucial;
others think the pupils' freedom to choose, plan, and act is
basic; still others single out the school hierarchy and its
inflexibility; and so it goes. Each view can be rationalized
by reference to this or that commonsense notion bolstered
up by a pseudo-technical vocabulary. This is a condition that
calls for caution as one thinks about and plans for school
reform. Surely any move to change the school should be
considered from as many angles as possible and made on
a trial basis with ample evaluation in terms of benefits to
both the individual and society. The better part of wisdom
would seem to be to approach the whole question conserva-
tively, working first with those variables that appear to be
closest to the learning process before trying more remote ones.
This approach is frankly eclectic, based partly on common
sense and partly on the research and conceptual constructions
of others. On this basis certain clusters of variables are
hypothesized as being more promising than others for school
reform.

The first set of variables consists of the content of instruction. In its most general form, the basic question is how to
decide what knowledge is of most worth for everyone. That
question has haunted the minds of pedagogues throughout
the history of Western education. The answer can be given

only in terms of the principle of utility. If one considers the utility of schooling in its broadest sense, no knowledge appears to be more defensible than the concepts and skills involved in reading and arithmetic. These not only facilitate further learning in all domains of knowledge but they also provide abilities for the individual to participate in a wide range of activities throughout life. In addition, their social benefits are not to be questioned. But the level of achievement in those skills and concepts to be prescribed for everyone is a question that has seldom been considered, let alone answered.

Beyond these concepts and skills, however, identification of knowledge that can be justified as a universal requirement for all pupils by its utility either to society or to the individual is uncertain. Some authorities hold that certain knowledge is necessary for anyone to function in the various roles he is required to play, e.g., a citizen, consumer, or producer. But this claim rests on more tenuous grounds than the claim for reading and arithmetic. Such knowledge is not universally useful in further learning. Also, the advantages it provides appear to vary so much from one individual to another as to render its general utility questionable. Even were its general benefits established, that fact would not imply that such knowledge should be learned in school, especially in the first twelve years. Nevertheless, these concepts and skills continue to be defended as fundamental because of their alleged social and individual utility. The probability of their general utility is entertained as hypothesis, and a way of testing it is suggested. The value of any other knowledge is hypothesized as depending upon the learner. Whatever benefits are derived from its mastery accrue to him. But social utility appears to be a different matter. The social utility of schooling beyond the mastery of the elements of reading and arithmetic is not content-specific. It is hypothesized that social utility depends upon the amount of time spent in school and the thoroughness of the learning. This means that the advantages of schooling to society do not depend upon any particular content of the educational program.

The notion of thorough learning leads one to the view that the second set of variables has to do with teaching. It is reasonable to suppose that the variables most closely associated with school learning are those involved in the interaction of teachers and pupils. Among these are the concepts and skills of the teacher. It can be said that these variables have already been tested and found wanting, but this is true only in a loose sense. The fact is that teaching performance has been equated with nonbehavioral variables, or with reports that certain procedures or approaches were followed. Data based upon such variables and accounts of performances are no longer acceptable. They show nothing about teaching effectiveness, only that pupil achievement is not related to such uncertain and static variables.

If the teacher can analyze pupil behavior and respond appropriately to the pupil's difficulty as he tries to learn, learning is likely to occur. Assuming this proposition to be plausible, the question then is what preparation will enable the teacher to identify and deal with learning problems. Teacher education, except in the areas of learning disabilities and diagnostic and remedial work in reading, has virtually ignored the question of how to identify and treat learning difficulties. For the most part, teacher training has emphasized various methodological formulas, analyses of objectives and other tasks involved in planning instruction, and a few weeks of apprentice teaching. This sort of program prepares the teacher none too well to teach even those who have few if any difficulties in learning. More advanced professional study does little to ameliorate the defects of this initial preparation. It is now time to formulate a program of teacher preparation in which specific concepts and skills, both descriptive and diagnostic, are taught by behavioral indicators rather than merely as verbal definitions supplemented by verbal instances, a program in which the public schools and the universities combine their resources to teach the concepts and skills needed to handle all sorts of learning problems. It must be emphasized that teachers now acquire their skills during a brief apprenticeship in the public schools, but neither the administration of these schools nor the teachers who conduct the apprentice training are accountable.

The notion that teacher preparation can be improved assumes a body of dependable concepts and skills adequate to underwrite an effective program. It must be admitted that the effectiveness of only a few concepts and skills has been demonstrated empirically. But these few plus those that make up the wisdom of the profession are sufficient to begin the reform of teacher training programs. Besides, it must be pointed out that the efficacy of concepts and skills cannot be determined until a sample of teachers becomes skillful in their use. The content of teacher preparation must therefore proceed slowly and experimentally, for only by training teachers in promising concepts and skills and then testing them can the current knowledge base be extended. As this sort of knowledge is determined and teachers are trained to use it, the competence of teachers will cease to be a subject of discussion.

Two erroneous beliefs have retarded the improvement of teacher education. The first is the belief that concepts and theories such as those in psychology can be applied directly to teaching. It has been assumed that if one knows how learning occurs, he thereby knows how to teach. If one knows the theoretical formulation of problem solving, he knows how to teach by the problem method. But teaching performance is not as simple as that. To go from conceptions and theories to performance in the classroom is to work out procedures and materials to bridge the gap between theory and practice. It is seldom possible to translate concepts and theories directly into practice. One must know the practical situation as well as he knows the concepts and theories if he is to design materials for training individuals to deal with the practical condition. Basic research is important and, in fact, indispensable in the advancement of practice. But it requires a middleman to work out the materials and procedures for applying the findings of such research to practical problems and for personnel training. This is just as true for teacher training programs as it is for instructional programs in the public school.

The second erroneous belief is the notion that a general theory of learning, once formulated and established, will give a complete etiology of learning. The causes of all pupil failures would then be known and pedagogy would thereby become a true science. Programs for the preparation of teachers have thus run the gamut of learning theories, beginning with Thorndike's S-R bond theory almost seventy-five years ago and coming down to Skinner's theory of behavior modification today. Between then and now one theory after another has appeared upon the scene—gestalt theory, topological theory, theories of purposive behavior, and a variety of genetic theories. But anyone who has tried to teach a concept, law, procedure, or skill to a pupil who is finding it hard to learn knows that there is more to learning and teaching than any learning theory has ever encompassed. The substitution of general theories of learning for knowledge of the barriers to learning encountered in the various subjects of instruction, in the linguistic and social adjustments to school, in complicated inference patterns, and in making emotional adjustments can only lead to defective teacher training programs.

However, an increase in teacher competence will be of no avail unless school conditions are favorable to its utilization. Performance of the most competent teachers can be reduced to trivial, routine behavior by the functionally ordered system generated by bureaucratic controls. In such a system each individual is assigned specified duties to be performed in particular ways, in fixed time frames, and under specified conditions. In the eyes of many teachers this is the school condition. Their performance necessarily fits the pattern as they see it. Since their perception precludes teacher initiative and productive thinking, classroom performance of both teachers and pupils tends to adjust to the level the system tolerates. To reform the school is in part to create the conditions essential to an optimum utilization of competence.

The import of the foregoing discourse is that reform of the school is only a part, although an important part, of the problem of renewing society through the education of each new generation. If one begins with the plight of children and youth, recognizing their social isolation, the poverty of their experience, and the boredom of their existence, and asks how society can be renewed by bettering their condition, one will begin to see the breadth and depth of the educational problem that faces the nation. One will then give quite different answers to questions about school reform than if one begins with the school, neglecting the plight of children and youth, and asks how the school can become more conducive to learning. The first of these is the approach taken in the following chapters.

FOOTNOTES

[1] John Dewey, *Democracy and Education* (New York: Macmillan, 1916), pp. 1–7. The tendency to identify socialization with schooling was noted by Counts over 40 years ago. See George S. Counts, *The American Road to Culture* (New York: John Day Company, 1930), pp. 11–22.

[2] Robert A. Dahl, *Pluralist Democracy in the United States* (Chicago: Rand McNally, 1967), pp. 1–24.

[3] There is an extensive literature on the plight of youth. The following will introduce the reader to it:
Maxine Davis, *The Lost Generation* (New York: Macmillan, 1936); Cellon Holmes, "This is the Beat Generation," *New York Times Magazine*, November 16, 1952; Howard Bell, *Youth Tell Their Story* (Washington, D.C.: American Council on Education, 1938); Peter K. Manning and Marcello Truzzi (eds.), *Youth and Sociology*. (Englewood Cliffs, N.J.: Prentice-Hall, 1972); Frank Musgrove, *Youth and the Social Order* (London: Routledge and Kegan, Paul, 1964); Joel Spring, "Youth Culture in the United States," in *Roots of Crisis*, by Clarence J. Karier, Paul Violas, and Joel Spring (Chicago: Rand McNally, 1973); Paul Goodman, *Growing Up Absurd* (New York: Vintage Books, Random House, 1956); Urie Bronsenbrenner, "The Origin of Alienation," *Scientific American*, Vol. 231, #2, pp. 53–61, August, 1974. For a comprehensive review of the youth problem today see Panel on Youth of the President's Science Advisory Committee, *Transition to Adulthood* (Chicago, Ill.: University of Chicago Press, 1974).

[4] Counts, op. cit.

CHAPTER II

The Eclipse of Adult Influence

The passage from childhood into adulthood is long and fraught with difficulties. It covers one-twelfth of an average lifetime if the adolescent period is counted as six years, beginning at 12 and ending with the legal voting age of 18. The passage is not only long but narrow, confined largely to the school and the home. To become an adult, an adolescent must first become a pupil in a school where the knowledge, skills, and values deemed essential to the performance of adult roles must be learned. To be unschooled is to be inadequate as an adult.

When the adolescent is neither at home nor in school, his life is largely limited to peer groups, some supervised clubs, and other informal groups and gangs. Associations with adults in productive activities and service functions are relatively infrequent and largely restricted to occasional part-time employment. Whether one considers the youth of suburbia, the rural village, or the central city, the circumstances vary only in degree, the latter having the least opportunity to engage in productive activities or in groups organized for their benefit.

The upshot of the situation is that the adult community wields no heavy influence upon youth as it did before the scientific technological revolution took over almost every activity of society. Increasingly in recent years the school has been assigned an ever larger share of the responsibility for shaping youth to adult roles. The purpose of this chapter is to describe how this state of affairs developed, to indicate how the school has attempted to respond to it, and to hint at the possible consequences of the failure of the adult community to share with youth its responsibilities.

How Adult Influence Diminished

How did the reduction of adults' socializing influence come about? The story begins 200 years ago with the introduction of the factory system and power-driven machinery.[1] Previously, production had been carried on in the household and small shops. Children and youth worked shoulder to shoulder with their parents and other adults or with a master to whom they were apprenticed. The introduction of machinery in the mid-1700s changed all this. The young were employed to tend machines. Their work was less related to adults than to the impersonal machine. What they learned from work was no longer a craft but rather the routinized performance demanded by mechanized production. The child lost not only its association with adults but also the educative value of its labor. Work that had been educative in both the guild system of the Middle Ages and in the more recent domestic system became exploitation for production and profit. The apprentice system, often abused but nevertheless educationally beneficial on the whole, became a means of gaining custody over large numbers of indigent children to supply factory labor.

By the early 1800s, a movement was begun in England to protect the health and morals of child laborers whose exploitation had become intolerable. Throughout the nineteenth century and the beginning of the present century, the struggle to protect the young continued. In 1938, the battle was won in the United States with the passage of the Fair Labor Standards Act. The federal law set the minimum age at 14 for employment in nonmanufacturing occupations. The minimum age was set at 16 for employment in work involved in interstate commerce, and at 18 for hazardous occupations. In the manufacturing industries, the young were thus reduced to a marginal status.

The farm was the last source of production to lose its formative influence. Mechanization of agriculture proceeded apace during the first half of this century, and the need for farm workers rapidly declined. In increasing numbers, youths were driven from the farm in search of employment in urban communities.[2] As the competition for jobs in the cities was hard, many young people became disillusioned and alienated. This was especially true of youths belonging to minority groups who wound up in the ghettos without jobs, handicapped not only by the meagerness of their education but also by deliberate discrimination against them. The farm youth, like the youth of industrial workers, came to share the same predicament— socially isolated, politically powerless, economically marginal, and alienated.

One fact frequently overlooked is the parent's absence from the home environment. The factory system and the corporate structure have created jobs that take fathers away from the home and the community. Consequently, children know very little about the work of their father; it is often abstract and remote from their experience. Under the impact of developing technology, large numbers of women also left the home for work in the factories and offices. During the Second World War and the post-war period, American mothers took jobs at an increasing rate. In 1948, 18 percent of mothers were gainfully employed. By 1960, approximately 28 percent of mothers of children under 18 years of age held jobs. Four out of ten (40.5 percent) of these mothers were employed by 1972. In 1960, about 18 percent of the mothers of preschool children were in the labor force. By 1970, 30 percent held jobs. By the beginning of the present decade, approximately

50 percent of mothers with children of school age worked outside the home.[3] With both parents at work and no other adult figures in the home, the child was denied relationships not only with his parents but also with other significant adults.

The development of child and adolescent psychology is not unrelated to social isolation. The fact that the interests of children are different from those of adults is attributable primarily to the fact that children are socially isolated and not to the limited extent of their years. The child who grew up on the farm in the last century would have been interested in the things that occupied his parents and other adults, for he would have worked side by side with them. By the same token, peer groups are born of social circumstances. Perhaps it is not too much to claim, as some have done, that the rise of adolescent psychology is grounded in the social context rather than in the nature of the youth itself. Be that as it may, it is certain that the development of adolescent psychology has arisen concurrently with the decay of the educative influences of the adult community.

The stability of youth is related to the distinctness of the path between their world and the adult world. Youths who are uncertain about their role in life are likely to become socially active in periods of social unrest, as was exemplified in the campus disturbances of the 1960s. Unrest was more extensive among liberal arts students, especially in the humanities and the social sciences. On the other hand, students in the professional schools—engineering, agriculture, business, education, law, medicine, etc.—were less involved in demonstrations and destructive conduct.[4]

Of course the liberal arts, nonvocational outlook is not identical to disenchantment and dissent. Most students in the social sciences and humanities, like those who are career-oriented, look forward to entering society as responsible participants. Nevertheless, this group yields the most activists and the most students who are disenchanted with American life. From this group come not only the most activists but also most of the advocates of meditation, astrology, encounter groups, and communes.[5]

A number of claims have been advanced to account for this difference between those who are career-minded and those who are not. It is said that the latter are more intelligent, more aware of social injustices, and less tolerant of social immorality than their vocational counterparts. These claims are open to question. The intelligence and general information about the social world among students of the professional and technical schools is hardly less than that of students in the social sciences and humanities. Surely the leaders of campus demonstrations, most of whom were in liberal arts departments, can easily be matched in mental acuity and knowledge by students from the professional schools. There is little reason to assume that students of the humanities and social sciences are more sensitive to social injustice than students in the technical and professional programs. Today there is too much communication, too much pretechnical and preprofessional preparation in all the various disciplines for the career-oriented student to ignore social injustice and immorality.

Perhaps the point of difference is not sensitivity but readiness to act on hunches and beliefs. The humanistic studies and to some extent the social sciences emphasize the role of intuition, impulse, conviction, and commitment in human action. The technical and professional curricula emphasize the importance of implications, consequences, and testing of hunches before committing oneself. Their students are hence less likely to act on impulse, to be possessed by beliefs, than their liberal arts counterparts. Be that as it may, the career-oriented student doubtless identifies more readily with political and economic institutions since they are his destination. The liberal arts student who has not yet found his path in life sees less in the social system with which he can identify. Students whose school objectives are vague and unrelated to life objectives are more likely to suffer from social unrest.

Substitutes for Adult Influence

What has replaced the influence of the adults? Fundamentally, nothing at all, for there can be no substitute for the educative weight of the adult community. Nevertheless, two things have filled the vacuum created by reduction of adult influence. The first is the school. During the last seventy-five years, school enrollments increased by leaps and bounds. Under the impact of compulsory attendance laws, the school became the repository for the young while fathers and mothers pursued their careers away from home and frequently outside the neighborhood. The total school enrollment today is staggering. Including higher education and private schools, it was 59 million in 1970; a school population greater than the population of France, Italy, West Germany, or the United Kingdom. If those 59 million students were a nation, it would be the ninth-largest in the world. Underlying this institutionalization of children and youth is the widespread belief that the school can shape character and civic behavior as well as cognitive development. When this belief has been shattered by youthful conduct, it is replaced by the firm conviction that the school relieves parents of the daytime burden of their children.

The second replacement for adult influence is the peer group. In their isolation from adult society, children and youth create their own groups and fashion in some degree their own views and rules of conduct. While the latter are still shaped somewhat by social institutions and mass media, they tend to be at odds with the beliefs and hopes of the adult society. This is the significance of what is referred to as the youth or counter culture. One of the basic elements of this orientation, especially among the more affluent youth, is an incipient disdain for productive work, particularly as an instrument of social and economic elevation.

While firm data on the attitudes of youth toward historic social values are scarce, a few points can be suggested. One account of the youth culture points out that youth today tend to live unto themselves, to feel attached to their own age group, to have a strong urge toward autonomy, to identify readily with the downtrodden, and to be strongly in favor of change.[6] According to a 1971 study, two out of three college students expressed themselves as willing to accept authority in work situations compared to one out of two in 1968.[7] This more positive view toward authority is probably due to the stable environment of youth in 1971 compared to 1968. If so, the 1971 expression is nearer the real attitude of youth toward authority on the job. While such attitudes are probably not stable, they nevertheless indicate the temper of youth toward authority relations.

This study also reported an increasing percent of the students were disposed toward less emphasis on working hard. In 1968, 69 percent agreed with the view that hard work pays off. In 1971, only 39 percent held that view. It must be recognized that these data pertain to the college population, those who have enjoyed the greater benefits of society. There is little reason to suppose that those who have had none of the advantages of affluence would look with more favor on the utility of hard work.[8] Nevertheless, four out of five college students still believe that a meaningful career is a significant aspect of one's life. These data are not readily interpreted. Do they indicate something about youth? Do they indicate a persistent change in attitude toward this small but important set of values? Or do they signify something about the world of work; that it is too often unchallenging, that opportunities for growth and advancement are being reduced by technology and bureaucracy?

Probably these beliefs are partly induced by the lack of jobs for college graduates and by the romantic notion that in the near future there will be an age of abundance for everyone, an age in which little labor will be needed, in which no one will be motivated to seek control over others and everyone will have a significant say in the decisions that affect society as well as himself. The elite will then be absorbed by the masses. In the foreseeable future, such beliefs can lead only to a dead end. They lead nowhere, certainly not into adult society, and the dreams of those who have such beliefs are likely to end with their youth. Those whose ambitions and life plans become inextricably committed to them are destined to join the ne'er-do-wells of society. Not all is lost; that outcome, too, pays social dividends. Many of these youths belong to affluent families. Their abdication will leave vacant spots in the social structure to be filled by others from the bottom. This circulation of youth will supply the nation's leadership with new blood to nourish its vitality.

The School and the Problem of Assimilation

What has been the response of the teaching profession to the declining influence of adults? Many responses have been given to deal with this situation. Only a few of the more important ones can be briefly discussed here. In general they can be grouped under the following headings: 1) programs to develop character and civic conduct; 2) programs to prepare the youth for work; and 3) programs to improve the quality of community life.

Teachers as well as the general populace have long associated schools with character development. This is evident in the claim made throughout the last century that the school's purpose was to develop the head, the heart, and the hand, or, as it was sometimes put, the mental, spiritual, and physical. Remarkable progress has been made in recent years. The current aim is to shape the cognitive, affective, and psychomotor behavior! Until the advent of experimental psychology and pragmatism at the beginning of this century, character was taught through moral stories, maxims, and study of great characters whom the young could emulate. All this was changed when schoolmen became convinced that an individual becomes what he does; that to practice proper behavior in life situations is to learn to behave as a person of good character and good civic conduct. Thus, the development of character through formal instruction and exhortation was displaced by group participation in the classroom and programs of extracurricular activities. These provided situations for the student to practice making decisions about correct behavior in a variety of circumstances. From such participation he was to become a more wholesome character and a better citizen. Character and citizenship were to be developed not by persuasion but by induction from objective circumstances.

This theory of conduct development posited that the most influential factor in shaping the character and civic behavior of the young was the quality of the school itself. As Dewey expressed it, the school should be an "embryonic community." By making the school a community where children and youth form their own government, run their own affairs, and take on some of the basic responsibilities typical of adults, they would grow into habits of right conduct; when school days were over they would become wholesome members of society. The idea of the school as a community also includes the classroom. School work is to be conducted in such a way as to involve pupils in choosing, planning, and evaluating their work in group and individual activities.[9] In this way they would acquire habits of cooperation as well as the ability to collect and assess facts, weigh alternatives, and choose among values. Although children and youth are denied participation in the adult community, they can create a replica of it in their school life and thus fashion themselves after the societal type.

The belief that the school's program can serve the assimilative function of society is not without merit. It has increased pupil participation in nonacademic affairs of the school and experience in a few types of community behavior. The school can foster, among other things, self-discipline, growth in personal interactions, and acceptance of group norms. Unfortunately, this belief is open to certain objections, and efforts to follow it in practice have been none too successful. The young are still isolated from adults except for their teachers, many of whom are barely older than their pupils and have themselves had little experience in life beyond the school.[10] The faculty holds the reins of power in the "embryonic community" of the school. To expect the young to learn more than a few habits of conduct required by an adult society in this rudimentary social system, under the control of superiors, is like expecting youths to learn to drive an automobile by manipulating a model while their trainers hold the wheel. Then, too, the school has tended to give pupils reassurance and personal warmth and to protect them from frustration in the hope of fostering learning and self-realization. When these practices are backed up by family affluence shielding youth from want, many of them are unable to accept hardship and disappointment as part of their lives or of the human condition. They do not know how to cope with the frustrations of uninteresting work and hard personal associations.

A second way that the school has attempted to bring youth and adults together is by involving youth in the world of work. Since the breakdown of the apprentice system, efforts have been made to devise some other way of preparing youth to enter the labor market. The motivation for these efforts is partly the belief that the school should give as much attention to the masses of children and youth who do not go to college as to the few who do, partly to the conviction that everyone should have the knowledge and skills required to earn a living, and partly to the need of industry and agriculture for skilled workers. Perhaps the earliest attempt to provide such preparation was the manual training programs that began in Europe and spread to America about a hundred years ago. This development was followed by the establishment of trade schools in the first decade of the present century. These schools provided training in such trades as pattern making, machinist and tool making, carpentering and wood working, plumbing and gas fitting. They were open to eighth-grade graduates and to those able to read, write, and calculate. The program of these schools deviated from the apprentice system only slightly. One of the chief differences was the emphasis upon academic work.

In 1917, congress provided for vocational programs in the

public school, acting on the report of the National Commission on Vocational Education, which found that out of some 27 million workers in agriculture and industry only about 2 percent had had an opportunity to prepare themselves. These programs included agriculture, trades and industries, commerce, and home economics. They flourished for several decades but have never reached more than a small fraction of the youth. In 1970–71, less than 10 percent of secondary school pupils were enrolled in occupational programs.[11] Changes in the nation's occupational structure reflected in the decline of employment opportunities on the farm, the development of an endless variety of service occupations, the automation of industry, and the decline in home activities have all but undermined the justification of the program as it was originally conceived. This program is being enriched today by work experience. The student works for pay in some business, trade, industry, or service where he is placed and supervised by the school authorities. Credit toward graduation is often given for the experience. The student learns to work with adults, to be punctual, to follow through on his responsibilities, and to do what the job requires.

A new program, "career education," is now on the horizon. It has certain features to commend it but it lacks integrating principles by which the program's supporters can identify their common ground.[12] At the elementary level the pupils engage in such activities as writing and staging a television program, running a classroom bank, building a radio-controlled airplane, and visiting industries and commercial centers.[13] This is all strangely reminiscent of the activity movement of the 1920s, a movement that emphasized construction projects in the classroom and field studies dealing with the community's problems of health, transportation, and countless others. In the course of studying these problems, pupils engaged in all sorts of activities, many of which are required by various occupations. The residue of the activity movement is still to be found in the schools in the form of projects, varied pupil activities, pupil-teacher planning, and pupil evaluation of work. Career education at the elementary level is apparently utilizing these earlier innovations. The objective is to acquaint the child with the world of work and to give him some experience in simple manual skills that have general utility.

If career education becomes a way to prepare the elementary pupil merely to do manual activities or to steer him into an occupational choice, it would be indicative of a simple utilitarian conception, one that would not justify the program. The program at this level can be justified by the contribution it makes to the child's understanding and appreciation of man's work, of the materials he has used and the principles he has depended upon in the course of his cultural evolution.[14] If this approach is ignored, the whole venture can turn out to be an ingenuity that is merely spectacular and results in distracting teachers from the primary task of developing skills of learning and basic concepts.

Career education at the high school level is also undefined. The program is still in a formative stage; to speculate about the form it may finally take is risky. Its controlling objective appears to be to sensitize youth to the range, significance, and opportunities of occupations and to provide youth with elementary skills for admission to a family of occupations. A program of this sort is not significantly different from the work experience program mentioned above, which is well-established in some schools. If this statement of purpose is correct, the program is open to the criticism that its assessment of the plight of youth is only partly correct. The separation of youth from the world of adults in every aspect of the social system, not just work, is prolonging their immaturity. Although productive work is an important experience, it is only one way of eliminating the separation.

Another move by the profession to fill the vacuum created by the separation of youths from adults is an effort to develop community education. This began as the community school movement. The aim was to make the school into an educational and recreational center for adults as well as for children and youth. The school would become a place where individuals of all ages could engage in joint activities, share the benefits that accrue from expansion of social relations, and pursue their interest in learning. The school would thus become the center of community life, open to all ages from morning until late evening.

This movement began in earnest in the 1930s when youth were adrift in overwhelming numbers, unemployment was rampant, and social cohesion was painfully in need of repair.[15] The movement has had its ups and downs, but it has continued with increasing support from various quarters. One example at Flint, Mich., was developed with the support of the Mott Foundation. Some 300 communities now boast of a program similar to Flint's. However, the concept of the community school has slightly changed. Today some of its advocates speak of "community education" instead of "community school" to signify that the school is only part of community education.[16] Beyond the school are business and industry, which have resources to broaden the experience of both children and adults. Many community and governmental agencies can also be coordinated to educational ends. In this notion of community education the school becomes the central agency through which the people come to recognize their needs and learn how to satisfy them.

Can the Profession Do the Job?

The purpose of the foregoing discussion has been to outline the profession's major efforts to cope with the problem of assimilating children and youth into the world of adults. However, these steps have inevitably fallen short of solving the problem. The profession has largely attempted to bridge the gap between the young and the world of adult experience by expanding the school's domain of operation. This is in keeping with the principle of residual function; namely, whatever needs of children and youth are not satisfied by other agencies are the school's responsibility. This principle is clearly evidenced by the programs of work preparation and also in the community education movement. Commitment to this principle has led the profession to accept one responsibility after another. Today, the school is supposed to solve the drug problem, improve family life, reduce unemployment, encourage temperance, reduce traffic accidents, improve public health, provide death education, and serve any other popular cause. Given today's social conditions, the logical outcome of this principle is that the teaching profession will become responsible for the complete socialization of youth.

Of course the home and the school can be effective as socializing agencies in the early years. During infancy and early childhood the family is the chief socializing influence. As the child enters school it comes under new influences— teachers, peers, and the wider world that school opens up. These influences are dominant during elementary school days. They require little supplementation if parents take their responsibilities seriously and are economically and socially able to provide a stimulating and constructive home environment. Where parents cannot do so or do not because they value other things more highly, the poverty of the child's experience can be pronounced and the effects of the school reduced. Beyond the elementary school age, the home and school must be extensively supplemented. This is because these institutions constitute only a small segment of the social world into which youth are to be inducted. Consequently, the gap between the experiences required to become a responsible member of the adult society and those provided by the home and school becomes wider and wider as the individual grows into adolescence.

The notion that the profession of teaching can take on the entire task of inducting youth into the adult society boggles the mind. The responsibility of preparing the youth for work, guiding them in choosing among occupations, and placing them in jobs almost overwhelms the imagination. One then must consider induction into political, recreational, and family life. Can the profession teach knowledge and skills and at the same time take on the task of preparing approximately

THE ECLIPSE OF ADULT INFLUENCE

45 million pupils for adult roles? Considering occupational
life alone, the task would be almost equal to preparing every
man, woman, and child in the United Kingdom for work,
helping them choose their careers, and placing them in jobs
every twelve years. No one can deny that youth must be
prepared for work or that they must be helped to find a
place for themselves in the complex social structure of today,
or that work experience helps to bridge the gap between youths
and adults. None of this is in question. The question to be
answered is: Who is responsible for doing the job?

Equally questionable is the view that the teaching profession
should be responsible for the formative influences of the
community. It cannot be denied that the school's program
should be adjusted to the desire of adults to occupy some
of their time in learning, although the junior college will
probably assume much of this responsibility. Nor is there
any good reason to suppose that the school should curtail
its programs of entertainment and recreation for adults and
children. The soundness of the view that the profession, even
with community reinforcement and supplementation, should
become the directing force for the coordination of the various
formative influences of community life is not so evident. Surely
to do this would be to exceed not only the competence of
the profession but also its social and political power.

These objections do not exhaust the criticism of the teaching
profession's efforts to deal with the occupational and social
disengagement of youth. The objectives of work experience
programs indicate that youth and adults are to share experiences primarily in work situations. This is a very limited
experience with the adult world. The adult responsibilities
in the work situation can be and often are perfunctory, leading
to a sterile experience for the young worker. Then, too, these
work programs typically neglect professional occupations and
the domain of social and political policy formulation, decision
making, and action. The spectrum of adult activities in which
youth should be responsibly involved is as wide as the total
range of functions performed in society. To deal successfully

with the plight of youth, it is necessary to work out ways of inducting youth into adult life rather than merely to find ways of inducting them into industry and commerce. Adults must be held responsible for making their interactions with youth educative. In the realm of work the aim should be to restore its educative influence rather than merely to develop marketable skills.

The attempt of the teaching profession to cope with the problem of assimilation has allowed an all-too-willing adult society to unload its responsibility. By paying school taxes, adults feel that they are relieved of whatever obligations the profession of teaching will fulfill. The tendency toward syndication of obligations in American society is all too evident. One contributes to the United Fund, Red Cross, or whatever, and ipso facto his obligations to charity are discharged; he pays his insurance premiums and a host of family and personal obligations are signed off; he pays his taxes, and he expects the school to house, supervise, and educate his children. The average family head pays hundreds of dollars per year for others to "worry" about him and his family— health, safety, unemployment, disability, education, property, investments, and death. This tendency to delegate responsibility to agencies is good in aspects of life that can be so assigned without loss of benefits. It frees the individual to do other things, relieves him of some anxieties, and provides services that can only be provided collectively in modern conditions. However, some things cannot be provided by syndication. The most important of these is the assimilation of youth into society. This function is broader than any institution or agency, more inclusive than the home, and more fundamental than schooling, and it cannot be performed adequately without the loyal involvement of all significant institutions and agencies. Youth can become adults in a social sense only by participating in adult activities with their elders. The nature of society and the inherent limitations of the individual's modes of development and learning prevent any substitute.

Much has been said about the increased knowledge of youth today. The schools are more effective, and the young pick up much information from mass media that once was available mainly through the school. But something more than information and knowledge is needed in the complex world of today. Youth need wisdom. Among other things, wisdom indicates an ability to exercise sound judgment in practical affairs, to judge rightly in personal relations and in complex social matters, and to time one's utterances and actions. Youth today are no more prudent than their elders were in their own youth, if indeed they are as wise. Neither the schools nor the mass media can teach wisdom. To say, "I am going to teach wisdom" would be odd. Wisdom comes mainly from hard experience whose consequences season the emotions and the mind: certainly little can come from the classroom or the college halls. The rapidity of change, the density and complexity of events, and the shift in values call not only for more knowledge and skill but also for greater prudence in their use. Since the development of wisdom is fostered by responsibility, the earlier the youth are involved in situations with adults, the greater the chances that more of them will come of age with greater wisdom than did their forefathers. When adults take on their responsibility for introducing each child into societal membership, infusing him with the spirit of constructive participation and cooperation, and opening the doors to information and experience, society will be deserving of its young.

FOOTNOTES

[1] Edward P. Cheyney, *Industrial and Social History of England* (New York: Macmillan, 1926), Chapter VIII and pp. 132–249. John Dewey, *The School and Society* (Chicago: University of Chicago Press, 1902), pp. 6–29.

[2] One person in 22 lived on a farm in 1972, or about 4.6 percent of the total of 207 million in the nation. Only about one-fourth (2,380,000) of the total farm population were children under 14 years. See U.S. Department of Commerce, Social and Economic Statistics Administration, Bureau of the Census; Series Census—No. 44, June, 1973. ERS, p. 2–27.

[3] U.S. Department of Labor, Bureau of Labor Statistics, *Marital and Family Characteristics of Workers, March 1972*, Special Labor Force Report 153 (Washington, D.C.: U.S. Government Printing Office 1973).

[4] Alan E. Bayer, "Institutional Correlates of Faculty Support of Campus Unrest," *Sociology of Education*, Winter, 1973, pp. 76–94; Roger M. Kahn and William J. Bowers, "The Social Context of The Rank and File Student Activist: A Test of Four Hypotheses," *Sociology of Education*, Winter, 1970, pp. 38–55; Richard E. Peterson, "The Student Left in American Higher Education," *Daedalus*, Winter, 1967, pp. 293–317.

[5] Kenneth Keniston, "What's Bugging the Students?" *Educational Record*, Spring, 1970, pp. 116–33.

[6] Panel on Youth of the President's Science Advisory Committee, *Transition to Adulthood*, op. cit.

[7] Daniel Yankelovich, *The Changing Values on Campus: Political and Personal Attitudes on Campus* (New York: Washington Square Press, 1972).

[8] Edwin Harwood, "Youth Employment—A Tale of Two Ghettos," *The Public Interest*, Fall, 1969, pp. 78–87.

[9] William H. Kilpatrick, *Foundations of Method* (New York: Macmillan, 1926), *passim*, see especially pp. 200–16.

[10] In 1956–57, 20 percent of beginning teachers had worked for pay outside of education. Of these, 32 percent had engaged in professional occupations and 43 percent in clerical. Only 10 percent had been involved in skilled and semi-skilled labor and only 2 percent in service activities. See Ward S. Mason, *Final Report on the Survey of New Teachers in the Public Schools 1956–57*, U.S. Department of Health, Education, and Welfare, OE 23009 (Washington, D.C.: U.S. Government Printing Office, 1961). In 1961, more than one out of four teachers were supplementing their salaries with income from summer employment. See National Education Association Research Division, "The American Public School Teacher 1960–61," *Research Monograph*, 1963, No. 2.

[11] Dianne B. Gertler and Linda A. Barker, *Patterns of Course Offerings and Enrollments in Public Secondary Schools 1970–71*, U.S. Office of Education, National Center for Educational Statistics, DHEW Publication No. (OE) 73-11400 (Washington, D.C.: U.S. Government Printing Office, 1972).

[12] Rue W. Harris, "Plan for Career Education," *Proceedings of the Eighth Invitational Conference on Systems Under Construction in Career Education Development* (Palo Alto: American Institutes for Research, 1971); *Comprehensive Career Education Models: Problems and Prospects*, Educational Policy Research Center, Syracuse University Research Corporation, June, 1971; *Career Educa-*

tion—*Prognosis for a Policy*, Educational Policy Research Center, Stanford Research Institute, December, 1971.

[13] Anthony M. Deiulio and James N. Young, "Career Education in the Elementary School," *Phi Delta Kappan*, February, 1973, pp. 378–80.

[14] Dewey, op. cit., p. 12–29.

[15] One of the earliest treatments of the community school is Samuel Everett (ed.), *The Community School* (New York: D. Appleton-Century, 1938).

[16] Clyde E. LeTarte and Jack D. Minzey, *Community Education; From Programs to Process* (Midland, Mich.: Pendell Publishing Co., 1972), pp. 3–29.

CHAPTER III

Toward Renewal of Socialization

The conventional meaning of "*rites de passage*" is of little use in mass society. No longer can it be a ceremonial event preceded by some profound experience, a feat of courage or endurance performed in a few hours or days. Today a youth demonstrates his fitness as a full-fledged member of society by attending to duties day after day, through every personal and occupational difficulty. It is not proving oneself in some contrived or chosen event that counts, but showing that one performs well day after day no matter how trying the circumstances. *Rites de passage* in this sense is a course, not an event. It is a demonstration that one is the kind of person that an interdependent society requires for the well-being of all, that one is dependable in varying circumstances over an extended period of time.

The *rites de passage* is not a well-defined process in mass society. It can be compared to one hunting for a way through the woods where the destination is uncertain and paths lead in all directions. In a simple society the paths are fewer, and one's destination more clearly marked. In today's complex society, there is a good chance of becoming lost in the quest for satisfactory adjustments to the roles one must play in life.

This is precisely the situation in America today. As the nation changed from an agrarian into an industrial phase and then into a highly technological and bureaucratic society, the likelihood of negotiating a satisfactory transition from childhood to adulthood became more and more uncertain. At the same time adults remained unaware of the changes in the influences that shape the young. How this state of affairs developed and the attempts of the teaching profession to cope with it were set forth in the preceding chapter. Providing the youth with social vehicles that can facilitate the transition to responsible adulthood can only be done with the participation of the adult community. This involvement is the subject of the present chapter.

Objectives of Socialization

Socialization goes on in all societies, industrial or agrarian, simple or complex. The problem of socialization in the technological, bureaucratic society today is not one of reinstituting the socializing process. It is to make adult influence again a main emphasis in socialization.

Socialization begins at birth. It is never finished, but it decreases when the individual begins to assume the roles expected of him by the adult community. Many behaviors must be learned in order to reach this point, among them the ability to support oneself, to provide for one's dependents, and to deal with untoward circumstances. To list all of these behaviors is to list the objectives of the socializing process. Studies of these have been made. Perhaps the most comprehensive is Havighurst's study of development tasks.[1] He divides these into three groups: infancy and early childhood, middle childhood; and adolescence, as follows:

Infancy and early childhood:
  1. Learning to walk
  2. Learning to take solid foods

3. Learning to talk
4. Learning to control the elimination of bodily wastes
5. Learning sex differences and sexual modesty
6. Achieving physiological stability
7. Forming simple concepts of social and physical reality
8. Learning to relate oneself emotionally to parents, siblings, and other people
9. Learning to distinguish right and wrong and developing a conscience.

Middle childhood:

10. Learning physical skills necessary for ordinary games
11. Building wholesome attitudes toward oneself as a growing organism
12. Learning to get along with age mates
13. Learning an appropriate masculine or feminine social role
14. Developing fundamental skills in reading, writing, and calculating
15. Developing concepts necessary for everyday living
16. Developing conscience, morality, and a scale of values
17. Achieving personal independence
18. Developing social attitudes toward social groups and institutions.

Adolescence:

19. Achieving new and more mature relations with age mates of both sexes
20. Achieving a masculine or feminine social role
21. Accepting one's physique and using the body effectively
22. Achieving emotional independence of parents and other adults
23. Achieving assurance of economic independence
24. Selecting and preparing for an occupation
25. Preparing for marriage and family life
26. Developing intellectual skills and concepts necessary for civic competence
27. Desiring and achieving socially responsible behavior

28. Acquiring a set of values and an ethical system as a guide to behavior.

This list includes social and psychological tasks.[2] If each is specifically defined, the list would be found to include the objectives suggested by the Panel on Youth of the President's Science Advisory Committee.[3] The panel suggests objectives consisting of three classes: self-centered, other-oriented, and unlabeled.

Self-centered:
1. Cognitive and noncognitive skills necessary for economic independence and for occupational opportunities
2. Capabilities of effective management of one's own affairs
3. Capabilities as a consumer, not only of goods, but, more significantly, of the cultural riches of civilization
4. Capabilities for engaging in intense concentrated involvement in an activity.

Other-oriented:
1. Experiences with persons different from himself, not only in social class and subculture, but also in age
2. The experience of having others dependent on one's actions
3. Independent activities directed toward collective goals.

Unlabeled:
1. The development of a sense of identity and self-esteem.

Havighurst's list differs in at least two respects. It includes objectives from infancy to adulthood and a wider range of abilities at each level of development. Greater specificity does not compensate for the lack of breadth of the panel's list. The items of each list will require extensive elaboration to be of use as guides either to program development or evaluation. Items 19 to 28 of the Havighurst list appear to place less emphasis on responsibility for others and experience with adults, but these are implicitly present in the list.

The school's formal program is designed to take care of tasks 14 and 26 and, to a lesser extent, tasks 15, 18, 21,

24, 25, and 28. The informal environment of the school, particularly the culture of the pupil body and extra-class activities, influences in varying degrees the remainder of the tasks in middle childhood and adolescence. These determinants taken together, however, are no substitute for the influences of an adult community. An individual who lives in a home and school life throughout his adolescent years, sheltered from participation with adults in the social, economic, and political functions of the community, will have no experience in coping with an adult role.

The influence of the school on nonacademic developmental tasks has received only meager study. Some evidence points to the paucity of the school's effects. For instance, vocational choices are more often made in terms of nonschool influences. If the high school seniors of Indiana can be taken as typical of the seniors of the nation, only about one-third are primarily affected by the school in their career choices.[4] In sharp contrast, about 42 percent report relatives and friends as being most influential, and work experience is credited as being most helpful by almost 13 percent. These choices are not stable, nor can one be certain that the pupil always knows who or what helped him most. For example, only 5 percent reported the counselor as most helpful, which may be attributable to the fact that counselors typically try to give information to the pupil and to stimulate him to decide for himself. The pupil may thus underrate the counselor's helpfulness. Nevertheless, it is clear that only a minority of the pupils perceive either the school's personnel or its program as the dominant influence in their career choices.

Socialization from birth to the end of the elementary school years is somewhat different from that of adolescence. Since the home and the school are the primary socializing influences during the elementary school years, the task of assuring proper socialization is one of providing homes and schools conducive to learning and to wholesome physical and emotional development. The import of the argument for nursery schools and programs of parental education is not just to facilitate school learning but to assure the ultimate shaping of the child for adult living. While his interests and experiences determine where the home and the school can best begin to further the child's development, the ultimate purpose is to advance him in the process of socialization. During the preadolescent and adolescent years, socialization requires an ever-increasing involvement of all social institutions, not just the home and the school. At this level the task is to mobilize the adult community to take on its responsibility for helping to shape youth to the societal type.

Master Plan for Socialization

The first thing to consider is the resources for socialization. They include all the avenues through which individuals can enter into the countless activities that maintain and advance the society. They are so varied that it is all but impossible to list them here. It is more useful to consider the social functions to which these avenues lead. If society is viewed as a set of functions performed by adults in their varied activities as members of the community, it is easier to see into what the young are to be inducted.

Social behavior is organized into systems called institutions. They are "organized systems of practices and social roles developed about a value or series of values, and the machinery evolved to regulate the practices and administer the roles."[5] A concrete institution, for instance, a particular family, is to be distinguished from the class of institutions called the family. Sociologists have grouped institutions into four classes, each serving particular human needs through the performance of certain functions. They are: political, economic, expressive-integrative, and kinship.[6] These are not mutually exclusive groupings. In some social systems an expressive-integrative institution may exercise the functions of a political institution as in medieval society when the church exercised political control and regulated commercial activities. Not long ago the church and the family were the agencies for dispensing charity.

Today the state has largely taken over this function in many societies. The family controls its members through the exercise of authority as does the polity, and it is also a producing unit, particularly in nonindustrialized societies. This overlapping of functions has led sociologists to formulate categories that embrace functions exercised in different ways by different institutions. For example, authority is exercised by the state, church, and family and is conceptualized as the *structure of authority*.[7] It transcends both particular institutions and classes of institutions. Nevertheless, it is useful for present purposes to treat institutions as organized social ways of meeting human needs.

The institutions and agencies that carry on the work of society can be grouped by function. For example, the quest for salvation is a social function in which millions of people are involved through a multiplicity of agencies and institutions. Among them are the churches of the various denominations and their ramified activities such as counseling centers, youth organizations, charitable operations, and recreational centers. If all the functions were determined, the range of resources for the assimilation of youth could be seen. They are numerous and fully adequate for the involvement of all youth with adults in responsible activities. The development of such a chart of resources is an essential step in planning a comprehensive attack on the problem of assimilating youth. Another step is to work out ways for the youth to engage with adults in each family of institutions or agencies, determine what activities they can engage in, and learn what supervision the enterprise can provide.

For the purpose at hand, it is sufficient to rely on the four main classes of institutions, to give instances of each class, and to list their functions:[8]

1. Political Institutions. In the United States these include national, state, and local governmental agencies—legislative, judicial, and executive branches including the police and the military. Their functions are to:

a. maintain internal order and protect against outside influences and attacks
b. administer justice
c. foster the general welfare—health, education, living standards, working conditions, parks, recreation, charity, etc.
d. foster and regulate the economy
e. protect persons, property, and resources.

2. Economic Institutions. Among these are labor, business, professional, industrial, commercial, and financial institutions. They function in order to:

a. produce and distribute goods
b. provide services—professional, technical, recreational, etc.
c. provide transportation
d. provide communication.

3. Expressive-Integrative Institutions. These include such organizations as churches, schools, museums, theaters, and philosophical and scientific institutions. These serve to:

a. provide for production and enjoyment of aesthetic objects
b. provide for expression of religious feelings and beliefs and man's search for his relationship to the supernatural
c. provide learning for the young and adults
d. produce and distribute knowledge
e. help man understand himself and life's meaning.

4. Kinship Institutions. In the United States this category is represented by the family, which serves primarily to:

a. regulate sex behavior and propagate the species
b. provide a social context for bringing up the young
c. protect its members in sickness, misfortune, etc.

One must be productively engaged in one or more of these institutions and not merely a recipient of their benefits to be labeled a functioning member of society. A retiree with no family duties and no productive outlet for his energies or a person completely on welfare and with no family responsibilities would not be functional members of society. The youth are nonfunctioning when they have no duties in any of these institutions, for they are then simply the beneficiaries of the families, schools, and other social agencies that minister to their needs. This is the predicament of a large proportion of modern youth of all social strata and cultural groups. The nonfunctional role is harmful enough for the aged, but its influence upon the youth is far greater as it debilitates their experience and dwarfs their development.

To be an informed member of society is not only to know about these functions but also to have experience in them. This experience is denied to most youths in the specialized, technological society of today. To share responsibility in these functions and to evaluate their performance is to behave as a citizen should. Of course, an individual can work all of his life in an institution or agency without developing a mental picture of these social functions just as he can study a function in the abstract and never understand its performance. This point emphasizes the importance of schooling in conjunction with socializing experiences. Social functions are suggested not as a basis of education, but as a frame within which to picture the range and kinds of contexts in which youth and adults can be associated. Work and schooling can be related through social functions. While work is rooted in these functions, the disciplines are their intellectual basis. For instance, economics has to do with the regulation of the economy, journalism and English with public information, and geography with resources. As will be evident in a later chapter, work and schooling can be seen as having common ground when their relations to social functions are made explicit.

Involvement of Youth

How are the youth to engage in these social functions? Their engagement can be entrusted to the automatic operation of social forces as it is now. To follow this course is to make no planned and systematic provision for the great majority of youth to take on the informal knowledge, personal commitments, and sense of responsibility for oneself and others expected of an adult. The alternative is to formulate plans and act upon them. Whatever plans are finally settled upon will necessarily include youth's participation in the occupational system, where adults participate in the functions of society and where youth can be significantly associated with them. The scenario of the plan proposed here is as follows: Suppose each social function is performed in a number of ways. For example, goods are produced in ways too numerous to mention and by the activities of a large proportion of the population. The same can be said of the production of knowledge, the administration of justice, the provision of services, and indeed all other social functions. If all productive activities engaged in by members of society were classified, they could then be coordinated with social functions. This coordination would constitute a master chart showing the range of functions in which youth can be involved and the possible activities through which their participation can be realized.

The participation of members of society in these functions is called work. The work of a housewife is to provide a wholesome environment for her family, the work of an artist is to produce aesthetic objects, and the work of a salesman is to sell a product. Some 40,000 forms of work are listed in the *Dictionary of Occupational Titles*,[9] grouped into twelve occupational categories. These, including instances of each, are as follows:

1. Professions: artists, librarians, nurses, surveyors, interpreters
2. Technical: auditors, radio announcers, airplane navigators, insurance underwriters, athletes
3. Managerial: city managers, store managers, public ser-

vice directors, airport superintendents, fashion coordinators, broadcasting program directors
4. Clerical: court reporters, proofreaders, cashiers, bank
tellers, stock clerks, bookkeepers
5. Salesman: insurance agents, home furnishings salesmen, food product salesmen, ticket brokers, routemen,
auctioneers
6. Services: chefs, barbers, ushers, exterminators, bridge
operators, detectives
7. Farming, Fishery, and Forestry: forest rangers, park
caretakers, sap collectors, greenskeepers, nurserymen,
fishing guides
8. Processing: enamelers, kiln operators, jewelry casters,
electroplaters, furnace tenders, dough mixers
9. Machine Trades: tool and die makers, gear inspectors,
press operators, bag sewers, auto mechanics, typewriter
servicemen
10. Bench Work: radio repairman, jewelers, dental cera-
mists, painters, seamstresses, paper pattern folders
11. Structural Work: welders, plasterers, pipe fitters, ditch
diggers, road oilers, roofers
12. Miscellaneous: logging, baggagemen, bookbinders,
waste disposal men, stationary engineers, blasters.

These categories are related to social functions. Farmers
produce goods. Librarians disseminate information. Some
occupations are connected with more than one function.
Political economists serve the government as well as private
agencies for production and distribution of goods and services.
Priests provide for the expression of religious sentiment and
also disseminate information.

Work is the primary means by which youth can participate
in social functions. When work is added to the family and
the school, the basic agencies of socialization are pretty well
exhausted, although the church, mass media, and many
voluntary organizations can be added. The influence of the
church is still strong even in the secular atmosphere that
prevails today. The mass media's effect on youth is controver-

sial; much evidence indicates that it is a countervailing influence.[10]

The work youth should engage in cannot be decided in blanket terms. Rather, each individual must be considered in reference to his abilities and interests and the character of various work situations. Occupations differ widely in their socializing influences. Some involve little contact with persons. They are object-centered rather than human-centered. A radio repairman works with things, and his association with persons is infrequent and impersonal compared to the work of a school counselor. The latter works with persons rather than objects. He is constantly in close association with other persons. The performance of workers in some occupations is programmed. Other occupations provide little structuring and leave a wide range of decisions to the individual. The development of a program of socialization requires that occupations be analyzed to determine the demands they make upon the individual and the range and kinds of experiences they make possible.* In addition, each youth must think about himself, his interests, his strengths and weaknesses, and his goals. His particular characteristics are to be considered in relation to social functions and their occupations. When all these factors have been taken into account by an individual and his advisers, he should then work out a program of socialization through work covering at least one social function of the political, economic, and expressive-integrative categories. The objective of an overall program should be to provide each youth with experiences in at least one occupation in each category of social functions.

The survey of social functions and their corresponding agencies, the determination of the ways youth can be engaged, and the mobilization, coordination, and placement of youth in these agencies is not something that can occur without extensive planning, management, and financial and public

---

*Fortunately, a considerable part of this analysis is to be found in the *Dictionary of Occupational Titles.*

support. How is this to be done? The interrelations in society are so numerous and complex that it would be hazardous to launch a national plan. Different plans serving as guides in the development of trial units are needed. It is likely that with adequate support and leadership one or more of these trial units could be actualized on a wide scale.

No attempt is made here to work out the details of operational plans, but some guiding principles can be suggested. The trial units should provide for activities in all social functions so that the youth can have access to the full range of adult responsibilities and experiences. Evaluation procedures should be an inherent part of the planning and operation of each unit. One set of evaluative criteria should be drawn from the developmental tasks and such elaboration of these as is necessary for clarification and behavioral specificity. Another set should be developed for evaluating efficiency of operation and the cost benefits to participating agencies, the society, and the individual youth. Ample time should be allowed for thorough planning and preparation before a unit begins to operate. Some trial units should be operated by the adult community and some by the school to determine the feasibility of different approaches.

The work program can be coordinated with the school program in at least two ways. The daily schedules of the school and work can be matched to provide time for both programs. The instructional program can be correlated with social functions to provide the youth with learning experiences appropriate to their work.

Consideration of Objections

Several objections are likely to be raised against this proposal for the assimilation of youth. One will probably come from those who are contemptuous of adjustment and scornful of compromises to make the social system work. Any adjustment in the system to improve the status of youth is likely to be viewed as selling out to the establishment. The old

Protestant ethic will be trotted out and kicked around again; the "corporate state syndrome" will be rehearsed.

A viable society must not only tolerate but encourage individuals who are primarily concerned about the future and consequently weigh present circumstances and tendencies against extraordinary ideals. Tney serve to keep the age aware of its potential and to warn of the shoals ahead. It is well to remember that they have no monopoly on the power to forecast the future. Whether the forecasters be intellectual giants or analysts of lesser stature is unimportant. They can speculate about the shape of the future, but they know nothing positively. It is all supposition. Data and laws of social dynamics are not available to forecast future states of society. Criticism of the present derives from one's ideas of history and his own intellectual standpoint. The best one has are a few facts about present conditions and tendencies. Forecasts made from such a precarious base are to be taken judiciously.

The socialization of youth, like schooling, is always bound by space and time. It can occur only here and now. It is risky enough to induct youth into a mode of life that is; it is downright foolish to attempt to induct them into one that is merely prophesied and in fact may never exist. The social functions mentioned above will most likely be performed in the future in about the same way as they are now. Their performance will involve the entire adult population in one way or another. The involvement of youth portends few evils compared with the failure to involve them.

A second objection is likely to stem from those who believe that business, industrial, agricultural, and professional enterprises are committed to making money and not to humanitarian objectives. Consequently, it will be almost impossible for these segments of society to commit themselves to an educational venture that has no direct financial return. It is true that some leaders in these enterprises resist proposals that negatively affect their corporate interests. However, it is a fundamental fact that industry, commerce, agriculture, professional, and service enterprises reap benefits from the socialization of youth. Without high-level performance of workers, wise consumers, and an orderly community, no enterprise is likely to prosper. Many business and professional people recognize this fact. They know that their obligation to foster the proper development of youth is no less than their obligation to serve the public.[11]

It is likely that spokesmen for minorities and the poor will claim that the proposal allows for further exploitation of these groups. Some will say that poor and minority youth will be placed in menial labor situations while their affluent counterparts will be assigned to advantageous situations. Their suspicion is justified, for discrimination has occurred in school programs. The chance of discrimination in the program of assimilation constitutes a problem, not a weakness in the proposal itself. Indeed, discrimination of this sort occurs in the present state of affairs. The chance of eliminating it is greatly increased in an assimilation program that embraces all youth. If there are unfair practices, they can be identified and dealt with explicitly. In the absence of a program, the discriminations go unattended because no one can be held accountable. The whole matter is passed off by some as an evil of the establishment and by others as the lot of the incompetent.

The greatest challenge to those who attempt to improve the processes of assimilation will be given by the youth of the rural slums and the ghettoes. This is because the institutions and agencies through which social functions are performed are not as available to these youth as to those in more favorable localities. Solving this unequal distribution of opportunities is a problem of great import. The requirements of its solution can be determined only by extensive investigation into particular cases. Perhaps no general answer will be possible. Complete solution may wait upon social and economic changes not yet in the political hopper, but a beginning should be made now no matter how adverse the local circumstances.

FOOTNOTES

[1] Robert J. Havighurst, *Human Development and Education* (New York: Longmans, Green and Company, 1953), pp. 9–41; 111–58.

[2] These tasks were worked out about twenty years ago, long before the drive to eliminate sex bias in the society. Item 5, 13, and 20 must now be considered controversial. If interpreted in the spirit of present-day context, they can stand.

[3] Panel on Youth of the President's Science Advisory Committee, *Transition to Adulthood,* op. cit.

[4] J. P. Lisack, *Changing Trends in the Plans of High School Seniors,* Manpower Report 73-1 (West Lafayette, Ind.: Office of Manpower Studies, School of Technology, Purdue University, 1973), p. 11.

[5] Edward B. Reuter, *Handbook of Sociology* (New York: Dryden Press, 1941), p. 113.

[6] Alex Inkeles, *What is Sociology?* (Englewood Cliffs, N.J.: Prentice-Hall, 1965), p. 68. See also Joseph S. Roucek and Roland L. Warren, *Sociology* (Patterson, N.J.: Littlefield, Adams and Company, 1962), for a simple discussion of institutional functions.

[7] Ibid., p. 68.

[8] The first workers to use social functions as an approach to program development were Hollis L. Caswell and Doak S. Campbell in the development of a core curriculum in the State of Virginia. See their *Curriculum Development* (New York: American Book, 1935), pp. 173–84. They used these functions to define the scope of the core curriculum. It is interesting to note their rationale. "This procedure is based on the assumption that the activities of children in school should be organized in such a way as to carry over with greatest ease to real life situations. This concept of organization of the instructional program suggests that the school program should provide in so far as possible for children to gain an increasing understanding of the issues and problems encountered outside the school, should aid them in developing desirable controls of conduct that operate in meeting such issues and problems, and should give them opportunity to participate extensively in such real situations. This procedure further assumes that an adequate program of education will provide for the introduction of the child to all of the important areas of activity in real life and will provide for his gradual induction into participation in these activities."

[9] U.S. Department of Labor, *Dictionary of Occupational Titles,* Vols. I and II (3rd ed., Washington, D.C.: U.S. Government Printing Office, 1965).

[10] An early summary of studies is found in Edgar Dale and Harold A. Wilson, "Mass Media," *Encyclopedia of Educational Research*, 3rd ed., pp. 794f. The findings reported there have not been discounted.

[11] Report of a special Task Force of the Secretary of Health, Education, and Welfare, *Work in America* (Cambridge, Mass.: The MIT Press, 1973), pp. 24f; 93–120.

CHAPTER IV

The Utility of Schooling

Youth gain adult modes of behavior by participating in the agencies that perform specific social functions. They acquire the norms, folkways, social skills, and aspirations that enable them to assume the roles of adults. The obligation of all social institutions is to provide for participation. However, there is more than this to socialization. The youth must also be introduced to the realm of systematized knowledge, aesthetic and moral traditions, and skills of communication. The school's unique responsibility is to provide this introduction.

As pointed out in the first chapter, the school, like the entire socializing process, is in need of reform. Its attempt to teach fundamental processes to all youth, while more successful than is generally recognized, falls far short of meeting the profession's goal; its failure to adjust to the poverty of youth's experience and its lack of flexibility are all too evident. The process of schooling, however, cannot be reformed in the abstract by some pedagogical formula grounded in indubitable principles. In the absence of systematic theory, an eclectic approach is more likely to be effective. Renewal is apt to be successful if it selects variables most closely

associated with the school's impact on learning and appropriately modifies these variables.

The first problem of school reform, however, is how to assess
changes in the school. The task is complex because the school
is a part of a social system, and changes in it must be evaluated
by reference to their effects on the system as well as on
individuals. Evaluation of pupil progress, it must be emphasized, is not the same as evaluation of changes in the school
itself.

The problem of how to determine the benefits of changes
in the school is almost completely neglected. One plan after
another is being advanced to make schooling more effective.
Measures that have been offered as cures for the ills of the
school and have turned out to be fruitless litter the trail
of educational history. Most of the reform literature of today,
like that of the past, gets its data from the predilections
of the authors. The authors believe they are stating and solving
an objective problem: What kind of schooling is more beneficial
than the present one? In fact, they are not solving an objective
problem at all but a subjective one: What form of schooling
best fits my predilections? They are encapsulated by their
own predispositions, certain that intelligent men and women
will share their view of what constitutes a good education
and how the schools should be improved. These reformers
are not aware of their subjectivity or the circularity of their
reasoning. They take as proven the very thing they are trying
to establish about the quality of schooling.[1]

The Meaning of Utility

How to deal with this subjectivity is the purpose of the
present chapter. In its most general form, the question is:
What is the utility of schooling? First of all, what is utility?
Simply stated, it consists of the benefits to the individual
or society that accrue from schooling. Utility is to be distinguished from objectives of instruction. Objectives can be stated

in terms of teachable objects.* Among these are concepts, laws, rules, procedures, values, facts, skills, explanations, and interpretations. These are knowledge forms that teachers deal with as they plan and conduct their teaching and that they expect pupils to acquire. The benefits from individuals' use of these learnings or the benefits to society that result from schooling individuals in them constitute their utility. Arithmetic operations can be taught and learned, but they are not utilities. If the individual is efficient in managing his income because of his knowledge of arithmetic, or if the national wealth is increased because of widespread ability in arithmetic, these can be counted as utilities. Utilities are not teachable. The teaching profession is not accountable for them, but it is responsible for seeing that the objectives of instruction are realized at levels that render them usable.

Lagging support of schools and the pressure to reduce compulsory attendance are enough to drive one to raise such questions as these: What are the advantages of schooling for society and for the individual? What level of schooling corresponds to the point of diminishing returns? Is the answer for society different from that for the individual? For different individuals? For different societies? For the same society at different stages of development? The notion that the compulsory attendance age should be lowered and that alternative forms of education should be provided are being advocated and defended by expedient arguments. The data base on which to make such decisions is woefully deficient. Criteria for assessing the benefits of schooling are few, and, except for studies in the economics of education, practically no empirical studies have been made of either the social or personal dividends of schooling.

To determine the utility of schooling, it is necessary to collect and organize data on the benefits of schooling to the

*The expression, "teachable objects," is taken from the works of Kenneth B. Henderson.

individual and society. To escape subjective biases, data should be collected by public criteria. The determination of these criteria is a complex process, and the collection and organization of relevant data are perhaps even more taxing. All that can be done here is to set forth some of the criteria found in the current literature and to indicate in a general way what their use would probably lead to.[2]

These benefits can be classified as follows:

1. Benefits that accrue to the individual
   a. Admission to the labor force
   b. Increase in income
   c. Multiplication of options
   d. Personal development
2. Benefits to other individuals
   a. Advantages to employers
   b. Enrichment of community activities
3. Benefits to society
   a. Advantages to a market economy
   b. Contributions to economic growth
   c. Contributions to political behavior
   d. Contributions to social cohesion.

The Criteria Problem: Admission to Work

The first issue to be considered is the utility of basic knowledge and skills. There is little question about the desirability of fundamental learning. Almost everyone agrees that children should be taught to read, write, calculate, and to understand basic concepts and principles. Anyone who fails to acquire these abilities risks exploitation throughout his life and an inferior level of life in his personal and social existence. These abilities are important to a nation whose populace works in a wide range of occupations and makes decisions about personal and societal issues. The school should guarantee that all pupils reach minimum levels of achievement in fundamentals. Exceptions to this standard should include only those few pupils whose learning potential is severely hampered by physical, mental, or emotional characteristics that render them incapable of achieving the minimum levels. These pupils should be included in as much of the school program as might be beneficial to them.

The level of achievement the school should accept as its goal must be determined. Several minimum levels of proficiency in one of the basic learnings, reading, have been suggested. One is that illiteracy should be eliminated. But what is illiteracy? According to one definition, a person who cannot read or write any language is illiterate. By this standard, 20 percent of the population of the United States was illiterate 100 years ago. Today the illiteracy rate in the population 14 years of age and over is less than 1 percent.

Another conception of illiteracy is called "functional illiteracy." It is defined in relation to amount of formal education.[3] This notion of illiteracy originated in the 1930s with the Civilian Conservation Corps. It was found that men with less than three years of schooling could not follow directions or perform tasks successfully. These men were classed as functional illiterates. During the Second World War, the army defined the functional illiterate as one who had had less than four years of schooling. The level of schooling set in the 1960s by government officials concerned with the problems of poverty was a sixth-grade education. It was estimated that about 8 million Americans were functional illiterates, most of them older members of the population. It has been pointed out that by this criterion Abraham Lincoln and a host of other successful Americans were illiterate.

The census data yield no reliable information about the number of persons who can read and write. The criterion of reading and writing ability is indefinite, and the census taker gives no test of the individual's ability to read and write. Because of these shortcomings, other ways of estimating the school's success have been followed.

Perhaps the most common criterion for deciding the school's success in teaching fundamental skills and knowledge is the grade norm. It has been employed to determine whether the benefits of schooling are equitably distributed among the regions and social groups of society. By isolating a target group, for example, the American Indian, and comparing its average achievement to the average of the total group, it can be determined if the school is adequately preparing the target group in basic skills. In this approach those above the grade norm are regarded as adequately served by the school. The pupils whose performance is below the norm are considered to be those on whom the school's influence has been less desirable. If a large proportion of a target group falls below the norm (say, 70 percent), it is concluded that the school is failing with that group.

One of the most frequently cited studies of the school's effectiveness in teaching basic skills to minority groups, using grade norms as the criterion, is the Coleman report on inequality. According to this report, reading comprehension of the average black nonmetropolitan student in the sixth grade is over two grade levels behind his white counterpart in the metropolitan Northeast. Compared to the metropolitan white student, the metropolitan black is 1.8 grade levels below the grade norm in the Northeast, 1.8 in the Midwest, 2.1 in the South, 2.1 in the Southwest, and 2.1 in the West. Mexican-Americans are 2.4 grades below; Puerto Ricans, 3.1; American Indians, 2; and Oriental-Americans, 1.[4] The retardation in mathematics is in the same direction and slightly larger. Furthermore, children of the poor tend on the whole to lose about .3 of a grade in achievement each year, and the loss is cumulative so that by the twelfth grade their schooling has been discounted by almost four years.

Not only are there differences in the effects of schooling upon the poor, the minorities, and the white affluent but there are also regional differences in the country. The inequities in school achievement as reported in the literature reveal that the lowest achieving pupils in the nation are found in the rural Southeast and the poverty-stricken inner city. At the other extreme, the suburban pupils in the Northwest and the West surpass the South, although neither region equals the achievement of its counterpart in the Northeast.[5]

The foregoing data on differences in achievement among regions and various minority groups are in themselves interesting, and one could make extensive studies to explain them. But what do they mean in practical terms? Do they indicate that the school is foundering in its efforts to teach basic skills? If one is concerned with the question of equality as between minority groups and the white majority with respect to achievement, he is likely to answer yes. But if he is concerned with the question of whether or not pupils in the lowest 25 percent of the grade distribution are learning enough to pursue further knowledge, to enter a gainful occupation, and to perform other activities expected of a member of society, his answer may be less positive.

Grade norms assume that pupil performance establishes standards against which to compare the achievement of individuals and groups. Schooling that results in higher grade norms is typically judged to be better. But reliance solely on an achievement criterion begs the question. The preference for greater achievement is left without justification except for the claim that achievement is good in itself. This position provides no external standard for judging schooling or for deciding how much formal learning a society should provide for its members. To ask if a particular level of pupil achievement is adequate is to ask an incomplete question; one must also question for what is it adequate. Without an external criterion, the answer must be that achievement is adequate in itself. This answer is pointless. To escape this circularity, an external standard for assessing pupil achievement must be found. The most satisfactory approach is to look for a measure of utility.

The matter can be put differently. The criterion should not be one that compares an individual with the average achievement of his age group. Rather, it should address the question of how much and what kind of learning the society should require of all individuals. Aside from societal maintenance and well-being, the purpose of schooling is to induce learning sufficient to enable the individual to assume an adult role. The criterion should specify an achievement floor in basic knowledge and skills below which none would be permitted to fall, except for cases of extreme disability. If the analysis in preceding chapters is correct, this floor should be the threshold to the realm of work. Those who reach it would thereby be admitted to the labor market without penalty for inability to read, write, calculate, and use fundamental knowledge.

Unfortunately, there is no empirical basis for such a criterion, although the utility of certain knowledge (arithmetic operations, for instance) was a subject of much interest in the early years of educational research.[6] Nevertheless, it is possible to approach it by using the judgment of competent persons. If the performance expectations of everyday life can be decided upon by a board of judges and the ability of pupils to perform these expectations can be measured by tests, then it would be possible to begin the development of a criterion of utility such as is suggested here. As pupils progress through school they would advance toward this floor each year. With an improved program it could be established empirically that by a specified time every pupil will reach the level of achievement agreed upon by competent judges. This is the position developed in the next chapter. It is by no means certain that a floor thus established provides admission to the world of work. It may still be so low that pupils who just reached it are ruled out of jobs because of deficient skills and knowledge. Only follow-up studies can validate the criterion set by expert opinion.

How can one determine that the level of achievement judged as adequate by competent persons matches the level of competence required by the world of work? To answer this question is to decide what knowledge and skills are required by some selected level of employment. Doubtless there are different ways of dealing with this question. Only the outlines of a possible way can be given here. Assume that occupations can be arranged on a continuum, with the most menial jobs at one end and the most intellectually demanding at the other.

For example, structural occupations (welders, plasterers, etc.) might be at the lower end and professional occupations (constitutional lawyers, research workers, etc.) at the higher end of the series. Suppose also that some group of occupations on the continuum is selected as the criterion group. Service occupations, for instance, may be selected because this group includes a large proportion of the labor force and because it falls near the midpoint of the continuum. Then tests should be designed to measure the performance expectations selected by competent judges as suggested in the following chapter. These tests can be given to a random sample of persons in the service occupations. Their test scores could then be used to set an achievement level. It would be assumed that anyone who reaches this level of achievement would be able to enter the labor force at and below the service level. This criterion is independent of the instructional program and emphasizes a basic utility of schooling.

This approach has certain shortcomings. For one thing, many individuals could undoubtedly enter the labor market even though they fail to attain the floor of achievement thus established. But this objection can be raised against other floors. The question then becomes one of deciding upon an optimum floor in terms of the range of occupations possible between the most menial labor and that for which the floor provides admission. For another thing, there are activities outside the world of work that require fundamental knowledge such as purchasing insurance, protecting one's rights, and managing money. But the problem of validating the judgment of experts in this case appears to be about the same as that in the case of arithmetic and reading. It may involve the selection of a different reference group, since there is reason to doubt that present-day occupational groups have sufficient knowledge to function adequately outside their positions of employment.

It can also be said that pupils are preparing for an adult life but that that life is not the same as that of today's adults. The youth will require standards and activities that adults have not experienced. Hence a floor of fundamental knowledge cannot be based on adult performance. There is some justification of this criticism, especially if the desocialization of adult society is not checked. But this objection is itself hypothetical and can best be confirmed by empirical studies. In any case, testing of adults as a check on expert judgment does not seem to be out of reason even if exclusive reliance on adult norms turned out to be inadequate. However, the techniques and procedures for empirically validating expert opinion are outside the purpose of this treatment of the topic.

The Criteria Problem: Other Individual Benefits

Once the individual enters the labor market, his income is associated with the amount of schooling he has had. It is to be understood that this relationship is based on averages and is not necessarily true for particular individuals. For large numbers, however, it is quite clear that income and schooling are positively correlated.

The individual forgoes wages while he is in school and thereby invests in his own schooling. On the other hand, he stands to gain higher earnings with schooling. Is there a point of maximum economic return from his investment? Perhaps few individuals look at their schooling in this way, but there is such a point. Some authorities report that on the average the greatest rate of returns on the individual's investment is derived from elementary school, the next from high school, and, finally, from college.[7] The maximum rate of return is apparently derived from elementary schooling. Of course, the rate of return will vary with the individual's ability, energy, and social status. Obviously, if an individual invests in schooling and social barriers preclude the use of his learning for economic gain, his investment is depreciated.

Schooling also increases the individual's options along a number of dimensions. It enhances his job opportunities. The band on the spectrum of occupations from which an individual may choose to seek employment widens with increased schooling. One who has just reached the achievement floor in basic knowledge and skills will be restricted in the jobs he can expect to get, while the individual who has completed more advanced levels has a wider range of job options.[8] In some cases schooling can also restrict the individual's chances of employment. A highly specialized person may find his job opportunities greatly restricted. A professional engineer may not be able to find employment in a job market oversupplied with engineers as readily as a person with only a high school diploma. Unable to find employment in his profession, the engineer will seek alternative jobs at a salary commensurate with his ability. Anything less would be a sacrifice of his training and ability as well as of the values of his life style. He is likely to seek work in service activities for which his specialized training is more of a handicap than an asset. The employer is apt to look askance at one who is overtrained for the level of occupation in which he seeks work. If this analysis is correct, there is a level of schooling at which job options are maximized.

Schooling not only increases employment opportunities but also options of life-styles. Many patterns of life are possible in an industrial society. For example, one can live a "life of carefree wholesome enjoyment," of "meditation and study," of "group participation and group enjoyment," and of "sympathetic concern for others."[9] On the average the range of choices among these styles is contingent upon the amount of schooling one has had. Ordinarily a high school graduate will have more options than an elementary school graduate, and a college graduate will probably have more than a high school graduate. Again the relation between schooling and life-style options is probably not linear. There appears to be no good reason to suppose that continuous increase in years of schooling will indefinitely multiply one's choices among ways of life. Perhaps one who settles for a bachelor's degree will have as many options, other things being equal, as one who completes a doctor's degree. Although one can hypothesize that a college graduate has more options, four years of high school may be as near the maximum as a college degree, for all we know.

The individual benefits from schooling in still another way. The school contributes to his development as a person. Every individual possesses potentials. The richer and more open the society the better are his chances to actualize his potentials. The school is dedicated to this end. This is a moral aim of schooling and is discussed as a form of equality in the last part of this chapter. Its utility is the individual's satisfaction resulting from his growth. This utility is associated with the humanistic tradition, which emphasizes schooling as a means of self-actualization, self-direction, and adequacy, although personal development may accompany all forms of learning regardless of their utility. The individual pursues knowledge because it gives him satisfaction. If self-fulfillment is the realization of one's aspirations through his own efforts, this benefit is associated with no particular knowledge or skill— academic, vocational, or otherwise. It all depends upon the individual's private sense of satisfaction. In the pursuit of learning for this benefit, is there a point of diminishing satisfaction with the expenditure of one's energies? Theoretically there is. But it could be true only for knowledge about particular things since one's appetite for learning shifts from time to time from one thing to another and is perhaps insatiable except for specific ends.

The individual is not the only recipient of the benefits of schooling. Others also benefit from it.[10] The profits of schooling spill over into various activities that affect other individuals. The employer who must depend upon the performance of his employees benefits from the work of the school. The success of his enterprise often depends as much upon the abilities and sincerity of those who work for him as upon his own efforts. The individual's schooling not only increases the quality of his labor but also helps to enrich the experiences of his neighbors. Their aesthetic life, as reflected in clubs, choral groups, art and flower shows, landscaping, care of the home, and social life are heightened in some measure by his schooling. A neighborhood of persons who have completed high school would be likely to be rated higher in terms of the quality of its culture than one whose schooling did not exceed the elementary grades.

The Criteria Problem: The General Case

Schooling can be beneficial to society as well as to the individual and his neighbors. The society can benefit in two ways: collectively and distributively.[11] In the first case the advantages accrue to society as a whole, but they affect individuals differently. In the second case the society benefits as a whole, and at the same time all individuals are affected in the same direction. Neither form of utility takes into account the needs of individual members of society.

A form of schooling that produces scientists and technicians to build an efficient military machine can work to the advantage of the society as an aggregate in its struggle with other nations. This can have differential effects on individuals, assuming limited funds for education. The lower classes can be affected deleteriously by this policy, since their learning may be neglected. The more affluent classes can profit because of the educational and economic advantages enabled by military education.

Educational policies that affect the nation collectively are likely to be controversial. If a nation faces the problem of whether to support extensive expenditures for the production of scientists and technicians to strengthen its position in relation to other nations or to emphasize schooling for the masses, the matter is likely to be unsettling. If one considers the nation's security and nothing else, he will decide that the sacrifice of the masses' schooling is beneficial. On the other hand, if another person takes into account only the benefits to the masses, neglecting any indirect benefits they may gain, he will conclude that sacrificing their schooling is morally wrong. It is nonsense to ask who is right in the absence of a criterion for rendering the two opinions comparable. In the absence of such a criterion, any discussion of the issue will only produce rationalizations that cover up the real motives.

A change in schooling can increase the school's utility for society and at the same time can benefit all individuals. This is utility for the society distributively. The expenditure of public money under the Smith-Hughes Act to advance vocational education was beneficial both to the society and all individuals. The society was strengthened in its relationship to other societies since a trained labor force enhances production. At the same time every member of society benefits, assuming an increased supply of consumer goods and a higher national income resulting from a more productive labor force. A change in the school that results in an increase in the gross national product would be beneficial to the society, and each individual would also benefit from the improved economic conditions. If the school were to increase the amount of political participation, it would thereby benefit the society distributively. In this form of utility, changes in the school can increase the advantages to individuals when affecting the society as a whole.

A polity will necessarily be concerned with the societal benefits of schooling. It assumes that the establishment of schools will enhance the society. In its early periods of development a polity is not likely to support schools merely for personal benefits such as self-actualization. When the concerns of the polity for societal benefits have been satisfied, the advantages of schooling for the individual can then be more readily sanctioned. It is likely that personal utility for every body *per se* is possible only under special circumstances of great wealth and optimum distribution, a condition that few societies are approaching. In technological societies, and in those that aspire to be so, the policy of gearing the school to the needs of society itself dominates.

The American government has tended to place great emphasis upon schooling for economic production and defense. This is evident in the various educational acts of the national government. The Morrill Act to support colleges, the Smith-Hughes Act to support vocational education, the Smith-Lever Act to diffuse information about agriculture and home economics, the Reserve Officers Training Corps, Army Training Programs, and recent efforts to launch a program of career education support this statement. In addition, states have enacted laws exercising control over the curriculum in the interest of collective advantages. For example, many states require American history in the schools to preserve traditions and promote patriotism. Meanwhile, schoolmen and educational theorists were committing the school to the production of certain societal results, expressed generally in the Cardinal Principles of Secondary Education: command of fundamental processes, worthy home membership, vocational efficiency, citizenship, worthy use of leisure, ethical character, and health.

The failure to distinguish between objectives of instruction and utility is a constant source of confusion in educational literature. All but one of the cardinal principles are utilities and not objectives. Achievement in the fundamental processes is not a utility, but learning that is useful because of what it enables the individual to do in life. The other objectives are societal benefits. The school can teach knowledge and skills that might enable an individual to be a worthy member of a home, a good citizen, and an efficient worker, but it can have only limited influence on the development of the kind of person who will use the knowledge and skill to these ends. This confusion lies at the base of the issues about the accountability of the school. The school can be held accountable for whatever can be tested, such as knowledge and skills. But it is not accountable for the uses they are put to, for the teacher cannot control the ends for which knowledge will be used.

Some of the societal ends to which schooling contributes, theoretically at least, were mentioned in the preceding section, specifically, maintenance of a market economy, economic growth, political wisdom, and social cohesion.

The market system in an industrial society is dependent upon the transmission of information. The vast system of communication—newspapers, books, magazines, and other media—by which human wants are stimulated and channeled underwrites the distribution of goods and services. This system is possible because of widespread literacy. What people want and what they strive to get is what they know about. The better informed they are, the more likely they are to choose wisely. They can thus affect the market itself. It is likely that this benefit begins to decrease at an undetermined level of schooling. For all that is known, little advantage along this line may result from schooling beyond the secondary level. But an extensive study of consumption patterns of different educational strata and their effects on marketing practices should probably illuminate this aspect of the school's utility.

For more than forty years the primary measure of the economy's status has been growth in the national income or the gross national product, which is approximately the same. One societal goal is to increase, or at least maintain, economic growth. Does schooling contribute to this end? Considerable research has already been done on the relation of schooling to this goal. While the research has not produced conclusive evidence on the relationship, it has given approximations and pointed the way to more adequate methodological procedures. How much does schooling contribute to economic growth? The amount of the contribution depends upon the level of the society's development. Roughly speaking, the investment in schooling in advanced nations enjoys about the same returns as investment in physical capital. In developing nations the payoff of investment in physical capital is less than for investment in schooling. The highest percent of return is from elementary schooling, while higher education yields the lowest.[12]

These estimates of the contribution of schooling to growth take no account of the content of schooling except as it is reflected in the educational levels. It is safe to assume that the content of elementary schooling consists in fundamental skills and knowledge. At the secondary and higher education levels, content can be extremely varied. Apparently the content of elementary schooling has a high payoff economically, since elementary schooling accounts for almost half of the contribution of schooling to economic growth.[13] At higher levels the comparative efficacy of one kind of content is indefinite. Using influence on economic growth as a criterion, data from a few developing countries faintly indicate no superiority of technical over general secondary schooling.[14]

An open society depends upon the political behavior and wisdom of its members. Their political beliefs and practices are acquired from a number of sources: participation in neighborhood and community activities, newspapers and other media, family associations, and so on. It is widely held that the school also helps to develop awareness of social and political issues, national goals, and basic values. In addition it is claimed that the school develops the ability to participate in the democratic process. The development of the individual along these lines presumably contributes to a stable, progressive society and thus benefits the social system as a whole as well as individuals.

Is this claim true? Does schooling enhance political behavior? Measures of political behavior are in their infancy, and their capacity as indicators of a healthy democracy is not yet determined. The indices are chiefly concerned with participation in political activities. Some of these are: active membership in political organizations, attendance at political meetings, support of candidates, voting, and influencing the vote of others. Data bearing on these indices show that the higher the level of schooling the individual attains, the more likely he is to become engaged politically in these ways.[15]

A society must have some degree of social unity in order to carry on its various functions.[16] It can undergo one dissension after another as long as there is common ground on which to stand while the struggles over issues and conflicting commitments are being settled. In an open society some of the ingredients of the common ground are commitment to procedure, belief in common virtues, traditions, ideology, and in the taming of all forms of power. Whatever values may characterize a society, it is watchful of its unity. A society always attempts to safeguard its cohesion by force, by control of communication, by schooling, and by such other means as may from time to time appear to be effective. The belief that schooling contributes significantly to the cohesion of society is deep-seated in advanced countries. It partially explains state laws specifying that American history and patriotism be taught in the public schools of the United States.

Does schooling contribute to the cohesion of American society? Leaders of the teaching profession sometimes claim that it does. It is said that the school teaches social values, that it inculcates a way of life, and that it disciplines youth in the procedures for identifying and criticizing values and resolving conflicts. These are what the school supposedly teaches. But that is not at issue. The basic question is: What are the indices of social cohesion? Clues to indicators of cohesion are hard to come by in the literature. Only a few suggestions can be given here. The degree of social cohesion may be indicated by the ability of a society to meet its internal and external conflicts constructively, the amount of like response to symbols, the amount of consensus on ideals, the ability to stand together in a social crisis, and the similarity of outlook across generations.

The contribution of schooling to social cohesion is probably conditioned by its purpose as much as by its quantity. A program of schooling that emphasizes economic returns on one's investment in schooling rather than other utilities is likely to yield a disintegrative effect in a prolonged or severe crisis such as the Great Depression of the 1930s. Furthermore, if this utility is highlighted in justification of higher education, a large supply of highly trained people who cannot find employment commensurate with their training can be a source of dissension and bitter opposition to the system.

The general problem of social utility can now be restated. Knowledge, skills, and attitudes are taught in the school. These entities are testable, except perhaps for attitudes, and thus teachers can determine how effective their instruction is. Assume that the instruction induced the desired learnings. At this point, the school is successful, judged by its internal standards. But is it successful when social dividends are considered? At the present time this question can be partly answered for economic utility; for other social returns the answer cannot be given. It is possible to state something of what an empirical answer would require. Assume that the goals of a society are identified. Assume also that the maximum and minimum effects of schooling upon society's progress toward these ends are determined. If numerical indices are then assigned to different levels of schooling that approximate the point of maximum return, it can be said that these indices are a measure of the utility of schooling.

To sum up, it is well to bear in mind that the suggested list of utilities is only partial and is not as important as the problem posed. An exhaustive list of possible utilities is not needed. The aim of research should be to establish a few crucial criteria by which to determine what schooling is most beneficial to society and the individual. Issues concerning what programs the school should provide, whether general or technical schooling is better, how much schooling should be compulsory, alternative forms of schooling, or alternatives to schooling itself are being discussed in a data vacuum. In the absence of external criteria to guide the collection and interpretation of data on these issues, one hears arguments based on personal experience, random observations, sentiments, and pedagogical and social doctrines. At best these issues are considered in the light of data bearing on dropout rates, achievement of poverty groups, equality of educational opportunity, adolescent interests and problems, changes in the character of school populations, and the like. Until research has established criteria for determining the benefits of schooling, basic educational policies will continue to be decided by idle and inconclusive arguments and inadequate data.

Some fundamental questions could be answered were a breakthrough on this problem to occur. How many years of schooling should be required? What should be the minimum level of achievement in basic skills and various areas of knowledge? What is the school accountable for? How much emphasis can be given to schooling for self-realization? Consider an abstract society in which progressive changes in the school continue to increase the level of schooling of the total population. Would the crucial social utilities of schooling reach a maximum? Theoretically, they would. The maximum would be the point where the benefits would no longer be increased by an increase in schooling for the populace. At this point there would be no reason to improve or extend the school for these utilities. The nation would then enjoy educational prosperity.

What about personal utility in this abstract society? An approach to this question can be made if it is assumed that the society must have economic and social well-being before it can devote energy to the ideal of self-cultivation on a universal scale. If this assumption were allowed, the society could turn to the utility of schooling for the personal development of every individual after the maximum of social utility is in sight. At last education could become its own end.

The Criteria Problem: The Moral Case

Neither the development of an achievement floor in fundamental skills nor the determination of the maximum social utility of schooling answers the claim that schools discriminate against minorities, women, and the poor. It is well established that the minorities fall behind the white majority in achievement and are unfairly treated by school personnel. It is incumbent upon anyone who proposes reform to show that these inequities will be corrected. The usual criterion of correctness is the principle of equality. This principle has been explicated in various ways, depending on the educational context. Four meanings of the principle dominate the literature: [17] Equality is a state of affairs in which:

1. any child is worth neither more nor less than any other child as an object of development;

2. the rules that apply to any child apply to all others alike;
3. any child has just as good an opportunity to learn as any other child;
4. any child acquires as much knowledge and skill as any other child.

These will be referred to respectively as moral equality, rules equality, equality of opportunity, and substantive equality. The first—moral equality—is the most fundamental in the sense that it is the end for which the others are means. One child may not be as capable as another of developing at the same rate, in the same direction, or to the same extent in a lifetime. But one human being is just as important as any other, not as a means but as an end; every person has his own potential, which must have proper conditions for its development. To thwart the development of an individual or social group is to commit the gravest social injustice.

If persons are equal in this moral sense, their development must be safeguarded. It can be done in three ways: equality of chances, equality of substance, and equality of rules. In the liberal tradition the approach is equality of chances and rules; in the socialistic tradition, equality of substance.

Consider first equality under the rules. Individuals are equal in a game in the sense that the rules apply alike to all players. To abide by the rules is to play fair; to have the rules applied impartially is to be treated as an equal. Rules equality is exemplified in courts of law where rules of evidence and procedure apply to all persons alike. It is exhibited in assemblies governed by parliamentary rules of order. It is manifested in schools when the rules are applied alike to pupils. It is found in all circumstances where behavior is governed by rules.

One must hasten to add that the rules themselves may be biased so that even their judicious application serves the advantage of some and the disadvantage of others. Perhaps one of the most serious types of discrimination is to be found in the fact that the rules of the game of life are often biased.

As long as one cannot live where he chooses, cannot be buried where he wishes, cannot get a job in occupations for which he is prepared, and cannot engage in any number of other activities of the society because the rules are not applied equally among men or because the rules are distorted or are made for ulterior purposes, he is denied rules equality. If a school treats a pupil differentially because of his social status rather than his potential or merit, the game is not being played fairly in that school. The rights of the individual are defined in terms of impartial rules; he has a right to those things to which rules entitle him as they entitle others.

Rules are often unstated. An individual may conform to a rule without being aware of it. A school counselor may constantly advise pupils from poor families toward certain types of occupations and affluent pupils toward others without being aware that he is conforming to a persistent decision pattern. The task of eliminating the discriminations and biases from the operation of the school necessitates ridding the personnel of its prejudices and the materials of instruction of the biases built into them. But the task is just as much a matter of cleaning up the rules and applying them alike to all pupils.

Consider next equality of opportunity or equality of chances. If A's chances to gain for himself the goods of life are neither greater nor less than B's, their chances are equal. They both have the same opportunity to develop as human beings. This is the classical liberal conception of equality. It was born in a period of protest against oppressive governments that regulated the social and economic activities of the individual. It therefore assumed that the removal of governmental restraints would free the individual to pursue his goals in his own way. With such freedom his chances in life would be the same as those of anyone else. It pictured the world as being out there for anyone and everyone, and every individual as having as good a chance as every other to turn it to his advantage so long as the government does not restrain him from doing so. Life is a race—if an individual does not place in the contest, if he does not get his share of the goods of life, if his plans go awry and his efforts come to naught, he has no one to blame apart from himself or Dame Fortune.

The classical concept of equality is formal. It simply says that one has a chance to do something for himself in life if the circumstances are favorable. In the classical interpretation, the circumstances are deemed to be favorable if the government does not interfere with one's activities. Strict interpretation of this conception would not include the establishment of public schools, as this would require the intervention of government guaranteeing a substantive contribution for the individual's benefit. Instead of the individual taking advantage of his opportunities in a *laissez-faire* society to gain as much learning as he wanted, the individual would be dependent upon the government for his schooling.

The classic conception of equality has always encountered troubles in practice because individuals begin life with all sorts of handicaps—economic, social, and political. Although it may have approximated reality on the frontier in early America, the social conditions assumed by this conception were always more fictional than real. This conception has rapidly eroded in recent decades and has tended to merge with the ideal of substantive equality: The notion that one person is treated as equal to another if he has as much of the material and cultural goods of life as any other.

It early became apparent that in society the chances were generally stacked against those who lacked basic skills and knowledge. Partly for this reason free schools were established. In time, even this was seen as insufficient. Teachers were not equally competent, and school facilities were poorer in some districts than in others. Steps were taken to remedy these inequities. The tendency has been to move ever more in the direction of substantive equality in order to equalize learning opportunities. Consequently, the ideal of equal opportunity has lost its original meaning. Opportunities are now considered to be equal only if the state intervenes to make the initial conditions for the race the same for everyone.

Educationally, this means that the quality of the school from community to community is to be made equal. If the personnel, buildings, laboratories, libraries, curriculum services, etc., of School A are of the same quality as those of School B, it is said that pupils in A have the same opportunities as pupils in B. When these conditions were approximated, however, it turned out that inequities in achievement still persisted. It was then hypothesized that these inequities could be reduced by de-equalizing the substantive conditions of opportunity in favor of the schools where underachievement is heaviest.

The principle of substantive equality is implicit in the policy of minimum wage laws, social security legislation, and in all welfare legislation that establishes minimum floors. Carried to its logical conclusion, this interpretation of equality would reduce to zero the difference between the floor and the ceiling in the material and cultural advantages of society. This is a state of affairs few would accept. Certainly no literate society has ever attained it. The policy of establishing floors has become one of the working interpretations of the substantive principle, justified on the grounds that it presses the ideal of equal opportunity closer to reality. In societies of advanced technology the principle is being accepted that to improve the well-being of the total population it is necessary to raise the economic and cultural floors for the people distributively.

The proposal that equality apply to the outcomes of schooling goes beyond the policy of national floors for wages, social security, etc. It would equalize the impact of identical environmental conditions upon individuals. This is not a practical possibility. Theoretically, there can be equality of learning: What X knows and can do is neither more nor less than what Y knows and can do. Equality of outcomes is a step in that direction, but as in the case of other social and economic floors, it can never be more than an approximation of the ideal without bringing everyone to the same level. That is neither possible nor desirable.

The classical principle of equality places the responsibility for learning upon the individual. If he does not learn, it is neither the fault of the society nor the school personnel but rather the failure of the individual to take advantage of his opportunities. This focus of responsibility has shifted with the growing emphasis upon substantive equality. This ideal of equality places responsibility for the individual's welfare upon the state. The parallel in education is the shift of the responsibility for the pupil's failure to learn to the school. By the classical principle the pupil is responsible; by the substantive principle the school is responsible. Both have their advantages. Until the individual reaches a satisfactory achievement floor, the burden of responsibility for his learning would fall heavily upon the school. Beyond that level, the obligation would shift increasingly to the pupil. This does not mean that at that point the school should become unconcerned; rather the school should continue to provide top quality instruction and guidance. It means that the pupil should have begun to develop his life goals, and to take increasing responsibility for finding opportunities to learn and for turning them to his advantage.

The problem created by the application of the principle of equality is not solvable when framed in terms of achievement among individuals. Nor is its solution immediately possible when the problem is formulated in terms of averages between the white majority and minorities or between different regions of the country. This is so because the achievement disparities are rooted in economic disparities and cultural differences. The ineffective pupils are concentrated among the poor of all racial and social groups. In absolute numbers, there are more low achievers among whites than among nonwhites. It may be more accurate to say that the problem of low achievement is more attributable to poverty than to racial discrimination. The unfair partiality of the school is against the poor of all races and cultural groups. The minorities bear an undue proportion because they suffer most from the burdens of poverty. The differences in school achievement among groups of the population can be expected to level off as the economic life of the minorities more nearly approaches that of the white majority. It may well be that cultural differences that influence school achievement will become less potent at that point.

Nevertheless, elimination of disparities in achievement among races and cultural groups will not take care of the problem of equal opportunity in responsible adult activities. It can only remove whatever stigma is attached to a social group that is lower on the average than the white majority. If equality in that sense were achieved, would it tell anything about the ability of pupils in the lower part of the distribution of the school's products to cope with the tasks of life? The aim to achieve equality for the poor would not be served by this equalization of achievement averages. The poor would still be at the bottom of the distribution. Their chances of entering the labor market or any other responsible social activity would still be few. To deal with the lot of the poor is to establish a floor of achievement high enough to enable everyone to enter the adult world unhampered by the lack of fundamental learning. Equality would consist in everyone having the same chance to enter that world insofar as their schooling is concerned. Equality beyond that premise is impossible except in the sense of equality of treatment by the rules.

To establish social, economic, and achievement floors prevents the ideal of equal opportunity from being an empty slogan. The individual can raise himself as high above the floors of learning and social well-being as his initiative, ability, energy, and luck will carry him. If these floors become the height of aspiration, the individual is likely to settle for less than his capabilities warrant. An advanced society that becomes overburdened with individuals of that level of initiative and hope is doomed.

FOOTNOTES

[1] The reform literature is extensive and covers almost the whole span of educational history. Reading of recent reform documents will be sufficient to support this

claim. Among these are: Arthur E. Bestor, *Educational Wastelands* (Urbana, Ill.: The University of Illinois Press, 1953); Charles E. Silberman, *Crisis in the Classroom* (New York: Random House, 1970); Theodore R. Sizer, *Places for Learning/Places for Joy* (Cambridge, Mass.: Harvard University Press, 1973); Peter Witonski, *What Went Wrong With American Education and How to Make it Right* (New Rochelle, N.Y.: Arlington House, 1973).

[2] John Vaizey, *The Economics of Education* (New York: The Free Press of Glenco, 1962), pp. 37–53, 125–35; Burton A. Weisbrod, *External Benefits of Public Education* (Princeton, N.J.: Industrial Relations Section, Department of Economics, Princeton University, 1964), pp. 69–99; George Psacharopoulos, *Returns to Education* (San Francisco, Calif.: Jossey-Bass, 1973), pp. 1–35; 111–25; Mark Plaug, *An Introduction to the Economics of Education* (London: Allen Lane The Penguin Press, 1970), pp. 23–101, 101–20; Charles Benson, *The Economics of Public Education* (New York: Houghton Mifflin, 1961), *passim*.

[3] Ben J. Wattenberg, *This U.S.A.* (New York: Doubleday and Company, 1965), pp. 226–29.

[4] J. S. Coleman et al., *Equality of Educational Opportunity.* U.S. Dept. of Health, Education, and Welfare. (Washington, D.C.: U.S. Government Printing Office, 1966).

[5] National Assessment of Educational Progress. *Preliminary Report 02-R-00.* Reading Summary. (Denver, Colo.: Education Commission of the States, 1971). Also Report 7, 1969–70 Assessment, 1971.

[6] Guy M. Wilson, "A Survey of the Social and Business Uses of Arithmetic" *Teacher College Contributions to Education,* No. 100 (New York: Teachers College Bureau of Publications, 1919); see also his *What Arithmetic Shall We Teach?* (Boston, Mass.: Houghton Mifflin, 1926).

[7] Psacharopoulos, op. cit., pp. 17ff.

[8] Weisbrod, op. cit. pp. 23ff.

[9] Charles Morris, *The Open Self* (New York: Prentice-Hall, 1948), pp. 73–96.

[10] Weisbrod, op. cit., pp. 30–39.

[11] Vilfredo Pareto, *The Mind and Society* (New York: Dover Publications, 1963), Vol. IV, pp. 1456–1500.

[12] Psacharopoulos, op. cit., pp. 87ff.

[13] Ibid., p. 13.

[14] Ibid., p. 70.

[15] V. O. Key, *Public Opinion and American Democracy* (New York: Alfred A. Knopf, 1961), *passim*.

[16] Louis Wirth, "Preface" to Karl Mannheim, *Ideology and Utopia* (New York: Harcourt, Brace and Co., 1936).

[17] R. H. Tawney, *Equality* (New York: Harcourt, Brace and Company, 1931), *passim;* T. V. Smith and Edward C. Linderman, *The Democratic Way of Life* (New York: New American Library, 1951); John Dewey, *The Public and Its Problems* (New York: Henry Holt, 1927), pp. 148–51.

CHAPTER V

Establishing National Floors

This chapter addresses the recommendation that every pupil should acquire at least minimum knowledge in fundamental learning.* This recommendation is a response not only to the fact that many pupils fail to acquire the fundamentals,[1] but also to the fact that fundamentals are a necessity if schooling is to have utility. If the schools meet the goals set forth in this chapter, people who previously represented the lower extremes in achievement will be elevated above the incompetence that resulted from inadequate provision for their schooling in the past. Members of future generations will have at least the minimum abilities required to participate in society.

Social Impact of Achievement Floors
Those who obtain the knowledge included in fundamental learning are better prepared to cope with the demands they

*Only those few students whose extreme mental and physical handicaps prevent them from coping successfully with this expectation should be exempt from this recommendation.

face in a technological, professional, service-oriented, bureaucratic society. However, the acquisition of knowledge and the
deployment of that knowledge are not the same. It is at this
juncture that the responsibilities to be faced by society become
paramount. There is no assurance that knowledge will be
used productively. The schools are in a less tenable position
than are other agencies to assure productive outcomes from
the acquisition of knowledge. [2]

Two problems in particular arise regarding the application
of knowledge. The first is that a more highly trained population
may not find useful outlets for its knowledge. The frustrated
scientists and engineers who lost employment because of
reductions in the space and airlines industries, the educated
but underemployed housewives whose abilities are unused,
or the qualified minority member who is offered less than
his training suggests may be multiplied by establishing a
minimum achievement level without provision for utilizing
improved human resources. Elevating school attainment will
call for ingenious utilization of a more capable citizenry rather
than caring for or adjusting to the incompetent and unquali-
fied. When one considers the heavy toll ignorance has levied
on individuals and society, concern with the problem of
capitalizing on knowledge is an attractive exchange. [3]

The second problem is that the relationship between the
schools and society must be mutually supportive or the chasm
between adults and youth may widen; each new wave of better
prepared youth will be a disruptive force in the social,
economic, and political system. Higher achievement will not
be put to good use unless the knowledge and attitudes acquired
in school synchronize with the expectations and requirements
of the society. The school can explain application of knowledge,
describe utilization of abilities acquired, and advocate uses
of knowledge that will encourage productive work, but to
expect the school to provide appropriate outlets for knowledge
without support from other community agencies is an unrealistic expectation. The school should guarantee that each pupil
acquires minimum abilities and knowledge, but the use of

knowledge and the application of skills depend on factors that are not exclusively within the province of the schools. Adults must share the task of inducting youth into society.

Substantive Aspects of Achievement Floors

The schools must do much more than teach fundamentals, but the special need to see that pupils reach minimum levels of achievement is an essential task. A testing program is needed to identify pupils who require assistance. Those who meet the minimum standard can be freed from further requirements, and those who fall short of the minimum can be given additional instruction until they meet the established floor.

Criterion-referenced testing is the best method to determine when a pupil has attained a level of knowledge that is sufficient for him to proceed to the next stages of learning. The criteria for testing must be based on the utility of knowledge as determined by factors that are both external and internal to the schools. Tests should measure the ability to perform functionally in the expectations of everyday life and to utilize the fundamentals to obtain additional knowledge. In meeting a minimum level of competence, the effectiveness of the schools can also be increased by eliminating redundancy for those students who require no additional instruction in fundamentals. For example, once a student has mastered the basic operations in mathematics, repetitive practice of these fundamentals is unnecessary. The student's time is better spent if he does not continue with the time-consuming practice of addition, multiplication, subtraction, and division. After he has mastered basic number relationships, he should make use of his knowledge rather than "relearning it regularly." The same principle applies in many other areas throughout the school system. However, until a student acquires these basics, he is handicapped in his pursuit of more learning.

For the purpose of this discussion, fundamental learning is defined as minimum knowledge required to function in this society. Advanced learning consists of elective knowledge a person may choose to pursue. Within the category of fundamental learning is a subclass of knowledge that is essential for further learning to occur. This subclass will be called basic knowledge and includes the essentials in reading and mathematics. The remainder of the fundamental learning is the knowledge and skills required of any functioning adult. Basic knowledge must be a requirement for establishing minimum floors of achievement because it is necessary for further achievement. Basic knowledge should be distinguished as a separate class treated differently from other fundamental knowledge and given the highest priority in the reform of schools.

An illustration can help make the distinction between basic knowledge and fundamental learning. A student who is unable to read is handicapped in his efforts to acquire additional knowledge. Reading fits the definition of basic knowledge since it is required for further learning. Fundamental learning that is not basic can be illustrated with an example of the preparation to perform social functions. One can easily realize that comprehension of the rights of a citizen of the United States is not a necessary condition to acquire additional learning. If knowledge about citizens' rights is critical for each citizen to function adequately, then it might be classified as fundamental learning, but it would not be classified as basic knowledge.

Advanced learning consists of knowledge that is not required by every individual to function in the society but that one might acquire out of personal choice. This learning is not viewed as superior, but rather as knowledge sought to meet the individual's interests in the development of his personal life. Advanced or elective learnings are described in Chapter VI and should be provided according to the recommendations made for their inclusion in the school program of studies.

If there were no restrictions on funds or qualified personnel, the nation might launch an intensive program of frequent testing and tutorial instruction to elevate all pupils to a point of maximum utility of schooling, but the nation does not enjoy the luxury of unlimited resources. However, with some increased support, certain steps should yield substantial returns. These steps include a procedure whereby criterion-referenced tests are administered at selected times in pupils' school careers. A nationwide periodic testing effort should be undertaken to identify students whose achievement in fundamental learning is subminimal. Instruction should be provided to lift those students at least to minimum levels.

The implementation of this program calls for increased school support to be provided where the greatest learning difficulties of pupils exist. This principle of distribution of fiscal resources is a departure from the practice in which resources have been distributed according to a level of poverty. It may be the case that low achievement and other factors such as indigence correlate positively, but if eradication of inferior achievement is one goal of the school, then resources should be focused on the schools and the individual pupils where low achievement is found. The location of a school or the presence of a high percent of minority pupils is not the critical factor. There are children in urban settings and children of minority groups whose academic performance and intellectual achievements are superior. They deserve the opportunity to rise to levels of excellence provided by the recognition of their superior achievement. There are also children in "good" schools from families of the majority whose learning levels are inadequate. They also require special help to escape the trap of ignorance. Descriptive data make it apparent that the average achievement level of pupils is lower in inner-city schools than it is in the suburbs.[4] Thus, a fiscal policy based on achievement would result in a tendency to give special help to inner-city schools. Support should also be provided for low-achievement pupils in rural and suburban areas. The basis for supplying special support should be the achievement of pupils rather than some other characteristic, such as poverty, that is assumed to be a reliable proxy for what a pupil knows. Inferring a level of achievement from extraneous indices has the double fault of falsely stereotyping

pupils and of giving inadequate assurance that the investment
in time, money, and effort is applied to pupils who are most
in need of help.

Development of Achievement Floors

The establishment and implementation of minimum floors
is complicated by the lack of experimentally derived and
externally validated subjects and minimum achievement
levels for the schools to promote. At the outset of establishing
minimum levels, there must be heavy reliance on the judgment
of those whose expertise gives reasonable confidence that they
can determine proper standards. Judgment enters in most
strongly in establishing minimum criteria and in ruling that
any particular knowledge is essential for the acquisition of
further knowledge or for functional behavior. After a period
of time the wisdom of initial decisions can be assessed against
the consequences in longitudinal research studies. The immediate task requires that objectives be selected to serve as
a guide in the development of the tests for acquisition of
minimum knowledge. Fortunately, a major program has begun
that provides considerable help in this undertaking: the
National Assessment of Educational Progress (NAEP).[5]

NAEP includes assessment of 9-, 13-, and 17-year-olds, and
young adults between the ages of 25 and 36. Throughout
the decade of the 1970s, the NAEP program is designed to
gather evidence on knowledge, understanding, skills, and
attitudes in ten subject areas: Art, Career and Occupational
Development, Citizenship, Literature, Mathematics, Music,
Reading, Science, Social Studies, and Writing. NAEP plans
call for periodic reassessment so that changes over time can
be determined.

The objectives selected in the ten areas of NAEP were
submitted for critical appraisal to three different groups. One
group included scholars in the discipline of the given subject
area, another included educators, and the third included
laymen. Scholars attested to the academic credibility of the
objectives; school personnel were concerned with the feasibility

and appropriateness of including the objectives in school programs; laymen were asked to rule on whether or not the objectives represented content necessary for participation in society. Thus, all objectives were subjected to review for academic respectability, rationality for inclusion in the school programs, and utility from the point of view of knowledgeable laymen. All exercises* developed for the assessment were referenced to the objectives that had been approved by the three panels.

An important characteristic of NAEP exercises is the provision of items that reflect nonschool tasks as well as in-school tasks. Some similarity does exist between NAEP exercises and other standardized tests, but many items included in NAEP relate to out-of-school circumstances. Because of this feature, the NAEP items are more compatible with the concept of individual utility than are tests designed primarily to measure and predict only school success. In the reading exercises, for example, items are included calling for: reading and interpreting road signs involving instructions to bicyclists and pedestrians; reading and interpreting TV schedules; analysis of advertisements on candy wrappers and dog food; and questions about a city map. These exercises require the pupil to respond to situations that he is likely to confront in his experiences out of school. In the field of science, elementary school pupils are asked to show that they understand certain basic principles that relate science to the world around them. They must associate day and night with the rotation of the earth; determine how to dress properly for sunny, 45° weather; and understand precautions in using acid. Each of NAEP's ten categories reflect this tendency to incorporate practical and out-of-school exercises in the tests.

NAEP organized the administration and analysis of its assessment to determine the relationship between perform-

---

*NAEP uses the term "exercise" instead of "item" to distinguish national assessment material from standardized tests. These two terms are used interchangeably in this chapter.

ance and numerous variables. Comparisons are made among geographic regions, parental educational levels, males and females, blacks and whites, and size and type of community. Because of the procedure employed in packaging the exercises used in NAEP, however, there is no way to identify any single pupil, school, or district and to compare that performance with national or regional standards. The major contribution made by NAEP to the establishment of minimum standards of achievement is that it has developed objectives and exercises clearly related to utility. These provide a pool useful in developing minimum requirements. The standards and specific items for assessing pupils remain to be determined.

The exercises in NAEP were administered to a sample of each age group, and results were reported by giving the percent that responded correctly to each exercise. For each exercise, NAEP lists the level of difficulty according to the national sample. For each exercise assessed, a weighted sample of 2,200 to 2,700 9- and 13-year-olds enabled NAEP to estimate the performance of approximately 4 million pupils in each of these age levels. Among 17-year-olds the weighted sample of 2,200 to 2,700 enabled an estimate to be made of the performance of approximately 3.5 million 17-year-olds. The adult weighted sample of 2,100 to 2,300 young adults provided data to estimate the performance of approximately 23 million young adults. A minimum level of acceptable performance in the schools can be initiated with considerable confidence by using these national assessment data.

Since the NAEP program does not include procedures for identifying individual pupils or classrooms for comparison with a standard or with each other, a bridge must be built between the data obtained in NAEP and the data needed to establish and test minimum floors. One approach might be to set a goal to increase the percent of pupils who correctly answer the exercises. For instance, if 40 percent of the NAEP national sample answered an exercise correctly, then the schools might plan to increase the percent of its pupils who answer correctly to 60 percent. In the application of this approach, a class of thirty pupils who reflect the national standards would initially have had twelve pupils out of thirty who successfully completed the exercise. The goal of increasing the number of pupils from 40 percent to 60 percent could be met in this average classroom if eighteen pupils supplied correct answers. The remaining twelve might not improve, but the improvement by the class would meet the established criterion. The advantage of this plan is that NAEP exercises and information could be used to set achievement goals without much additional alteration or extension of NAEP procedures. The disadvantage is that improvement of the class performance may reflect improvement only among those whose achievement is minimally deficient. If batteries of tests, clusters of test items, or any other selection of exercises based on this approach were used, the effect would be to improve the pupils who are on the borderline of minimum floors and to leave the extremely low achievers untouched. This approach is unacceptable as it fails to attend to all pupils who perform below standard.

Another plan to set minima would be to select NAEP exercises according to the criterion of individual utility and then develop tests consisting of those items. All pupils who successfully completed such items could be classified as pupils who have met the minimum standards. Those who did not answer the exercises correctly could receive special help until they also perform satisfactorily. One goal of school reform would be to elevate all pupils above the set standard. Although this approach is preferable, it is also more difficult to develop and carry out. The tasks in this approach are to determine the percent of correct answers required to meet an acceptable minimal level of achievement and to select and prepare exercises that are appropriate for criterion testing.

To answer the question of item difficulty, we can choose a cutoff point on exercises and analyze the consequences of the selection. Suppose items answered correctly by 75 percent of the sample were selected to test for minimum achievement. Selecting the 75 percent level of difficulty assumes that pupils

Table 1
Random Distribution of Answers on Ten Exercises
Exercise Number

Stu-dent	1	2	3	4	5	6	7	8	9	10	Per-cent
A	x			x			x			x	40
B	x	x		x	x		x	x		x	70
C	x	x	x	x	x	x	x	x	x	x	100
D	x	x	x	x	x	x	x	x	x	x	100
E	x	x	x	x	x	x	x	x	x	x	100
F	x	x	x	x	x	x	x	x	x	x	100
G		x	x		x	x		x	x		60
H		x				x			x		30

x Indicates correct response

who are currently in the lowest 25 percent on the NAEP distribution should be identified and elevated to the level that is currently occupied by the upper 75 percent of school-age youth. If the program of elevating basic achievement is successful according to this standard, then the frequency count of pupils who achieve in the current lowest quartile would be reduced to zero. In actual practice the statistics do not hold up as precisely as this statement implies because all items selected would not be exactly 75 percent in difficulty. A perfect performance on all tasks is not recommended as a requirement for all pupils either, but the principle of elevating lower achieving pupils to higher levels is maintained. To see an illustration of how this approach could be employed, examine how eight pupils might be distributed randomly on ten items that are each at the 75 percent level of difficulty as shown in Table 1.*

*The use of eight pupils and ten test items for these examples is only for illustrative purposes. In no case will ten items be a complete test battery, and the number of pupils involved will invariably be much larger than eight. The illustration and discussion are provided to present the background that supports recommendations that follow on the selection and interpretation of test items.

In the illustration in Table 1, each exercise was answered correctly by six (75 percent) of the students. If the standard for minimum levels was set at 100 percent, then four pupils would be classified as meeting the standard and four would be classified as not meeting it. However, an examination of other factors in this distribution suggest additional considerations in determining the criterion level. In the distribution, if pupils C, D, E, or F had carelessly missed one item, they would not have met the 100 percent criterion. Missing an item through carelessness is not the same error as missing an item because of lack of knowledge. Some allowance needs to be made for this difference. For this reason, the criterion level should be less than 100 percent. This raises the question: If a test is employed in which the usual average of correct responses is 75 percent, what percent of correct answers is regarded as an acceptable level of individual performance? There is no scientific solution or mathematical formula that will give a precise answer to this question, but we recommend that 90 percent be considered an adequate criterion to begin the testing program. The 90 percent standard should be high enough to identify pupils who lack the knowledge being tested but should also retain flexibility to allow for errors due to occasional carelessness or extenuating circumstances.

It is unlikely that correct answers would be randomly distributed as shown in Table 1. It is more probable that pupils who answer one item of a given type correctly are also likely to answer additional items, and those who fail to answer any given item will miss additional items of that same content. The distribution in Table 2 is a more realistic expectation from administering the test to eight pupils than is a random distribution of correct answers.

In this illustration, each item was also answered correctly by 75 percent of the pupils. However, when the performance of each pupil is calculated, the distinction between those who performed well on the test and those who performed poorly is obvious, with the exception of pupil H, who scored 80. Pupils D and F, who each scored 20 percent, were clearly

Table 2
Distribution of Answers on Ten Exercises
Exercise Number

Stu-dent	1	2	3	4	5	6	7	8	9	10	Per-cent
A	x	x	x	x	x	x	x	x	x	x	100
B	x	x	x	x	x	x	x		x	x	90
C	x	x		x	x	x	x	x	x	x	90
D			x					x			20
E	x	x	x	x	x	x	x	x	x	x	100
F							x			x	20
G	x	x	x	x	x	x	x	x	x	x	100
H	x	x	x	x	x	x		x	x		80

x Indicates correct response

below the others in the distribution and are candidates for additional instruction; pupil H could be treated as a special case and given additional help according to factors known best by the teachers who work with him. The test scores serve as a supplemental aid to that analysis. If scores of 90 or higher were considered acceptable, then five of the eight pupils would meet the criterion, and three would be classified below standard. The interpretation of these data enables the school to identify pupils who fall below the minimum and also to locate pupils who require no additional instruction in the area being tested.

The difficulty level of NAEP exercises selected for tests needs further discussion. In the illustration given, the difficulty of each item was assumed to be 75 percent. In actual practice, the difficulty of the items will range over a continuum. One approach would be to select items whose median percent of difficulty is 75 percent. This approach would allow for some difficult items as well as some easy items to be included. However, to expect a pupil to perform at a near-perfect level such as 90 percent or better when difficult items are included defeats the purpose of criterion testing as advocated here. Pupils who possess the knowledge needed to meet the standards in each objective should have the potential to answer all items correctly. Therefore, no items should be included that are not clearly within the reach of any pupil who possesses the knowledge being tested. It would be better to include relatively easy items initially to determine if pupils possess the minimum knowledge rather than items that might include subtle or difficult discrimination that only the most knowledgeable pupils could make. Thus, items that have been answered correctly by approximately 75 to 100 percent of the sample of each age group should be considered for inclusion in the examination for minimum achievement in the basic learnings. This standard should help identify those pupils in the lowest 15 to 25 percent of the current pupil population for additional instruction.

The use of objectives that have been validated on the basis of factors external to the school may result in tests that identify different pupils from those who are identified by using only in-school factors. Since reform of the school should include provision for more successful entry into the community, this external factor becomes important in establishing the content of the achievement tests.

Individual pupils who are in schools with generally high achievement but who require special help should also be identified and given additional instruction. Individuals who attend schools where general school achievement is low but where their individual performance is high should be identified and encouraged to progress at a rate commensurate with their ability. The development of examinations according to the above approach can help identify these pupils.

As an illustration of what to expect in this program, consider the following distributions of pupils in two different settings. In the first illustration, in Table 3, an example is presented of a distribution in which ten items of varying difficulty ranging from 75 to 100 percent might be administered in a school setting that has pupils whose performance is typically

Table 3
Distribution Among Above-average Students
Exercise Number and Percent of Difficulty
Item and Difficulty Level

Stu-dent	1 (75)	2 (80)	3 (90)	4 (87)	5 (95)	6 (77)	7 (86)	8 (92)	9 (94)	10 (86)	Per-cent
A	x	x	x	x	x	x	x	x	x	x	100
B	x	x	x	x	x	x	x	x	x	x	100
C	x	x	x	x		x	x	x	x	x	90
D	x	x	x	x	x	x	x		x	x	90
E		x	x			x		x			40
F	x	x	x	x	x	x	x	x	x	x	100
G	x	x	x	x	x	x	x	x	x	x	100
H	x	x	x	x	x	x	x	x	x	x	100

above national averages. The number in parenthesis is the difficulty level of the item.

In this example, seven of the eight pupils met the criterion of 90 percent. Pupil E, with a score of 40 percent, fell below the criterion. When any pupil in the class scores below the criterion on the test, the fact that the class average is above the criterion should not exclude this low-achieving pupil from receiving special help to overcome his deficiencies. Seven pupils scored at or above standard. They should be provided with opportunities to utilize their knowledge in the pursuit of additional learning.

In the second illustration, which follows in Table 4, eight hypothetical pupils are described from a school that has a large percent of pupils who typically score below national norms. The distribution that follows could occur on the same test items that were included in Table 3.

In the situation illustrated in Table 4, one pupil met the criterion and another pupil was on the borderline with a score of 80. The latter pupil might reach the standard with some additional help. The remaining pupils fell short of meeting

Table 4
Distribution Among Below-average Students
Exercise Number

Student	1 (75)	2 (80)	3 (90)	4 (87)	5 (95)	6 (77)	7 (86)	8 (92)	9 (94)	10 (86)	Percent
A	x				x			x			30
B	x		x								20
C	x	x	x	x	x	x		x	x	x	90
D			x			x	x	x			40
E	x	x						x			30
F	x	x		x		x	x	x	x	x	80
G		x									10
H						x		x			20

the criterion and require remedial attention. The one pupil who scored at the criterion level should be given the opportunity to advance to the level of the seven in the previous example who all met it. This pupil should not be held back from advanced learning even though he is enrolled in a school where the majority of pupils need a slower pace and more work on basic learning. The application of this testing procedure will help to identify those who are exceptions to the school norm.

On the basis of the foregoing discussion, the following recommendations are necessary to implement this program of reform:

1. Exercises from the National Assessment of Educational Progress with a difficulty level within the range of approximately 75 to 100 percent should be employed on the tests for minimum achievement in the basic learning.

2. When more items than are available from NAEP are needed to provide an adequate measure, additional items should be constructed based on the NAEP exercises as models.

3. Any pupil who scores 90 percent or higher on a set of exercises tied to a specific objective will be classified as one who has met the criterion in respect to that objective.

4. Any pupil who scores 80 to 89 percent on a set of exercises would have his case reviewed to determine if he needs additional help or should be allowed to continue with those who have met the criterion.

5. Any pupil who scores below 80 percent on the set of exercises will receive additional instruction to acquire the knowledge represented by the minimum standard.

6. All retesting of pupils should take place only after the teacher who works with them recommends given pupils for retest.

Additional questions remain in respect to the subjects that should be included as fundamental, procedures for implementing testing of the chosen subjects, retesting of pupils, and scheduling of examinations.

Elements of Fundamental Knowledge

One issue in the selection of subjects for minimum achievement is to distinguish between fundamental knowledge and advanced areas of study. The curriculum includes some subjects that are linear in content. For instance, in mathematics the content begins with simple number relationships and progresses to algebra, integral calculus, and higher levels. Basic learning in mathematics is necessary to obtain more knowledge, but basic learning also has utility for those who do not pursue advanced learning. Mathematics is a subject that contains knowledge that is both fundamental and advanced. Other areas of study cannot be classified as linear because the content is not sequenced into fundamental and advanced knowledge. Nevertheless, the content in these areas may be vital to functioning in the adult world. The area of career and occupational development includes information that is required to cope effectively with one's vocational decisions. Career and occupational development is not a linear subject to study like mathematics or science, but its content should not be ignored in determining what knowledge has general utility and is classified as fundamental.

The selection of areas that contain fundamental learning

is likely to be controversial. A practical and sensible solution is to limit the choices initially to those areas included in the work of NAEP that contain fundamental knowledge. The NAEP list does not encompass all the current offerings in today's schools. Additional areas of study may eventually be added to the list, but the problem of launching a program of minimum floors is the reverse—namely, to reduce the number of areas to a manageable number and to include the most essential learning rather than to enlarge the list. The NAEP list is useful for making an initial selection of the areas to be included.

The areas recommended for inclusion in the establishment of minimum floors are reading, mathematics, citizenship,* science, social studies, writing, and career and occupational development. To specify that minimum floors be established for civics, science, social studies, writing, and occupational development is not to recommend that they become required courses. The knowledge represented by test items in any of these areas can be acquired from a number of sources—radio, television, news media, everyday experience, school studies, and the like. All that is intended is that these titles designate the domains for which objectives and test items are to be formulated for the purpose of developing floors of achievement. However, any pupil who falls below the floor in any area will be expected to work in that area until his weakness is removed.

Within this list, the subjects of reading and mathematics are set apart as basic subjects. They should receive highest priority in initiating the program of minimum floors. The approach used in developing minimum standards for reading and mathematics should follow the recommendations discussed in the previous section of this chapter. A slightly

*The knowledge and skills in the domain of civics in its broadest sense has the same degree of individual utility that one would acquire from other fundamental subjects such as mathematics and science. Therefore the term civics seems as appropriate as the term citizenship and is preferred by the writers, and it will be used in subsequent discussions.

different approach is required to establish minimum requirements in the remaining areas. The difference can be illustrated
by contrasting an exercise in reading with an exercise in
science. One exercise in reading calls for 9-year-olds to view
four doors with the names "principal," "nurse," "cafeteria,"
and "library" written on them. The pupil is asked to designate
the door where he would send a visitor who wanted to see
the person in charge of the school. In the NAEP sample,
94.5 percent of the 9-year-olds answered the item correctly.
This item could qualify as a test item, and about 5.5 percent
of the 9-year-olds who failed to respond correctly would be
headed toward classification as pupils who require additional
instruction. Using this relatively easy item helps identify
pupils who lack essential reading ability. The cumulative
effect of using items such as this one should identify pupils
who need additional instruction to acquire basic knowledge.

Now consider the area of science. It is no longer feasible
to rely only on exercises that are relatively easy as a basis
for selection of test items. Basic learning is knowledge that
is required for the pupil to obtain additional knowledge. Other
fundamental knowledge includes useful information that
heretofore may not have been mastered but will come within
the ability of all pupils with higher achievement in basic
learning or is identified as essential for normal functioning
as an adult. Using an example from the science exercises,
this point can be illustrated. It was found that only 61 percent
of the 9-year-olds knew how to connect a bulb properly to
a flashlight battery. According to standards for selection of
exercises in reading and mathematics, this item in science
would not be included because it would be considered too
difficult. However, if this knowledge is considered essential
for everyday living for 9-year-olds it might be appropriate
to include it. In fundamental learning beyond the basics in
reading and mathematics, it would be preferable to include
some items whose difficulty is below the 75 percent level
but whose content is functionally necessary.

It is therefore recommended that essential content in reading and mathematics be regarded as basic learning and that standards for minimum floors be established at the 90 percent level of accuracy on exercises chosen from the difficulty range of approximately 75 to 100 percent. Examinations for minimum achievement in the other areas should include items that are judged minimally essential to function adequately in society and should be selected from the entire range of difficulty of items included in NAEP. On these items, the 90 percent standard should still be applied for students to demonstrate that they have attained the minimum level of achievement. The assumption behind this recommendation is that minimum levels of achievement in reading and mathematics can be assessed by limiting the requirement to relatively simple standards that can be applied to all pupils. After this basic learning is mastered, the remaining fields of knowledge contain information that is not necessarily known to even the best pupils but should be a part of the knowledge of all who are expected to function adequately in society.

Undoubtedly, some will contend that this list of required achievement levels has failed to include other areas of study that might be equally or more important. When a given area such as mathematics is listed as basic and fundamental and another area such as art is excluded from the list, mathematics is not being considered more valuable than art. Certain universal learnings are the special responsibility of the schools. Guarantees must be made to assure that the schools meet those responsibilities. Many additional subjects and areas of study should be incorporated in a school program that must become more flexible than is currently the case. The establishment of minimum levels of achievement is intended to facilitate the acquisition of knowledge in other fields rather than to restrict the program to a narrow range of offerings.

In regard to the areas selected, it is evident that schooling and education for an individual require that he be able to read. The frequent reliance on the printed word and the transferability from the printed form to other ways of using language permeates the culture. The high positive correlation between attainment of levels of schooling and adult success have been documented.[6] A cause-effect relationship between reading and school achievement is not as firmly established as the correlational relationship, but the obvious need to possess reading facility in order to acquire knowledge makes a good case for promoting reading as a basic requirement.

The case for including mathematics as basic learning is similar to the justification for including reading. The activities of youths and adults in managing themselves and in calculating and comprehending events such as employment, personal budgets, building a home, paying taxes, planning a vacation, or retirement are but a few of the common occurrences that require basic mathematical ability. The problems that require fundamental comprehension of numbers and basic mathematical principles are legion. Anyone who faces the decisions of living without such basic knowledge has little chance of avoiding problems that arise from unwise judgment where numbers and simple calculations are involved.

Another reason for selecting reading and mathematics is that reviews of the pupil achievement nearly always include measurement and interpretation of performance in reading and mathematics. The analysis of these findings shows a wide discrepancy among pupils in their attainment in these two areas. If surveys of pupil achievement in these two areas revealed that all pupils achieved equally, then the reasons for wide differences in their eventual attainment should be attributed to factors other than reading and mathematical knowledge; however, wide discrepancies between different subdivisions of the nation's school-age population have been reported in the literature. In the most recent report of NAEP, reading contrasts were drawn between Extreme Inner City (EIC) and Extreme Affluent Suburbs (EAS), and, without exception, the median percent of correct responses of EIC pupils was lower. The median score of EIC children on written directions was 72 percent; that of EAS children was 92 percent. On drawing inferences, EIC children scored 59 percent and EAS children 83 percent, and on critical reading the averages were 60 percent for EIC and 78 percent for EAS. Since there are wide differences in attainment in these areas and the connection between eventual attainment and acquisition of fundamentals in reading and mathematics is a logical relationship, there is a good case for elevating pupils in the lower levels of reading and mathematics above their present levels as a means of improving their lot.

Achievement in reading and mathematics does not guarantee that an individual will remain in school or obtain productive work as an adult, but to fail to achieve minimally in these areas considerably reduces his chances in life. In addition to basic learning, one must consider the fundamental areas—science, writing, social studies, civics, and career and occupational development. All can make significant contributions to the lives of pupils, and there is no objective basis on which one might be designated as more essential than another. If the essential learning in each area is identified as minimum levels of achievement for all pupils, and if all pupils reach this level, then the performance of the total population should be elevated to a level where the social and private returns from education are enhanced.

The entire program of studies should receive periodic scrutiny to add or delete subjects for minimum standards. If it becomes apparent that the program of studies is hampered by inadequate fundamental preparation, additional areas, objectives, and tests should be added to the list. The designation of seven areas of minimum essentials does not restrict the school program to these fields of study. This designation of minimums is recommended to enable all pupils to acquire the knowledge that will enable them to profit from the more diverse and appropriate program of studies that should accompany school reform.

An Approach to the Selection of Objectives

Some objectives listed in NAEP are general objectives from which more specific objectives and test exercises must be derived. Other objectives may not be appropriate for use in establishing minimum levels of achievement. NAEP's approval of an objective does not automatically justify its inclusion in the list for selecting exercises for minimum achievement. Some objectives might be desirable but not essential; minimum floors require that all pupils should acquire the learning that represents the essential objectives.

Another caution in selecting the list of objectives from National Assessment without further evaluation is that some objectives may be too vague to be directly translated into specific outcomes with clearly specified test items or exercises. For example, one of the objectives in the area of reading is for the pupil to draw appropriate inferences from the material by "reading between the lines." This objective provides considerable latitude for interpretation, and it may be impossible to prepare test items that will determine when pupils have met the objective. Also, this objective may not be regarded as fundamental and may be rejected for this reason. Another reading objective is given as the ability to "decode printed words." Among the components of that objective is the statement that students should be able to recognize and identify letters, numerals, and symbols. If it is agreed that decoding printed words is both functional and essential, then the tasks included in it (such as recognizing and identifying letters, numerals, and symbols) define the objective sufficiently to enable selection or construction of items that will allow for examination of pupils and, therefore, determine if they have met the objective.

The best approach to developing test batteries is to select a panel of authorities in each subject area to specify minimum floors of achievement and assign the panel the task of selecting objectives from NAEP. Another task of the panel will also be to select the exercises that pupils should be expected to complete to prove their attainment of the achievement required. Further, the panel should develop additional items to add to the pool of exercises available from NAEP. New items should be developed as needed to create a larger sample of pupils' ability and to provide a more comprehensive selection of items. The larger array of items has the advantage of providing a more thorough examination than is likely from the limited items released by NAEP and of providing additional items for retesting pupils after a period of time.

NAEP follows the practice of releasing half the exercises from the first administration and keeping the other half confidential for the second administration. In the case of the released exercises in reading, the items answered correctly by 75 percent or more of the sample at each age level included forty-one exercises for age 9, eighty exercises for age 15, and seventy-six exercises for age 17. This pool of exercises should be a sufficient base on which to develop test batteries and to write additional items. Released exercises are currently available in science, writing, citizenship, literature, social studies, and mathematics.

The procedure recommended for the establishment of specific objectives and items in the subject field included in minimum achievement requirements is to form a panel of several people in each area whose expertise qualifies them to make judgments in their field. They will 1) select or rewrite objectives from the NAEP objectives that they regard as vital for all students to possess, 2) select exercises that conform to the objectives and purposes of the evaluation of pupils, 3) prepare or oversee the preparation of additional exercises beyond those available in NAEP, and 4) organize objectives and exercises into two or more equivalent examinations for testing pupils at different age levels.

Administration of Measurement and Analysis of Results

Several considerations enter into the administration of the tests. One factor is that pupils should be examined within a broad level of schooling (elementary school, junior high school, or high school) and at a time of the year when the school can act on the results of the testing. It would do little good to examine students in their last semester of high school and then attempt to remedy weaknesses. Testing must be done early enough in the schooling of the pupil at each level to provide time for assisting students who need help. This is not to suggest that final testing of high school seniors is unimportant. It is only to suggest that for the purposes of measuring the attainment of minimal achievements, the timing should be appropriate to capitalize on the information obtained. The best time and grades to utilize the testing would be in the spring of the third, seventh, and tenth years of schooling. The spring is preferable because that schedule leaves time after the testing to analyze and interpret results and to prepare individual schedules for pupils when they return for the beginning of the school year. Schools that operate on different calendars might test at different times but retain this principle. The third, seventh, and tenth years of schooling coincide closely with the ages in the samples selected for NAEP and also allow two or three years for additional instruction at each level of school as the systems are usually organized. Whenever a pupil performs above or below his expectations during the year after testing, he may be retested on the basis of teachers' recommendations. Retesting would apply in cases where a pupil improves sufficiently to warrant a retest or if there is doubt about a pupil's retention of minimum knowledge that he previously displayed.

Each pupil should have a profile prepared of his achievement and academic record specifying the minimum objectives he is expected to meet and whether or not he has succeeded. With the test information on each pupil, the school can assess its own effectiveness and can also individualize the program for each pupil in the school according to his strengths and weaknesses. Such testing and analysis should enable the school to isolate and remedy problems in basic learning.

Summary
The recommendations presented in this chapter provide a starting point for the tasks of identifying students who need remediation and monitoring the effects of instruction in overcoming current weaknesses. Admittedly, these recom-

mendations may include flaws in respect to choice of subjects, measuring instruments, target audience, testing schedule, and others. No combination of answers to these matters will receive unanimous approval. This plan for establishing and acting on minimum achievement levels has been offered, and the recommended next step is to carry out the plan, evaluate its effectiveness in identifying impoverished learners, and supply remedial help to elevate all pupils to a level where they can function in today's schools and eventually tomorrow's adult world.

FOOTNOTES

[1] National Assessment of Educational Progress, *Reading Summary*, Preliminary Report 02-R-00 (Denver, Colo.: Education Commission of the States, 1971). Also, Report 7, *Science;* Report 9, *Citizenship;* Report 10, *Writing.* Cf. U.S. Department of Health, Education, and Welfare, Office of Education, *Equality of Educational Opportunity,* by James Coleman (Washington, D.C.: U.S. Government Printing Office, 1966).

[2] Carl Bereiter, "Schools Without Education," *Harvard Educational Review,* August, 1972, pp. 390–413; Cf. James Coleman, "How Do the Young Become Adults?" *Phi Delta Kappan,* December, 1972, pp. 226–30.

[3] U.S. Department of Health, Education, and Welfare, Office of Education, "Education and Income" in *Digest of Educational Statistics, 1969* (Washington, D.C.: U.S. Government Printing Office, 1969), p. 14. Cf. U.S. Department of Commerce, Bureau of the Census, "Money Income—Percent Distribution of Families by Income Level by Years of School Completed; and Race of Head; 1961 and 1968," in *Statistical Abstract of the United States, 1970* (Washington, D.C.: U.S. Government Printing Office, 1970), p. 325. Cf. Joseph P. Cangeui, "Life Chances: A Comment on the Dynamics of Education and Money," *Journal of Negro Education,* Fall, 1967, pp. 424–27. Cf. Robert M. Frumkin, "Education and Mental Illness: A Preliminary Report," *Educational Research Bulletin* 36: 212–14. Cf. U.S. Department of Commerce, Bureau of the Census, "24 Million Americans: Poverty in the United States" in *Current Population Reports, Consumer Income, 1969* (Washington, D.C.: U.S. Government Printing Office, 1969). Cf. Charles B. Nam, (ed.), "The Relationship of Education to Unemployment," in *Population and Society* (Boston, Mass.: Houghton Mifflin Company, 1968), p. 619.

[4] National Assessment of Educational Progress, op. cit. Equality of Educational Opportunity, op. cit.

[5] The remainder of this chapter relies on the information supplied by the National Assessment of Educational Progress. Their publications include over fifty documents that describe areas under inquiry, newsletters, objectives, exercises, results, and analysis of their work.

[6] See Chapter XI.

CHAPTER VI

Social Utility and the Curriculum

The present chapter suggests adjustments in the school to satisfy social utilities. Ideally, nothing should be said about changing the school program until measures of the school's contributions to basic forms of utility have been worked out. These measures would make it possible to determine the advantages of changes in the school, but unfortunately, they are barely in an incipient state of development. In the meantime it is worthwhile to hypothesize what changes would maximize the societal benefits of schooling.

Program Dimensions and Social Utility
Three basic dimensions of the school program can be identified: amount of schooling expressed as time spent;[1] kinds of subject matter expressed as scientific, humanistic, and technical; and thoroughness of instruction and learning expressed as measures of achievement. Although these dimensions can be combined in a number of ways, the most plausible hypotheses to be generated from them are as follows: The

societal benefits of schooling are maximized by increasing: 1) the amount and thoroughness of schooling or 2) the amount and thoroughness of schooling in specified subjects. These hypotheses differ in that the first proposition makes the school program flexible since no particular subjects are required, and the second prescribes particular kinds of content.

The question of subject matter has been a perennial problem since adults first began to instruct children. Each society has had its own conception of what is significant for its children to learn. Whether one considers the ancient Egyptian, Greek, or Judaic cultures or the culture of the age of steam, electricity, and atomic power, the question of what to teach the young has been of considerable importance. A practical content seems to have prevailed in Egypt; linguistic and literary content dominated in Greece and Judea. The age of power has been characterized by a constant triangular struggle among linguistic and literary subjects, sciences, and practical studies. In the latter part of the last century the sciences were in the ascendancy and claiming an increasing amount of the school's time. The sciences have now become a prominent part of the curriculum, and the humanists are currently increasing the claims of their disciplines. These controversies over the relative worth of various studies are struggles within the affluent strata about their own values, not controversies about what is of most worth to society either as a whole or distributively. The justification of values claimed for different studies are typically couched in language depicting universal gains, for the "haves" unwittingly equate benefits to themselves with benefits to society.

Certain considerations favor the view that the utility of schooling for either the individual or society is independent of any particular content once the achievement floor has been attained. On first view, however, the proposition that various utilities of schooling can be affected by the content of instruction appears to be true. What can be more certain than that one's behavior is changed by the knowledge he acquires? If a pupil learns to type, obviously he will perform differently when he wants to use a typewriter from what he would have done previously. If a pupil learns the elementary concepts and principles of mechanics, he will be able to talk about mechanical efficiency, whereas before he probably could not have done so.

If individual behavior is changed by particular knowledge, why are the social utilities of schooling not also affected? The answer is not far to seek. Some behavior is content-specific. If an individual practices medicine, works as a secretary, or is a dairy farmer, a competent analysis can readily identify much of the knowledge he possesses. But if the individual engages in political activities as a citizen, his knowledge is not as evident. Assume, as indicated in the preceding chapter, that the amount of participation varies directly with the amount of schooling. How much of his participation could be attributed to learning acquired in the social studies program? It seems reasonable to assume that such behavior can be attributed to the content most closely associated with it. But what is reasonable is not necessarily the case. Political participation could be associated with a mass of information acquired from different disciplines. It could be generated by knowledge derived from scientific sources, the study of literature and other art forms, or from the whole complex of school studies.

In fairness, however, it should be noted that history and civics have been required of every pupil for several decades. Increased political participation with increased schooling may be attributable to involvement in these studies. It would seem that elementary school graduates participate less than high school graduates because they have had less exposure to history and civics. However, the connection between the content of these studies and political behavior is tenuous. One must ask why individuals participate in political activities. Is it because of a sense of duty generated by instruction in history and civics? Is it because of the knowledge of history and government they acquired in school? Do they participate because of the network of economic and social connections

in which they are involved as citizens and workers? When
one considers the vast complex of forces that play upon the
individual, it seems improbable that a few hours of instruction
in one or two school subjects could account for his political
behavior. Nevertheless, the question must remain open, for
relevant data are not available.

Some social utilities are not dependent upon the behavior
of individuals *per se* but rather are social phenomena involving
countless kinds of behavior of myriad individuals. Economic
utility is an example. The chain of influence linking it to
any particular content is long and devious—if indeed the
chain exists at all. Claims are often made that certain academic
knowledge classified as general education has universal value
and thus should be required of every pupil. The available
evidence, scant though it is, lends no support to such claims
when measured against the criterion of economic growth.[2]
It is likely that the *level* of schooling attained in a society
is more closely associated with economic growth than is a
particular *kind* of schooling.

Social cohesion is another utility that does not depend upon
the behavior of individuals. There is apparently no cohesive
behavior *per se*. At first glance, however, it would appear
that social cohesion is associated with schooling that emphasizes social values and political knowledge. A great deal has
been made of the importance of values and the contribution
of the humanities to the development of a value system,
but it is a far cry from this claim to social cohesion. Commonly
held values are undoubtedly essential to a society's stability.
It does not follow, however, that such values are either
generated or sustained by instruction in the humanities.
Rather, common values are in all probability developed by
participation in conjoint activities and sustained by institutions.[3] Furthermore, social cohesion may depend upon the
image of society possessed by its members. The development
of such an image may be influenced more by the total school
program than by a particular part of it. The following observation by Louis Wirth helps to elucidate this point:

A society is possible in the last analysis because the individuals in it carry around in their heads some sort of picture of the society. Our society, however, in this period of minute division of labor, of extreme heterogeneity, and profound conflict of interests, has come to pass where these pictures are blurred and incongruous. Hence we no longer perceive the same things as real, and coincident with our vanishing sense of a common reality we are losing our common medium for expressing and communicating our experiences. The world has been splintered into countless fragments of atomized individuals and groups. The disruption in the wholeness of individual experience corresponds to the disintegration in culture and group solidarity. When the bases of unified collective action begin to weaken, the social structure tends to break and to produce a condition which Emile Durkheim has termed *anomie,* by which he means a situation which might be described as a sort of social emptiness or void. Under such conditions suicide, crime, and disorder are phenomena to be expected because individual existence no longer is rooted in a stable and integrated social milieu and much of life's activity loses its sense and meaning.[4]

If Wirth's analysis is correct, there can be no doubt of the need to strengthen the forces of social integration. The task appears to be of such magnitude that one must question the contribution that a particular content of the school program can make. The matter cannot be settled until measures of social cohesion are available and ways of ascertaining the advantages of schooling have been worked out.

What about methods of teaching and curriculum designs? Do they influence the utility of schooling? If they influence achievement, perhaps they do. Types of curricula and methods of instruction are repeatedly advanced as significant influences upon achievement. A number of surveys of research literature contravene this claim. Walker and Schaffarzick have made one of the most extensive analyses of curriculum research, covering twenty-three studies made since 1957.[5] They strongly suggest that the new curricula are not superior to the traditional curricula when the content bias in the achievement tests is taken into account. They observe that "different curricula are associated with different patterns of achievement" found in the curricula themselves.

Their guarded conclusions are in agreement with those reached by others, particularly by Wallen and Travers, who reviewed research on methods and found that methods apparently made no difference,[6] and by Stephens, who concluded that such variables as methods, team teaching, programmed instruction, and a host of other variables fail to show consistent differences in achievement.[7] While these analyses do not show conclusively that such variables have no influence upon achievement, they certainly indicate that fundamental conceptual analyses and empirical studies based thereon must be made before one can be reasonably certain about the effects of curriculum types and methods of teaching. In the meantime, it seems wiser to assume that neither of these factors is associated with individual or social utility of schooling.

It is interesting to note what Walker and Schaffarzick have to say about content:

> If the designers of the studies we have reviewed realized that the curricula they were comparing would have different patterns of outcomes, why did they try to compare these outcome patterns with an agglomerate achievement test yielding only one composite score? And why . . . is there no systematic apparatus at local, state, regional, or federal levels of school policy-making for considering the merits of various items of content that might be included in the school curriculum or in tests used to judge the success of students, teachers, or curricula? Why is it virtually impossible to find research which attempts to discover the consequences of studying different items of content, when there is so much research on the consequences of different media, methods, or strategies of teaching? And why do schools and funding agencies spend so much on organizational and technological innovations that have not been shown to produce different patterns of achievement and relatively little on innovations in curriculum materials?[8]

The relation of particular types of subject matter to the social utilities of schooling is a fundamental curriculum question, and one on which much research must be done.

It is not improbable that the use of various criteria of utility against which to evaluate curriculum content would go a long way toward answering the perennial question: What knowledge is of most worth? It could turn out that some information now in the curriculum has little utility and that some not included has great utility. It seems just as likely, however, that the total impact of the school determines the social utility of schooling rather than any specifiable content.

Were the latter surmise confirmed, it would give an empirical justification for a completely elective program of studies except for those studies (chiefly reading and arithmetic) required by the national achievement floor. It would also lead to a different approach to curriculum development. The prevailing approach is to consider the question of educational goals as basic to all other curriculum questions. The concept of utility would undercut the quest for goals by providing a new way of viewing the school's function. The social benefits of schooling could be empirically determined and the long and fruitless effort to define the goals of education and to justify the content of the curriculum by references to those goals would be obviated.

The school program is more flexible now than it was two or three decades ago. This is especially true in the larger schools, where the course offerings have been expanded extensively and the required subjects have been typically reduced to American history and English. Today the secondary schools collectively provide over fifteen areas of study consisting of approximately 900 courses.[9] A considerable number of these courses are designed to provide preparation in various occupations; others, to prepare students for college and to meet popular demands. Yet the belief that English, history, science, and mathematics are more important than the arts, vocational subjects, and physical education is still dominant in the minds of teachers, parents, and pupils.[10] It might be said that academic tyranny has shifted from program requirements to the minds of teachers and parents. This is attributable largely to the fact that the favored subjects lead to college and university work, and more prestige is attached to college attendance than to involvement in the labor force.

In view of the foregoing analysis, it is not unreasonable to favor the hypothesis that the amount and thoroughness of schooling as a whole contributes as much to the social utilities of schooling as the amount and thoroughness of schooling in particular studies. This view has another point in its favor. About 94 percent of school-age youth are enrolled in school. Their interests and capacities are as varied as those of the nation's total population. To assume that it is possible to identify a particular study suited to the interests and capacities of every pupil in such a diverse population is to engage in fantasy. While an imposed study can kindle the interests of pupils who would never otherwise enjoy it, such an imposition can also alienate as many others.

Freedom from Program Requirements

While the instructional program necessarily includes objects of knowledge such as concepts, principles, procedures, skills, facts, and values, it does not necessarily include any specific set of objects except those involved in the achievement floor— skills of communication and computation and basic concepts and principles. The skills and knowledge that make up the achievement floor are prescribed for all pupils because they are necessary for participation in American society and not because they are inherently superior to other knowledge and skills or because they are identified with the values of any social class. It follows from the hypothesis advanced in the paragraphs above that if a pupil has mastered everything up to and including the achievement floor, he is to be freed of all prescribed knowledge and skills regardless of his age or level of schooling. From that point, what he does with his school hours is to be decided by the pupil in consultation with his teachers, work supervisor, counselor, and parents. The school must impose no further curricular requirements for any purpose whatsoever. Whatever restraints are laid upon his choices will be those of career requirements and personal satisfactions.

Hypothetically, the extent of this flexibility can be seen by reference to the following diagram for basic learnings only.

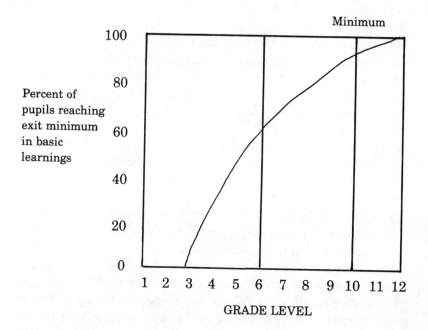

The school program is divided into three periods corresponding to elementary school, junior high or middle school, and high school. These divisions have no special merit; the purpose here is to illustrate the flexibility of the program. By reference to the diagram it can be seen that the elementary school provides for about 60 percent of the progress towards reaching minimum floors and that the secondary school assumes responsibility for the remaining 40 percent.

The diagram suggests that elementary school children are not likely to achieve the minimum until they have reached the third year of schooling, but at that time it is likely that a few of them will meet the standard. After the sixth grade only about 40 percent of the pupils will need further work in order to reach the achievement floor. By the tenth grade only about 5 percent will still be below the floor. This means that almost all of the senior high school pupils will be free to take all their work in the consumer curriculum if they choose to do so. The number of junior high school pupils who are entirely free is only slightly less.

Aside from the influence of parents and teachers and the narrowness of the curriculum, the main deterrent to freedom of curriculum choice is college entrance requirements. Many pupils are virtually forced to take college preparatory courses on the chance that they may want to go to college. This contingency can be reduced by eliminating all specific subject requirements for college admission. The experience gleaned from waiving conventional admission requirements for veterans and other groups makes it apparent that college success is determined more by the range and depth of experience, ability to read and compute, clarity of goals, and self-discipline than by knowledge of particular subjects. The deficiency in preparation for college is not lack of knowledge as much as it is the students' abysmal lack of experience and understanding of the adult world, its work, responsibilities, problems, procedures, and values. This deficiency helps to account for some college students' lack of goals, weak motivation, and inability to see the significance of what they study. If experience in adult responsibilities and a program of meaningful learning can be provided, college success can be just as assured as it is today with all the entrance requirements. The possible exceptions are to be found in the few areas where ability to do the work is demonstrably dependent upon prerequisite knowledge as, for example, in mathematics.

One must consider the possibility that college entrance requirements will not be relinquished. The history of colleges leads one to expect only slight changes rather than complete abandonment of admission requirements. This possibility may be of little consequence if the tendency of youth to discount college education continues. More and more youth tend to look forward to the labor force rather than to college. This discounting of college education will enable the youth to expand their perspectives on career opportunities and free them to take advantage of the options in an extended program of studies.

A great deal is being said nowadays about the irrelevance of school.[11] In the interest of clarity one must ask: Irrelevant to what? A pupil can say that the content of a required course is not useful to him; it must mean something to him, or else it is valueless. With all subject requirements removed, this case should not arise. If it does arise, the responsibility will fall no less upon the pupil than his advisers. A pupil who is concerned about inflation can hardly claim that economic facts and theories about the regulation of the economy are irrelevant. He can only claim that what he wanted to know about inflation was not in the course or that he had to learn material that did not deal with inflation. These can be legitimate objections. They indicate a need to package knowledge in units smaller than semester courses so that the pupil can have easy access to what he wants. If the pupil means irrelevance in some other sense, he can only have reference to the poverty of his experience. He does not know enough about his environment to see how a bit of knowledge illuminates the conditions affecting himself or others. This is probably the import of the assertion that the school is irrelevant. Part of the answer, of course, is adequate participation of youth in adult activities. The problem of relevance is as much a matter of reducing the poverty of experience as it is of selecting and organizing knowledge.

Social Functions and the Instructional Program

The traditional school program restricts the pupils' choice of studies and supports their isolation from the adult world. As noted above, about 900 courses are offered by the secondary school. In the larger schools this number may be approached, but in the smaller schools only a few courses are offered.

Even this vast number of courses, however, reflects glaring omissions of significant areas of knowledge. A program for all youth should leave no important area of knowledge untouched and should be organized in such a way as to emphasize the relation of schooling to the adult world. The purpose of this section is to set forth the spectrum of knowledge and to show how it is related to the spectrum of significant social functions.

It should be noted that knowledge in relationship to social functions can work in at least three ways. It can enable an individual to acquire further knowledge, it can enable the inquiring mind to create new knowledge, and it can render social functions more intelligible. The latter is the intellectual meaning of the injunction to relate the school to life. The task of increasing the individual utility of schooling consists partly in identifying the knowledge most closely related to the network of social relationships affecting the individual, and the first step in this direction is to determine the range of possibly useful knowledge defined by reference to categories. By comparing the school offerings with these categories, it is possible to identify those parts of knowledge neglected by the school and to see what knowledge is most relevant to social functions.

A pedagogically useful classification of knowledge has been developed by Tykociner in his work on *Zetetics*—the science of research and artistic creation.[12] In this work Tykociner developed a taxonomy of the sciences that appears to cover the domain of systematized knowledge and to give a fundamental basis for determining not only the actual but also the possible scope of the curriculum.

The taxonomy comprises twelve areas of knowledge, each area embracing a number of sciences having a common function. These areas are as follows:

1. *The Arts.* The sciences included in this area are architecture, choreography, dramatics, graphic arts, industrial design, landscaping, literature, music, painting, and sculpture. The

arts serve a number of purposes, among them to increase
the aesthetic quality of the objects comprising the environment, to advance and enrich communication, to encourage
creativity, and to sublimate unused energy resulting from
leisure.

2. *Symbolics of Information.* These include language, linguistics, mathematics, logic, and information theory. These
sciences make it possible to reason systematically. They
facilitate communication among persons in different cultures
as well as within a particular culture. They also make it
possible to handle abstract concepts and relationships and
to order and interpret information.

3. *Hylenergetics.* This area is made up of the sciences of
matter and energy, and it consists of physics, chemistry,
astronomy, geology, and mineralogy. These are frequently
referred to as the basic sciences, especially chemistry and
physics. They treat the building blocks of the universe (such
as atoms and smaller particles) as well as its structures and
superstructures (earth, solar system, galaxies). Their function
is to supply precise facts about the cosmos that enable man
to turn the environment to his advantage.

4. *Biological Area.* This area of knowledge comprises bo-
tany, zoology, taxonomy, morphology, cytology, genetics, and
physiology, typically called the life sciences. Its function is
to supply basic facts about forms of life, the dynamics of
forms, life processes, and mechanisms of communication and
controls within an organic system.

5. *Psychological Area.* This area chiefly constitutes experimental, developmental, abnormal, animal, and industrial
psychology. It deals with the dynamics of behavior, abilities,
capacities, behavioral development, and aberrations. Its
purpose is to provide basic facts and their relations in the
realm of animal and human behavior.

6. *Sociological Area.* Included in this area are sociology,
demography, social institutions, human ecology, and ethnolo-
gy. It supplies basic facts about the structure and dynamics

of social institutions, relations among individuals and groups, distribution and makeup of populations, comparative populations and cultures.

7. *Exeligmology.* The sciences that make up this area are those that deal with the past. These include the studies that treat the history of the world at large such as the historical aspects of cosmology, geology, biology, the past of human groups, and the history of the cultural evolution of man, his arts, sciences, technologies, and philosophies. These sciences are alike in that each attempts in one way or another to construct the past from data in the form of residues from transpired events. Their function is to provide various pasts in perspective.

8. *Pronoetics.* Among the sciences of this area are agriculture, medicine, technology, and national defense. These sciences are directed to the question of how man can take care of himself now and in the future, providing the necessities of life, health, and community.

9. *Regulative Area.* The primary regulative sciences are jurisprudence, political science, economics, management, and administration. This area contains the knowledge that has to do with the problems of regulating society and its institutions and keeping them in a state of viable equilibrium. The significant variables of society are constantly changing in number and magnitude so that maladjustments naturally arise. If one takes the position that these variables are mutually adjusted by automatic mechanisms controlled by natural law, then this area of knowledge is of little significance. In the recent past, this was the view of the economic system held by leading economists. Today the notion of automatic adjustment is in ill-repute, and great importance is being attached to the need for deliberate regulation of the economy. The political aspects of society and the operation of particular enterprises involve variables that also require deliberate control.

10. *Disseminative Area.* Among the sciences of this area are education, journalism, mass communication, and library.

These sciences are responsible for the collection, preparation, and communication of information. They accumulate and transmit the cultural heritage from one generation to the next and provide public information.

11. *Zetetics.* Among the sciences in this area are zetegny, taxology, problematology, and general methodology. It was pointed out years ago that man has not only made discoveries but, more important, he has discovered the method of discovery. Today he systematically goes about the task of increasing the amount and quality of knowledge. These sciences are concerned with the question of how knowledge is increased.

12. *Integrative Area.* The sciences concerned with this area are philosophy, theology, and general systems. Man is forever in search of unity, for a complete picture of reality, for his ultimate purpose and destiny. This area has been dealt with by philosophers, theologians, and prophets. A vast literature extending back to ancient times gives testimony to man's eternal quest for answers to fundamental questions about the world and himself, sources of his knowledge, his origin, the nature of nature, death, and where it all leads. As Wittgenstein put it, "Not *how* the world is, is the mystical, but *that* it is."[13]

In addition to these twelve areas, Tykociner also listed a number of sciences that connect them. For example, social psychology connects the Psychological to the Sociological Area; biophysics and biochemistry lies between Hylenergetics and the Biological Area; anthropology between the Sociological Area and Exeligmology.

The twelve areas of knowledge were grouped by Tykociner into five supercategories, which he referred to as series.[14] In this way he summarized the areas and gave their general functions as set forth in Table 5.

These areas of knowledge set the possible scope of the curriculum; they cover the totality of systematized knowledge in its present state of development. The curriculum has never reflected this total spectrum; the actual scope and the possible scope have never coincided. Even a cursory review of the

Table 5
Functions of the Areas of Knowledge

Series		Area	Function
I.	**1.	Arts	To develop systems
	*2.	Symbolics of information	of symbolic representations of perceptual and cognitive activity for purposes of communication
II.	*3.	Hylenergetics	To systematize
	*4.	Biological	knowledge of basic
	**5.	Psychological	facts and their
	**6.	Sociological	relations
III.	*7.	Exeligmology	To systematize
	**8.	Pronoetics	knowledge of the
	**9.	Regulative	past, project future
	**10.	Disseminative	needs, and regulate activities
IV.	***11.	Zetetic	To promote the growth of all arts and sciences
V.	***12.	Integrative	To create an all-embracing synthesis

*These areas comprise the major offerings of the high school program.
**These areas are only slightly represented in the high school program.
***These areas are completely ignored.

curriculum as it is today will reveal that the primary emphasis is upon Areas Two, Three, Four, and part of Seven. While Area One is given some attention, it is considered to be of minor significance, except for literature. Some aspects of Areas

Five, Six, Eight, Nine, and Ten are also included. On the whole, Series IV and V are completely omitted in the public school curriculum. The regulative, disseminative, and pronoetic sciences are short-changed, as are the psychological and sociological areas.

Moreover, the youth of today are exposed to fewer explicit moral guides and models of good character than perhaps any generation in recent history. The teaching profession has all but eliminated explicit attention to the moral development of children and youth. Parents and teachers are themselves often in doubt about what is the right and proper way to shape the character of children. This is due partly to the multiplicity of doctrines about child rearing that have bombarded parents and teachers in recent years and partly due to basic changes in man's relationship to man. Nowadays the individual must often deal with corporate entities, and the moral rules that apply in face-to-face situations do not carry the same commitment when applied to impersonal relations.[15] It is deplorable that the school continues to ignore the integrative sciences.

These restrictions upon the scope of the curriculum have at least three consequences of far-reaching importance. Any effort to utilize the interests of pupils is circumscribed since a considerable proportion of them would be more likely to have their interests awakened by the regulative, disseminative, and pronoetic sciences than by the physical and biological sciences. Others would find themselves more easily involved in the integrative sciences and the various arts than in other areas of knowledge. To speak of meeting pupil needs in a curriculum reflecting only a partial view of the domain of knowledge is unrealistic. The belief that all pupils can or should find interest in a curriculum that emphasizes only those aspects of knowledge familiar to teachers is one of the fetishes of the academic mind.

Specialization of labor has become one of the dominant features of advanced societies. While it increases production, specialization induces social illiteracy and apathy. Specialized

activities tend increasingly to shape the individual's experiences, his experiences shape what he knows and values, and
these in turn give scope and form to his perspectives. The
individual in a highly specialized society is likely to see life
narrowly and to weigh and consider alternatives in terms
that do not serve his personal welfare.

This would not be objectionable in a world that required
no collective action. The fact is that specialization creates
interdependence, and interdependence requires cooperation,
for specialized activities must be synthesized into a total
operation. Thus, the paradox that when men are required
to cooperate, plan, and act together to survive as they are
required to do today, their activities limit their experiences,
narrow their vision, and stunt their wisdom. To help counteract
this poverty of experience, foresight, and wisdom, experience
in a wide sample of social institutions should be available
as well as school studies that emphasize significant social
variables and their relationships. These studies are to be found
in the regulative, pronoetic, disseminative, and integrative
sciences, the very areas of knowledge so conspicuously depre-
cated by the school program.

Finally, the possibility of relating the school program to
what is going on in society is dependent upon the scope of
the curriculum. If the program consists primarily of the basic
sciences of physics, chemistry, biology, symbolics of communication, and a study of mankind's past, the relevance of the
program to the adult world will be very truncated. If the
domain from which the program of studies is selected consists
of the twelve areas of knowledge, the program of the school
can be articulated with all the social functions. In this way
the socializing experience of youth in the adult community
and their school experiences can become genuinely compli-
mentary.

Up to this point, the discourse has dealt with the areas
of knowledge and the fact that the school program includes
only a part of the total range of knowledge. A more adequate
program would consist of studies that include knowledge from

all areas adapted to pupils and to social functions. The task of relating the areas of knowledge to social functions requires far more care than can be given to it here. A suggested approach may help to illustrate a way to show the relationship between the curriculum and the world of adult activity. In Table 6 the axes are areas of knowledge and social functions.

An X indicates that an area of knowledge is related to a social function. For example, the arts contribute to the functions of providing services, communication, aesthetic objects, and expression of religious feelings. They provide services by producing entertainment as in the theater; they evoke pleasure through perceptual communication; they produce aesthetic objects as in buildings and landscapes; and they provide the aesthetic expression of religious sentiments as in religious songs and paintings. The regulative sciences have to do primarily with the functions related to the daily operation and maintenance of the total social system. The pronoetic sciences are concerned with the functions that provide for physical welfare. The integrative and disseminative sciences serve the functions that maintain cultural continuity and personal stability. Zetetics looks to constant cultural renewal.

Areas Three to Six inclusive appear to be unrelated to social functions because they are, in fact, not directly connected to them. This is what is meant by the expression "basic sciences." They undergird the sciences in Areas Eight, Nine, and Ten and impinge upon Areas Eleven and Twelve. They are therefore related to social functions through the contributions they make to these areas of knowledge. For example, the impact of physics and chemistry upon social functions is made through developments in technology, medicine, agriculture, and national defense, which partly depend upon the knowledge base provided by these two fundamental sciences. A similar observation can be made about the biological, psychological, and sociological sciences if one bears in mind that these areas are basic to Areas Eight, Nine, and Ten.

In spite of the fact that Areas One, Eight, Nine, Ten, and

Table 6
Social Functions and Areas of Knowledge

	to maintain internal and external order	to administer justice	to foster the general welfare	to foster and regulate the economy	to protect persons, property, and resources	to produce and distribute goods	to provide for services	to provide for transportation	to provide for communication	to provide for production of aesthetic objects	to provide for expression of religious feelings	to provide learning for the young and adults	to produce and distribute knowledge	to help man understand himself and life's meaning	to regulate sex behavior and to propagate the species	to provide a social context for bringing up the young
Arts						X		X		X	X					
Symbolics								X					X			
Hylenergetics																
Biological																
Psychological																
Sociological																
Exeligmology														X		
Pronoetics						X	X	X	X							
Regulative	X	X	X	X	X	X	X	X	X							
Disseminative						X		X				X	X	X		X
Zetetics										X				X		
Integrative												X		X	X	

Twelve are closely associated with social functions, they are the ones most consistently slighted by the school. Since the fundamental sciences are related to life activities primarily through these areas, it is easy to understand why the exhortation to relate instruction to life is so uniformly disregarded. The subjects through which their contribution is made are seldom found in the school's program. Consequently, about all a teacher can do is to give a few examples of practical applications of basic knowledge.

Toward a Consumer Curriculum

The answer to the question of how to represent these neglected areas of knowledge is not to add new subjects but to add a multiplicity of minicourses of two, four, or six weeks' duration. This coincides with the efforts of some schools to change the distribution of instructional time by breaking semester courses into smaller units. Minicourses can cover significant topics in the various areas of knowledge as these relate to social functions. The functions of political institutions and Area Nine will yield such minicourses as:

—your rights on being arrested
—military services and their opportunities
—courts and how they operate
—how local taxes are administered
—what you should know about wills
—pupils' legal rights
—control of the economy
—how your wages are fixed
—welfare agencies
—control of mass media
—income taxes
—conservation of natural resources
—laws regulating employment of youth.

Areas Eight and Nine and the functions associated with economic institutions will supply minicourses such as:

—how utilities are provided
—how to analyze a homeowner's insurance policy

—how to buy life insurance
—how to borrow money
—how to buy or rent a home
—how to buy transportation
—how to buy medical services
—language of data processing
—unions and what they do
—medical insurance
—production of news
—sources of energy
—dental work
—the drug industry
—food processing
—the meat industry
—physics and chemistry of communication
—mechanics of heating and air conditioning.

Areas Ten and Twelve in conjunction with economic and integrative institutions will yield such units as:
—control of schools
—how the school's program of studies is decided
—effect of mass media on children and adults
—how you learn
—what makes for contentment
—man's nature
—sources of knowledge
—moral conduct.

Some authorities will object to minicourses on such complex subjects and insist that no knowledge is better than half-baked information. These objections miss the point. The purpose of minicourses is not to give a quick overview of a subject; it is to select an important aspect of a subject of use to the layman and to deal with it in such a way as to make it understandable and beneficial to the pupil as a worker and a citizen and not as a student of economics, law, or whatever. For example, a minicourse on the variables involved in the maintenance of equilibrium in the economy would be enlightening to the pupil as a worker no less than as a citizen, for he can easily see how economic disequilibrium can affect him. The legal rights of an employee in industry, the legal rights of a pupil, the legal aspects of a will, or what a citizen should know about insurance can be treated in minicourses. Stripped of legal jargon, they can be adequately understood and appreciated by any high school pupil who has reached the achievement floor and has participated with adults in responsible activities.

The youth of today no less than yesterday are concerned about fundamental questions that can be treated in minicourses. The suggested minicourses given above are examples of the reorientation of the curriculum that must take place if the program is to have utility for individuals as workers, citizens, and persons in a complex and puzzling society. The minicourse curriculum should be viewed as an alternative to the long, drawn-out subject curriculum. However, the subject curriculum is not to be discarded. Extended study is necessary for pupils who wish to master systematically the concepts, principles, and procedures of particular disciplines. The conventional subject curriculum is appropriate for that purpose.

The belief that anything worth studying is worth studying for at least a semester should have been discarded long ago. The tenacity of this belief can be attributed to the fact that the program of studies has been considered as a linear structure: the study of one course preparing for the study of another and the whole structure ending in the graduate departments of the university. The temporal size of the units was thus determined by convenient breaking points in the various sciences and historic divisions of the school year. Had the program of studies been coordinated with the utility of knowledge in the adult world, a horizontal structure would have emerged, and the units of instruction would have been smaller and functionally oriented. To package knowledge in such minicourses and to make all courses above the achievement floor elective is to create a consumer curriculum, a program oriented to the pupil as a consumer of learning.

It should be noted that there are good reasons for smoothing the articulation of the secondary school and the community college. As high school youth become increasingly involved in community life, some may wish to enroll in afternoon or evening college classes to acquire new skills or to advance their general knowledge. Youth and adults will then be enrolled in the same courses. The practice of grouping by age brackets will be broken, and the socializing benefits from participation with adults increased. Such a merger of programs for youth and adults is likely to meet with widespread approval. In time, more adults than ever will be in school along with the youth. The changing nature of occupations and the growth of knowledge will render schooling a lifetime activity. The work week and day will become shorter. It is not unlikely that industry, commerce, and the professions will establish within a few years a system of sabbatical leaves for schooling and other modes of occupational adjustment and self-fulfillment.

Any program of schooling is controlled by structures that set limits to what can be done. The structure of the daily schedule, the system of credits and examinations, and the allotment of time are typical examples. Perhaps the most important of these is the pattern of time distribution. The present timetable calls for early childhood, kindergarten, elementary, and secondary schooling in an unbroken sequence, although this pattern is not conducive to the development of a program of socialization in the adult community. There is also a fixed amount of time in the yearly schedule for each course, typically sixteen to eighteen weeks. The content is packaged accordingly, regardless of whether it is useful to the consumer. This way of distributing time leads to inflexibility. Some of the ways of dealing with such inflexibility are now being developed in various school systems throughout the country and need not be discussed here.

Retreat from Compulsory Schooling

The length of required school attendance is a question now being debated in the press, educational circles, and legislative bodies. The question is relevant to the foregoing discussion. If a youth is permitted to decide his program of schooling after he has achieved the minimum floor, why not take the additional step and allow him to decide whether to stay in school at all? It is pertinent to review the arguments against compulsory attendance although the matter is not a pedagogical question. The arguments can be classified under these rubrics: motives, ideology, enforceability, pedagogy, and economy.

One argument emphasizes that compulsory schooling was established more to remove youth from the labor force than to develop educated workers and citizens.[16] Another argument holds that compulsory schooling resulted from the belief that school was the proper agency to Americanize the children of the vast horde of immigrants in the closing decades of the last century. Since the school functioned poorly as a melting pot and the need to keep youth from the labor market is not defensible, compulsory schooling should be abandoned. These arguments have at least one thing in common: Compulsory attendance is no longer justified because the reasons for its enactment are vulnerable.

The soundness of a policy does not necessarily depend upon the reasons or goals that led to its establishment. Arguments that discount a policy because its original goal is vulnerable are valid if that goal is the only important one served by the policy. This is seldom the case. One's experience will readily yield instances of policies whose original goals are less desirable than the goals that evolve as the consequences of the policy become evident. To show that the reasons of the policy makers are vulnerable is not to show that the policy itself is vulnerable. If this were not true, it would be almost impossible to establish equitable rules, regulations, and laws since all sorts of reasons move men to act as they do.

The basic ideological argument holds that because the school is an arm of the state it is an agency for the elite to control the mind of the masses. Compulsory attendance is thus a coercive instrument by which the upper classes appropriate children for indoctrination. Teachers are subordinates paid to do the bidding of the elite. To free the youth of schooling is to remove them from the coercive influence of the elite and thereby liberate their minds for revolutionary ideas. Deschooling of society is an instrument of revolution and not a plan for reforming the school.[17] This argument is quite familiar, for it is an application of Marxian thought to the educational system.

This whole line of thought can play into the hands of those who oppose the schools because they are costly. If youth do not go to school, the propertied element of the population is relieved of the tax burden for schools. In developing nations the argument supports the wealthy class in its resistance to public education for all children and youth. After all, the elite does not need the school for ideological purposes because they already own and control the press, television, radio, and all other instruments for molding the public mind.

This ideological position assumes either that a society can exist in the absence of an elite or that a new elite is necessary to right the current injustices. As for the first assumption, it is nonsense to hold that a society can organize and operate without leaders. There will always be individuals who occupy positions of power and will use that power to the advantage of themselves and their social class. As for the second assumption, any new ruling class will be as ruthless and cold-blooded in their struggle to maintain power as the class they liquidate. There is little justification for belief in the goodness of a ruling class *per se*. Whatever advantages the masses enjoy are to be attributed to social institutions and what these institutions enable the masses to exact from the elite through the exercise of their collective actions, established political procedures, and techniques. The major political difference among societies is not that some have an elite and others do not: All have an elite. The difference is the degree to which the masses have the institutional means and the organized capacity to tame the power of the ruling group and to turn it to their advantage whenever the opportunity arises. The open societies of the West provide institutions conducive to the welfare of the masses. Among these institutions is the public school.

Another ideological argument holds that the individual has a right to make mistakes.[18] This is an odd way of putting the matter since mistakes are not a right but a characteristic of the human condition. What is probably meant is that institutional regulations and laws should not rob the individual of the right to make decisions about things that affect him personally. One who holds this position would likely insist that a law requiring an individual to use a seat belt in an automobile is not justifiable for it infringes upon the individual's right to decide the matter for himself. The same logic seems to be applied to the question of compulsory attendance.

Is the amount of a youth's schooling something he should decide? This question requires one to consider the conditions under which an individual may be said to have the right to make decisions independent of others. The basic condition is that the individual be able to recognize and weigh the consequences of his decision. If not, few would hold that he should have the right to decide. However, other conditions must be considered even if this condition is satisfied. These additional conditions pertain to the types of decisions. One can distinguish three types: personal, private, and public. A personal decision is one that affects only the individual who makes it. If two or more persons make a decision and the consequences affect only the decision makers, the decision is private. If the decision is made by one or more persons and the consequences affect the decision makers and other persons as well, the decision is public. If a person decides not to use a seat belt as he drives his automobile, the decision appears to be a personal one. If he has dependents, or if his death in an accident is attributed to failure to fasten his seat belt and insurance rates are thereby increased, the personal character of the decision is questionable. Ordinarily, these sorts of considerations are not taken into account when the right of an individual to make a decision is considered unless the public character of the decision is significant. The claim of a driver to decide what he will do at a street intersection is denied because of the traffic disorder he might create and the danger to others that his decision could produce. It is partly to protect individuals from the decisions and actions of others that rules and laws are made.

Should a 14-year-old be given the right to decide whether or not to continue his schooling? The first point to consider is whether or not he or she is capable of understanding and weighing the consequences of his decision. For a person of college age to see the advantages and disadvantages of further schooling is difficult enough. It is placing a tremendous burden on a very limited experience to trust a 14-year-old to make such a decision. Parents decide countless things for their children because the children do not know enough to decide for themselves. Parents and teachers in increasing numbers are encouraging children to develop the ability to make wise decisions. The ones in which this ability is least developed are the ones who would most likely drop their schooling at the earliest opportunity. The question at issue is not whether children should have the "right to make mistakes" but rather what mistakes they should have the right to make.

Thirty-eight states including the District of Columbia now require school attendance to the age of 16, seven to the age of 17, and four to the age of 18. In some of these states the pupil can drop out of school at 16 only with parental consent. If such consent were required at the age of 14, the argument against reducing compulsory attendance on the grounds of immaturity would be discounted. If the compulsory age were dropped to this level, the children of the inner city and the rural slums would be the hardest hit. The more fortunate parents will send their children to school even without attendance laws. The children of the poor are those who stand to lose the advantages of schooling because their parents are the ones who are least likely to see the benefits of schooling.

Still another argument holds that secondary schooling is unnecessary for many jobs.[19] This is a valid point. But not all the benefits of schooling are to be assimilated to success on a job. To be sure, the ability to perform on a job is a necessary condition for a satisfactory life. However, other benefits must be considered: quality of life in the neighborhood and community, life-style, political participation, one's image of society, and the ability to manage one's affairs. By hypothesis, all of these are influenced positively by secondary schooling.

A position advanced by some educators and laymen is that compulsory attendance would be unnecessary if the schools were attractive, stimulating, active centers of life and work.[20] If compulsory attendance were abandoned principals and teachers would make the schools into attractive centers of life. Compulsory attendance now protects the teaching profession in its conservative bent. This view has little to support it. The more likely outcome is that the schools would gradually adjust their faculties to enrollments. This is precisely what the universities, colleges, and private secondary schools do. There is no good reason to suppose that the public high schools would follow a different course. Furthermore, as the pupils who are not doing well in their studies drop out of school the curriculum will become more academic because such a curriculum is cheaper and would satisfy the remaining pupils and their parents.

No one can reasonably oppose the view that schools should be models of social life, stimulating and inviting to youth. Some of them are. Some youth would quickly drop out under the best conditions, however. What an individual decides to do is the result of many forces that play upon him. An attractive school can only be one such force. And, no matter how strong the school's pull may be, many 14-year-olds would choose to be idle rather than face the challenge of an exciting school.

Finally, it is argued by some opponents of compulsory

schooling that attendance laws are not enforceable.[21] They point out that high school attendance has fallen sharply, as much as 15 percent in some communities. This is taken as evidence that the enforcement of attendance laws is practically impossible, and hence they argue for repeal. This line of thought is questionable.

In the first place, it appears that attendance data are open to question. It is claimed by some school authorities, especially in the big cities, that some pupils do not report for roll call in their homerooms, although they attend classes. This is said to be true in cases where the homeroom teacher is disliked and the homeroom activities are perfunctory. In addition, it is claimed that some pupils attend only the classes they like. Enrollment data are also unreliable as evidence that children of school age are actually in school. There are doubtless many children and youth (one estimate suggests at least a million between the ages of 7 and 15) who are not enrolled in school at all.[22] In some areas the estimate of nonenrolled pupils runs as high as 40 percent.[23] But like attendance data, these estimates must be taken with caution.

In the second place, the observance of any law by everybody is probably an impossibility. That is why the police system and courts were established. The question is how many violations are to be taken as evidence that a law should be repealed? Should it be repealed if 5 percent of the people break it? If 15 percent break it? Or what have you? The opponents of compulsory attendance provide no answer to this question. It does not necessarily follow that a law should be repealed because large numbers of people violate it. Many laws were violated at rock music festivals and in street and campus demonstrations of the 1960s. Yet no effort was made to repeal these laws. Why? Probably because these events were judged to be ephemeral, and the better part of wisdom seemed to be to contain them while they played themselves out. Who can say that nonattendance at the high school level is not a passing phenomenon generated by the current temper of youth and the blight of life in the inner city and the rural slums? Little attention has been given to the enforcement of attendance, probably because of the overcrowding of schools in the years of great population growth. A continued decline in the birth rate can lead to an increasing concern that all children be in school.

It should be said that a few youths should not be in the public school. The identification and diagnosis of such cases should be made by a staff of counselors, psychologists, social workers, physicians, teachers, and administrators. As Morrison noted long ago,

> We have to distinguish critically between the undeveloped pupil who is not yet positively vicious and who is still an appropriate object of general education and the pupil who has passed into the field of legal delinquency—the thief, the inebriate, the youthful rake. Such individuals are likely to be instances of outright social pathology requiring separation from the school and treatment outside the school.[24]

The foregoing analysis of the arguments against compulsory attendance is not an explicit defense of such attendance. The burden of proof is on those who oppose compulsory attendance laws. The point of the analysis is that the arguments are vulnerable and in some cases flimsy. Surely the repeal of attendance laws should be based on substantial and cogent arguments. The future of a large number of youth is at stake. To abandon compulsory attendance is not to improve their lot. They would not thereby be provided with the opportunity to make something of their lives nor would society be insured against the loss of the social dividends of secondary schooling. Youth must be provided with a more distinctive *rites de passage* than they now enjoy. Merely releasing them from the obligation to attend school will not provide it. The program of socialization and schooling suggested in the foregoing chapters is an attempt to provide a constructive entry of youth into the adult world.

FOOTNOTES

[1] For an exploration of the importance of this factor see J. B. Carroll, "A Model of School Learning," *Teachers College Record*, Vol. 64, 1963, pp. 723–33; and David E. Wiley, *Another Hour, Another Day: Quantity of Schooling, A Potent Path for Policy*, Studies of Educative Processes, Report No. 3, July, 1973.

[2] Psacharopoulos, *Returns to Education*, op. cit., p. 70.

[3] William Graham Summer, *Folkways* (Boston, Mass.: Ginn and Company, 1906), pp. 1–119.

[4] Wirth, op. cit., p. XXV.

[5] Decker F. Walker and Jon Schaffarzick, "Comparing Curricula," *Review of Educational Research*, Winter, 1974, pp. 83–111.

[6] N. E. Wallen and M. W. Travers, "Analysis and Investigation of Teaching Methods," in *Handbook of Research on Teaching*, N. L. Gage, (ed.), (Chicago, Ill.: Rand McNally, 1963), pp. 448–505.

[7] J. M. Stephens, *The Process of Schooling* (New York: Holt, Rinehart and Winston, 1967). Stephens reached about the same conclusion from an analysis of research studies made in the first three decades of this century. See his *The Influence of the School on the Individual* (Ann Arbor, Mich.: Edwards Brothers, 1933).

[8] Walker and Schaffarzick, op. cit., p. 98.

[9] Dianne B. Gertler and Linda A. Barker, *Patterns of Course Offerings and Enrollments in Public Secondary Schools 1970–1971*, U.S. Office of Education, National Center for Educational Statistics, DHEW Publication, No. (OE) 73-11400 (Washington, D.C.: U.S. Government Printing Office, 1972).

[10] Ibid., *passim*.

[11] Harry S. Broudy, *The Real World of the Public Schools* (New York: Harcourt Brace Jovanovich, 1972), pp. 176–98. See also Carlton E. Beck et al., *Education for Relevance* (New York: Houghton Mifflin Company, 1968), pp. 233–48; Walden B. Crabtree, "An Age of Irrelevancy," *Educational Theory*, Winter, 1971, pp. 33–41.

[12] Joseph T. Tykociner, *Outline of Zetetics* (Philadelphia, Pa.: Dorrance, 1966), pp. 29–90.

[13] Ludwig Wittgenstein, *Tractatus Logico—Philosophicus* (London: Routledge and Kegan, Paul, 1922), p. 187.

[14] Tykociner, op. cit., p. 51.

[15] Karl Mannheim, *Man and Society in an Age of Reconstruction* (New York: Harcourt, Brace, 1940), pp. 51–75.

[16] Howard M. Johnson, "Are Compulsory Attendance Laws Outdated?" *Phi Delta Kappan,* December, 1973, pp. 226–32.

[17] Ivan Illich, *Deschooling Society* (New York: Harper and Row, 1970), *passim.* See also Joel Spring, "Deschooling As a Form of Social Revolution" in *Roots of Crisis,* by Clarence J. Karier, et al. (Chicago, Ill.: Rand McNally, 1973), pp. 138–47. For an analysis of these arguments see Richard Pratte, *The Public School Movement* (New York: David McKay Company, 1973), pp. 98–122.

[18] Carl Bereiter, "Must We Educate?" *Phi Delta Kappan,* December, 1973, pp. 233–36.

[19] Johnson, op. cit., p. 227.

[20] Brown, op. cit., p. 229.

[21] Johnson, loc. cit.

[22] "An Interview with Mariam Wright Edelman," *Harvard Education Review,* Vol. 44, No. 1, 1974, p. 56.

[23] Ibid.

[24] Henry C. Morrison, *Practice of Teaching in the Secondary School* (Chicago, Ill.: University of Chicago Press, 1926), p. 427.

CHAPTER VII

Preservice Teacher
Education

One of the hypotheses advanced in the preceding chapter
is that the social utility of schooling is associated with the
amount and thoroughness of schooling. One can best begin
with the commonsense notion that the thoroughness of
schooling is associated with the pedagogical knowledge and
skill of the teacher and his knowledge of the subject taught.

Unprecedented advances have been made in teacher
competence and in research on teaching since 1900, enabling
progress of major importance to be made provided the application of research to teacher training is understood. The heart
of the argument set forth in this chapter consists in the
proposition that it is seldom possible to go directly from
research results and theories to pedagogical practice. Problems
at the level of practice must be solved. To solve them, one
must know as much about the practical situation as he knows
about the theory and research to be applied. In addition, the
solution of these special problems involves the development
of materials and procedures from which the practitioner is
to learn to perform, and their development presupposes that

the concepts and skills to be used in on-the-job practice are known. All this entails developmental research. No attempt is made here to set forth these skills and concepts. Rather, the general direction considered desirable for developmental research in teacher education is explored.

To Train or Not to Train

Before turning to the purpose of this chapter, however, it is fitting that an attempt be made to clear the air of the claims and counterclaims about the value of teacher training.

The school achievement of an individual is contingent upon six sets of factors: native endowment, previous learning (both school and nonschool), school facilities, peers, his efforts, and instruction. During the last decade, the winds of doctrine, fed by studies that purport to show the school's effectiveness, have blown in the direction of the first two. It is claimed that what the child brings to school almost completely determines what he will take away. If he brings little, he takes away little. The teacher's influence counts for practically nothing in the acquisition of basic skills and elementary knowledge.[1] It is not surprising that some persons have concluded from these studies that teacher training is a futile enterprise. Those who oppose this appraisal cite studies that purport to show that the teacher's influence is a potent element in determining achievement.[2] But on a number of counts these studies, both pro and con, are unconvincing.

First, they use nonbehavioral teacher variables—degrees, academic marks, intelligence scores, experience, personality scores, supervisory ratings—whose zero or nearly zero relation to pupil achievement has been known for almost half a century.[3] Teaching is the exercise of social, intellectual, perceptual, and manipulative skills under the control of conceptual knowledge. To know the effectiveness of a teacher is to know the consequences of his use of these concepts and skills. To know the effectiveness of teacher training is to know how well it develops these aspects of teacher behavior. Naturally, studies that investigate the effects of nonbehavioral variables can yield conflicting results, for such results will be produced by the obtrusion of unknown behavioral variables.

It is surprising to find that nonbehavioral variables continue to be used at this late date in studies of teacher influence. Perhaps they are used because of their convenience. The more likely explanation is that researchers assume that degrees, academic grades, experience, and the like are indicators of training. This assumption is wrong. Teaching abilities are attested by none of these variables, because teacher education programs are highly concentrated in verbal cognition and very weak in training in the performance of teaching skills. The inadequacy of the training program is the heart of the problem.

The findings of the prestigious Coleman report have been variously interpreted. In most cases they have been taken to mean that the teacher has little impact on pupil learning. On this point it is interesting to note the following appraisal of that interpretation:

> Those who have drawn the conclusion that teachers make no difference, from the evidence reported by Coleman and others in *Equality of Educational Opportunity* (1966), have misunderstood the nature of the data analysis they employed in that study, and overlooked the ambiguity of the word "difference." What studies of the Coleman type may (or may not) have shown is that measured *differences between* teachers are not closely associated with measured *differences between* pupils. What such a finding might mean is very difficult to understand, but it certainly does not mean that teachers do *not* affect pupils and it does *not* indicate in any way how much they affect their pupils. It should not take large-scale research studies, or sophisticated regression analyses, to indicate that children who are taught to play the piano, do rather better at piano playing than children who have never received any lessons.[4]

Second, the studies do not distinguish among types of pupils. Many pupils will learn without instruction if they are given assignments and materials and the opportunity to help each other. Many others will learn under the same conditions with a modicum of assistance from the teacher. Many students, however, cannot learn without diagnosis and appropriate help. These are pupils with learning difficulties. They are the ones who test a teacher's competence.

Programs of teacher education poorly prepare the teacher to deal with learning difficulties and disabilities. He knows very little about the diagnosis and treatment of pupils' problems in learning or in social and personal adjustment. College programs have prepared the teacher to work effectively with pupils who learn quite well if they are given assignments, materials, encouragement, a little help. A comparable program in schools of medicine would prepare physicians to treat patients who would get well on their own or who would recover with minor treatment.

If a teacher cannot cope with learning problems, he is inadequately trained regardless of his professional degrees. The test of the teacher's professional competence as well as the adequacy of his training is whether or not he can identify and alleviate the difficulties of pupils so as to release their potential for learning. The test is not the degree to which pupils approach the average of some reference group. If learning difficulties can be alleviated, pupils will attain the achievement floor and exceed it as time and circumstance permit.

Finally, one is led to ask, what do those who discount teacher training really mean? Do they mean that teacher training is impossible because the behavior of teachers cannot be changed? Do they mean that teaching can be done by anyone who knows a subject? Or do they mean that not enough is known about problems of teaching and learning to develop a reliable training program? If the opponents of training intend to suggest that teacher behavior cannot be changed, they are wrong. To answer them one need not stand on the general proposition that human behavior is modifiable. Specific studies of teacher behavior clearly show that the behavior of teachers, even those whose behavior is stabilized by experience, can be changed with materials and procedures designed for that purpose.[5] Furthermore, the change persists.

If they mean to claim that anyone with sufficient knowledge of content can teach successfully without training, they are wrong. It is well known that knowledge of an academic subject is no guarantee that one can teach the deaf or the blind to read, correct speech defects, or cope with the behavior problems of disruptive pupils. The opponent of training can reply that he did not intend his claim to cover the unusual. But this is just the point. Learning difficulties are unusual in the sense that they are not recognized by the untrained. They include not only handicaps due to physical dysfunctions but also those rooted in emotional problems, teacher-pupil discourse, motivation, background deficits, divergent cultural orientations, faulty inference patterns, perceptual troubles, and difficulties associated with the characteristics of the knowledge to be learned. In all probability, at least a third of the pupils at all levels suffer from one or more learning difficulties. These are the pupils who fall behind and either drop out or end their schooling with reduced life chances because of deficient achievement.

The opponents of training may take the position that the knowledge base for a reliable training program does not exist. If they do, they are wrong again. They either apply an inappropriate conception of knowledge or do not know the status of educational knowledge. It is readily admitted that educational knowledge does not consist of universal propositions (such as Newton's law of gravitation) that are applicable to an indefinite range of problems. Nor is education able to draw upon other disciplines for such universals, as engineering can draw upon physics. The nearest thing to an instance of such a resource for education is the principle of conditioning.

It is important to recognize that the lack of universals is of no consequence because educational knowledge, like the bulk of knowledge in all professions, holds for the context of particular types of problems. The knowledge of how to cope with learning difficulties rooted in depressed motivation is not the same as that required to handle perceptual problems.

It is specific to the type of problem. Furthermore, like knowledge in other professions, educational knowledge is probabilistic. If the symptoms are such and such, then the difficulty is probably this. If the difficulty is this, then the chances are that it will be overcome if you do thus and so. The knowledge about diagnosis and treatment resulting from research and practical experience of teachers bulks large.[6] It covers all sorts of problems in conduct, motivation, disabilities, reading and arithmetic, and to a lesser extent in certain content fields. Nevertheless, the need for additional knowledge is ever present, a need that calls for more research and the systematization of professional wisdom. However, the development of a reliable program of training is now possible. It can be undertaken only if those responsible for teacher education come to grips with the problems that children have in learning and concentrate teacher training on diagnosis, prognosis, and ways to cope with the difficulties.

The studies that have been made of the influence of teachers can be of value if they are seen as blind alleys and are taken as evidence of the need for a new approach to the problems of teacher preparation and the evaluation of the impact of schooling. To reject teacher training either as a matter of principle or on the basis of the foregoing claims, rather than to demand its redirection and the research to underwrite its progressive improvement, borders on the irresponsible. There can be no doubt that teachers trained to cope with the learning difficulties of children will make the entrance of youth to adult society easier and more secure. This fact makes it irresponsible to opt for zero training in a society still suffering from deficiencies in the basic skills and knowledge of its youth. What must be done is to declare a moratorium on talk about the futility of training and to get on with the solution to the problems that obviously and directly face those responsible for training the nation's teachers. Some of the more important of these problems consist in the identification of the concepts and skills that enable teachers to succeed with pupils who cannot learn without help, and to engage in the development and operation of a school program flexible enough to develop the potential of every pupil. They consist also in the development of materials and procedures and the institutional arrangements for training teachers in these concepts and skills.

The Redirection of Training

A profession renders a service; it does things for people that they cannot do for themselves. The character of teacher preparation in almost all institutions leads teachers to render service to those who need it least. The school houses pupils with varying degrees of need of teacher knowledge and skill. Despite the fact that the kinds and distribution of such needs are not fully catalogued, all can agree that the preservice program is harnessed to the average pupil.

The claim that little preparation is needed by teachers beyond a command of their subject matter is not without reason, although it has no justification in the case of pupils suffering from learning difficulties. A teacher can be effective with a considerable number of pupils if he knows the subject matter and is reasonably skilled in ordinary human interaction, because many pupils can learn with very little instruction. This fact and the fact that current programs of teacher preparation advance the teacher's skills only a little beyond those of the educated layman supports the criticism of education courses being made by academic faculties. The superiority of the professional over the nonprofessional is evidenced in cases that cannot be successfully handled without him—not in cases that can get along fairly well in his absence. If a profession cannot cope with cases that need help, its reliability is likely to be questioned.

The amount of professional knowledge and skill needed to teach effectively is inversely proportional to the development of the learner and directly proportional to the range and severity of his learning problems. The teacher in the primary and intermediate grades requires far more knowledge of human development, learning difficulties, and teaching

than a teacher in a graduate department. Almost fifty years
ago, Morrison distinguished among the segments of the educational ladder by the principle of increasing ability to learn
independently.[7] At the elementary level, the child is acquiring
the tools of learning. He is dependent on the teacher. When
he has mastered these tools, he is a secondary school pupil
and is less dependent. He passes from the secondary level
when he has acquired the ability to learn on his own. This
is undoubtedly an oversimplification of the matter, but it
contains the germ of the proposition that the teacher's need
for professional knowledge and know-how decreases as the
pupil's intellectual maturity increases. If preservice preparation is to contribute significantly to the competence of
teachers,* it must be reoriented; it must be turned away
from over-occupation with the average pupil and slanted
toward the pupil who suffers from learning difficulties, dis-
orders, and dysfunctions.**

The notion that the curriculum of teacher training should
include a study of diagnostic and remedial procedures and
materials is not new.[8] A few courses in remedial reading
and arithmetic have been included in programs of teacher
education almost since the first investigations into the acquisition of reading and arithmetic skills almost fifty years
ago. But no college of education has ever made diagnostic
and remedial work its central concern. Only one or two courses
in the treatment of learning difficulties are offered today
in the curricula of colleges of education. These are typically

---

*The definition of "competence" assumed in this discourse is stated in Criteria
2 and 3 of Turner's formulation in *The Power of Competency-Based Teacher
Education*, edited by Benjamin Rosner (Boston: Allyn and Bacon, 1972), p. 5.
Criterion 2 is acceptable for instructional skills. Criterion 3 is acceptable for
conceptual knowledge and for skills of diagnosis, planning, evaluation, and the
like.

**In a 1973 survey of teacher needs, diagnostic problems were rated as the
fourth important need among twenty difficulties faced by teachers. See "A
Comparison of Teacher and Educational Leader Assessments of Teacher Needs,"
National Education Association, March, 1973.

in reading and arithmetic and are limited mostly to elementary teachers. Usually they are not required. One would presume that pupils have no problems of learning in social studies, English, science, arts, or technical subjects.

Much has been said in recent years about the training of teachers through clinical experience. This is not to be confused with systematic training in diagnostics, prognostics, and remediation. Strictly speaking, clinical experience has to do with training based on observation and treatment of patients who need the care of a physician. But the practice in education consists of learning by observation and practice how to carry on instruction geared to pupils who need the teacher least. The clinical method of training is indispensable, but if it does not deal with the problems of learning, it is just another name for student teaching.

Naturally, teachers need to be prepared in the skills and concepts relevant to instructional situations that do not involve learning difficulties. Effective learning conditions must be created and maintained for all pupils, the autonomous pupils no less than those who must have help to succeed. To do this, teachers must be skilled in planning and evaluation, in the conduct of classroom work, and in the concepts that give technical meaning to their performance. Programs of preservice training have been somewhat successful in training prospective teachers in the techniques of planning and evaluation. Training in classroom performance has been relegated to the public school. Of course, this should have been done. The universities do not have facilities to provide training in classroom performance. But in the absence of proper preparation for the transference of this aspect of training to the schools, little training in specified skills has been provided. The trainees learn as best they can from unsystematized observation and practice in the classroom with feedback determined largely by what they must learn in order to survive. Concepts comprising the theoretical orientation that teachers need to act intelligently are taught and learned verbally. The trainee acquires no clear idea of what the concepts mean in terms of either teacher or pupil behavior.

This state of affairs can be explained in a number of ways. Part of the university program bears little relation to the tasks of the teacher because some professors hold that the school is antiquated, serving only the status quo, and that improvement can come about only by wholesale change. Hence, teacher education must be directed to the task of producing a new kind of teacher for the new school that is sure to come—if not today, then tomorrow. The problems of teaching here and now are neglected. Instead of dealing with problems daily faced by teachers, many courses in schools of education emphasize social and educational reconstruction and ideologies together with pedagogical doctrines believed to be compatible with these social and educational persuasions.

This is not a new development in teacher education. It first emerged early in this century and became pronounced during the Great Depression. It has gone by various names, depending upon the particular ideology. It is beneficial to any profession to encourage and protect its critics and its visionaries. There are aspects of the profession's responsibility that lie outside the concerns of the practitioner and the research worker, and the critics and the seers open these up for consideration. It can be damaging to programs of professional preparation when the critical and prophetic attitude plays a heavy role over an extended period, however. If the college faculty becomes overcritical of the public schools, teachers are likely to react negatively. In this atmosphere of discord the effectiveness of the college's program of instruction is likely to be reduced.

Efforts to orient teachers to ideal schools in the hope that they can somehow bring about a new system of schooling are doomed to fail. Too often, the beginning teacher experiences frustration and despair when he sees the job. Instead of viewing the difficulties as challenges to be met, such a beginner is likely to see the situation as hopeless and to flee from it at the first opportunity. If one may take the liberty to paraphrase one of Broudy's pungent sentences in a different context, it is mischievous, deliberately, to maladapt a teacher to the school, for those who are so maladapted cannot survive in it, let alone reform it.

A more basic consideration is the fact that the gap between research and theory, on the one hand, and practice, on the other, has never been bridged in programs of teacher training. Faculties of education have loudly criticized school personnel for failure to apply pedagogical theory and research results. At the same time, they have been equally amiss in using their own knowledge of theory and research in training teachers. The oft-made criticism that education faculties do not teach by the methods and techniques they expound is not the point. Be that as it may, the gap between research knowledge and practice exists in a more significant way. Education faculties have not used their knowledge of theory and research results in designing programs of training. They have incorporated only a smattering of such knowledge in training programs and have disregarded it in shaping the training process.

To bridge this gap is the major task of education faculties in this decade. How is it to be done? What are the connecting spans? One must begin with the footing: the empirical knowledge and wisdom of the profession. From these must be extracted the concepts, principles, and skills that will form the content of the program. The materials and procedures to be used in teaching this content must next be developed, tried out, and tested by their effects on teacher behavior. If the intended effects are confirmed, the next step is to test the effects of the teacher's behavior on pupils. The concepts and skills that stand this test will make up the part of the program that has to do with the development of classroom competence.

What does the development of these materials require? This question has been answered in bold outline above. But a more detailed account of the procedure is in order. For the sake of illustration, consider the development of materials to train prospective teachers in the ability to handle discipline problems. It is well known that maintenance of order in the classroom is of primary concern to teachers in training. They fear the time when they will confront disruptive pupils. To prepare materials to train teachers to manage classrooms, one must first determine the concepts and skills to be taught. The first move is to turn to empirical studies of classroom discipline to learn whether or not there are empirically established concepts with which to begin. If there are none, one must turn to systematic theory—for example, behavior modification. If such a source does not exist, one can turn finally to professional wisdom. In any event, the first step is to identify the concepts on which to build the training materials.

Kounin's study of classroom discipline resulted in four concepts: "*Withitness* (demonstrating that the teacher knew what was going on); *overlapping* (attending to two issues simultaneously); transition smoothness (absence of dangles, flip-flops, and thrusts); and programming for *learning-related variety in seatwork.*"[9] Materials to teach these concepts and the skills they entail must be partly audiovisual. If they consist only of questions, readings, discussion, written exercises, and the like, no training in ability to handle discipline situations will occur. Even when these activities are augmented by classroom visits and student teaching, acquisition of these concepts and skills is unlikely. The density of classroom events is too great and their tenure too fleeting for a trainee to learn concepts from classroom observation or skills of classroom control from practicing them as they are called for intermittently in the classroom.

Audiovisual materials are needed for effective training, although reading, questions, and discussion will still be helpful or, in some cases, necessary. These materials must be specially designed to exemplify the concepts. Consider *Withitness.* The behavioral indicators of this concept can be identified by reference to Kounin's analysis of what a teacher who is *withit* does. The specifications and script for a film to portray these indicators in the classroom can then be developed and the film produced.[10] The film should be short and to the point, probably eight to ten minutes long. It will show the behavior of a teacher at points where he knows what is going on, who is involved, and who is responsible. The film could also show by contrast the behavior of a teacher who does not know what the pupils are doing. The film can be studied and discussed until the performance of the trainee on a test of his ability to recognize the behavioral indicators meets a criterion score. The trainee will then be ready to practice the behavior in the classroom. If the behavior is already in his repertoire, the trainee may have learned enough from studying the film to perform fairly well at the outset. A modicum of practice and review of his behavior from video-tapes may be sufficient to clinch the skill. If the behavior is novel, the trainee will need considerable practice in small groups with feedback from video-tapes of his performance before he is ready for classroom practice.

Before the materials are incorporated in a training program, however, they should be tested. Do teachers in the field who are having discipline problems have fewer instances of disruptive pupil behavior when trained with materials based on Kounin's concepts? The developer must put his materials to this test. If they satisfy it, their use in a training program can be justified. If they make no difference, then they make no difference, as William James said about concepts.

The foregoing is an abridged discussion of the materials that development requires. Materials must be tested with children from different social strata and cultural groups, under various school conditions, and so on. Furthermore, not all concepts relate to classroom performance. Some have to do with school policy, others with interpretation of the behavior of parents, colleagues, the social environment, and data. Some of these can best be taught through films, while others can be acquired only in symbolic form. But the selection and classification of the concepts and skills for a training program must be made systematically, incorporated in appropriate materials that stand up under test conditions, and then used in programs of teacher preparation. Any other course of action is speculative.

To build a supply of audiovisual and verbal materials adequate for preservice and inservice training of school personnel will require the expenditure of millions of dollars over a period of at least ten years. The procedures and techniques—the know-how—for developing these materials are now known, and steps toward their development have already been taken by projects initiated and supported by the United States Office of Education.[11]

Diagnostic Concepts and Skills

When one is asked to list the concepts and skills of teaching, his thoughts most readily turn to those pertaining to such items as planning, questioning, reinforcing, evaluating, and many others before he comes upon diagnosis and remediation. If one turns to texts on the teaching of social studies, science, mathematics, and other subjects, he finds scant treatment of learning difficulties. It is interesting to note that one of the most, if not the most, seminal collections and classifications of teaching skills lists only a few skills related to this aspect of the teacher's work.[12]

What are the problems of learning, and how are they to be identified and treated? This is among the first questions to be answered as teacher education is remodeled. The answer cannot be given here, but its shape can be suggested. From research and practical experience, it is evident that learning difficulties are rooted, as noted above, in the properties of what is to be learned, teacher-pupil discourse, emotional disturbances, deficient motivation, and physical dysfunctions. These are general categories, and aberrations or problems in each category are to be expected. Nevertheless, a few observations about each category will indicate the flavor of the learning difficulties to be encountered.

Consider first some difficulties associated with properties of subject matter. The elements of subject matter are equivalent to the objects of learning and are referred to as skills, facts, concepts, principles, values, and procedures. These typically contain hard spots for pupils who try to learn them. In learning manuscript letters, first-grade pupils have more difficulty with the letters q, g, p, y and j than with others. The learner of arithmetic encounters the same sort of difficulty. Many years ago Thorndike opened up this aspect of learning and teaching by showing that it was harder for children to learn 7 + 9, 16 − 7, and 6 × 8 than such combinations as 3 + 2, 4 − 3, and 2 × 2. In reading, children often confuse words similar in appearance such as "can" and "car" or fail to distinguish similar sounds as in the case of "pen" and "pin." While the confusion of words involves properties of the words themselves, it may also be attributable partly to deficient visual perception or auditory acuity. To pinpoint a pupil's difficulty may therefore require consideration of factors in addition to the characteristics of the subject matter.*

More complex characteristics of the subject matter are found in the structure of the content. One idea can be related to another idea, or an operation to another operation, so that one must be learned before another can be learned. This is what is meant by "prerequisite knowledge." A pupil must grasp the earth's shape and a sense of parallelism before he can understand latitudes. If he has trouble with multiplication and subtraction, he will find long division insuperable. Countless instances of points where prerequisite learning is required can be identified in any subject manner. These are always potential learning difficulties.

A subject matter may call for inference patterns that a pupil is unable to perform. Piaget has investigated the generic patterns experimentally,[13] but they have not been studied in the context of the various subject matters. However, any perceptive teacher can readily supply examples of difficulties

---

*A distinction implicit in this discussion should be pointed out. There are two kinds of difficulties: learning difficulties and difficult learnings. The cause of the first is either physical or psychological; that of the second is some characteristic of the knowledge to be learned.

occasioned by inference patterns. For example, pupils ordinarily have little difficulty with direct proportion, but inverse proportion baffles some students. They do not grasp how one variable decreases while another increases. It becomes even more difficult when they must think inversely while keeping in mind that other variables are constant. Another form of inference difficulty is some pupils' tendency to continue to cope with a problem in the same way despite repeated failures.

Many pupils are handicapped because of their misunderstanding of language. Their thinking becomes bound by a tendency to identify verbal statements with reality. Among other things, they confuse definitions with descriptions of how things are; they fail to distinguish between inferences and observations. For instance, a pupil may mistake the killing of an individual for murder. Killing is an act; murder is a judgment about the act. In a discussion of race horses, the teacher says: "Suppose we say a flat race horse originating in England we choose to call a thoroughbred." The pupil replies, "No. We don't choose to call it a thoroughbred; that is what it is." If the teacher becomes involved in an effort to decide whether this, or any other, definition is true, he wastes time. Definitions are useful, but not true empirically. Teachers who do not understand the uses of language often waste hours of class time in fruitless discussion, as can easily be substantiated by a few classroom observations.

A second source of learning difficulties is the fact that the conventions of communication are not always shared by teachers and pupils.[14] In some cases the barrier to learning is related to bilingual factors, in others to dialects. While these barriers are still somewhat speculative and controversial, the progressive accumulation of evidence is beginning to establish a few points that warrant attention. For example, the claim that black dialect interferes seriously with cognitive learning is not established,[15] but there are good reasons to believe that teachers who do not appreciate the dialect or understand it are handicapped as they try to teach black children. The differences between nonschool and school discourse can cause misunderstandings between teachers and pupils, resulting in problems of adjustment and learning. While research is needed to clear up points of controversy and to develop knowledge of linguistics in relation to teaching, enough is now known to justify explicit attention to this area of learning problems in training programs.

A third area of diagnosis and treatment is that of learning difficulties stemming from emotional disturbances. It has been estimated that as many as 10 percent of school-age children are disturbed.[16] The teacher must be prepared to identify cases that need attention and to refer serious cases for diagnosis and treatment. The teaching of seriously emotionally disturbed children requires not only an understanding of such disturbances but also skill in setting a proper classroom climate and in working with these children. The teacher should be prepared to recognize the emotionally disturbed, to know when to refer them for further assessment, and to work with them if the diagnosis indicates that treatment should be carried on in a regular classroom. Pupils who are seriously disturbed require special treatment and can, of course, be handled only by specialists in collaboration with physicians, psychologists, and social workers.

Associated with the preparation of teachers to work with the emotionally disturbed is the preparation required to deal with disruptive behavior. Overactive pupils can be a source of classroom disturbance. These pupils will not always respond favorably to the ways of handling ordinary misconduct. Some pupils exhibit paranoid behavior such that the teacher is viewed with suspicion. These cases may require referral and treatment under more therapeutic circumstances.

In addition to cases of disruption that stem from emotional disturbances are those arising from the tendency of pupils to transfer their normal out-of-school conduct to the classroom. The normal conduct of pupils from environments whose rules of conduct differ from those of the school can be incongruous with classroom activities. Yet the pupil may not realize that his normal way of acting is inappropriate. This is less apt to be the case with the behavior of pupils from families of middle America, since their culture is more likely to be compatible with what the school accepts.

Finally, there are cases that spring from inappropriate teacher behavior, classroom conditions, and willful disregard of school rules by pupils. Teachers can prevent or control this type of misbehavior by handling classroom events appropriately. For example, a teacher who can attend to two or more situations occurring at once or negotiate transitions from one classroom activity to another will have fewer instances of misconduct.

The growing body of scientific literature on the diagnosis and treatment of disruptive behavior is making it possible to prepare teachers to deal effectively with the various types of misbehavior.[17] The knowledge is now available for systematically developing competence in this long-neglected area of teacher education.

Pupils without motivation for school work suffer from one of the most tenacious conditions of depressed achievement. These pupils typically come from environments whose stimuli are weighted not only against school but also against a viable future for themselves. A pupil's social medium is the agency affecting his hopes and aspirations. If the social medium in which a pupil lives has no horizon, he will have little or no hope beyond his day-to-day existence. What one aspires to is contingent upon what he perceives as possible. If he sees little, he will strive for little. If he does otherwise, frustration attendant upon failure will depress his aspirations. The next time he will try for less. That is the status of an overwhelming number of children in urban and rural slums today. If a pupil comes from such social circumstances, his achievement is likely to be low because he either aspires to little, is ill-prepared to do school work, or both.

Not all pupils with little or no will to do school work come from an environment that is debilitating because of its hopelessness. Some come from an affluent social context. An environment with unlimited horizons, rich with possibilities for the pupil, can be just as debilitating if his needs are met through little or no personal effort and responsibilities are lifted from his shoulders. He is likely to have grievances because he has never had a grievance. He thus finds little interest in the patterns of life that nourished him. The youth of both the top and the bottom strata of society thus are sometimes alike: They see little value in school; they have no serious aspirations and no life plan.

Deficient motivation is more likely to be found among pupils in the upper grades and high school than in the elementary years. The elementary pupil from a poverty-stricken environment is not mature enough to recognize that the doors to a viable future are closed to him; nor has the affluent elementary child built resentment against the environment that robs him of initiative and responsibility by responding to his every need. These elementary pupils are therefore apt to be interested in learning at least until they are well on the way to the achievement floor.

The identification of pupils who lack motivation is not easy despite the accessibility of their social medium. If there were a one-to-one correspondence between environmental variables and aspirations, the task would be simpler. But it is well known that out of the least favorable social conditions sometimes come individuals of considerable stature and achievement. The teacher must learn not to jump from the fact that a pupil's social medium is poor to the conclusion that his failure to learn is caused by low motivation. It can be due to other conditions such as emotional problems, lack of prior learning, inadequate inference patterns, or physical impairment. But once the social conditions of the pupil's life are pinned down as the debilitating influence, the question of what to do arises. The stock answer impressed upon the teacher in training is that the school program must be adjusted to the pupil's needs and abilities. This is at best a partial answer, for the root of the difficulty is the failure of socialization. While an adjustment of the school program is essential, it alone will make little difference. The problem belongs to the adult community. Unless the pupil can participate in the social functions that give meaning to an individual's efforts, teachers will typically be unable to do anything for him no matter what adjustments are made in the school program. If the adults of the community open the doors to a future full of possibilities for debilitated youth to use its energy constructively, schooling becomes possible and beneficial.

Another area of learning problems stems from handicaps. These disabilities include deficiencies in visual and auditory perception, speech defects, mental retardation, and dysfunctions due to anemia and other bodily conditions. Training in the recognition and treatment of these disabilities is now required only of teachers concentrating in special education. The more advanced aspects of the work should still be reserved for the specialists, but every teacher must be trained in the elements of these disabilities. To be able to identify pupils suffering from these dysfunctions, one must be trained not only to recognize symptoms immediately observable but also to use appropriate instruments for preliminary screening of pupils who are suspected of having such disabilities. The teacher should be able to identify these pupils in order to refer them for assessment and treatment. This reason alone is sufficient justification for the teacher to be given basic information about these types of problems. He should also be prepared to deal with them in the classroom if thorough diagnosis and prescribed treatment so indicate.

Skills have been identified and classified to enable teachers to establish and maintain learning conditions in the classroom; to handle the subject matter in such operations as defining, explaining, and valuing; to organize and direct pupil activities; to plan instruction; and to evaluate pupil progress.[18] This fact makes it possible to develop materials for training in these skills. The task of identifying diagnostic and remedial skills has barely begun. This task must be undertaken systematically if materials are to be developed to train teachers to cope with the problems of pupils who are not profiting from the school. The research required for this undertaking will require extensive financial support and the cooperation of research workers and teachers whose experience and insight have endowed them with the wisdom of the profession.

The Role of the University

The jurisdictional questions about teacher education have never been settled. What is the school's role? What is the role of the university? What is the responsibility of the state educational agency? The division of responsibilities for teacher education between the schools and the universities cannot be determined arbitrarily without risking incompetence. It can and should be decided in terms of the resources of these institutions. Teachers must be prepared in the content of instruction, in professional knowledge, and in the skills of diagnosis, instruction, evaluation, classroom control, and the like. The questions to be explored are: What part of this preparation are the universities equipped to provide? What part can the schools give? If one considers the experience of the last fifty years of teacher education, the task of preparing teachers must be shared. Neither the universities nor the schools can do the job alone. Each has a special role to play.

The universities, along with the great corporate laboratories, are the primary sources of knowledge in the contemporary world. The universities are also the primary agency through which knowledge is communicated to the professions, industry, agriculture, and commerce and through which high-quality professional, artistic, and scientific personnel are prepared. In this view of the university's role in society, one of its responsibilities is to prepare teachers in the subject matter of instruction and in basic professional knowledge at pre- and inservice levels.

Colleges of education provide instruction in the concepts and principles that make up the pedagogical sciences such as diagnostic and prescriptive studies, educational sociology, educational psychology, evaluation, educational economics, educational history, and philosophy of education. Preparation of the teacher in these sciences is a function that the university can perform effectively and the public school cannot do. Through its academic departments, the university also provides basic elements of the subject matter of instruction. These particular roles of the university are as old as university preparation of teachers. Critics claim that preparation in the disciplines is often unrelated to the teacher's objectives and that the pedagogical sciences are overly abstract and unrelated to the real world of the teacher. This criticism is partly correct, but the problem is not inherent in the disciplines themselves. With audiovisual and other forms of materials, these objections can be overcome.

Turning now to the domain of skills, the question is whether or not the university has the resources in either personnel or material to train teachers in classroom performance. The fact is the colleges of education have claimed training in skills as their responsibility. For many years such training was provided in demonstration or laboratory schools, usually owned and operated by the university. When enrollments in student teaching grew beyond the capacity of the demonstration school, the university took student teaching to the public schools. Here began an uneasy partnership in which the university retained control over the management of the practice program and the schools provided the actual training. To be sure, the university did provide a supervisory staff, but its personnel was occupied primarily in managing the program and in conducting concurrent courses in methods of teaching and classroom management. This program was seldom satisfactory, and as discontent with the schools has grown in the last few years, it has suffered considerable criticism. It is said that the training is neither systematic nor extensive enough to be effective; that the classroom teachers are not themselves prepared to train teachers; and that the supervising teachers from the university are either inadequate or are overburdened with travel from campus to schools.

The procedures and the focus of responsibility for skill training are being reconsidered. Recently a group of schoolmen

science, etc.—can be better treated in courses on diagnostic and remedial instruction in the subject itself where learning difficulties are often related to the content.

The supervision of student teaching is another area of staff utilization to be reconsidered. The supervision of student teaching in the public school by college personnel has been largely outdated by the emergence of a large number of public school teachers capable of working with interns, even though many of them could profit from a systematic study of how to work effectively with trainees. The college supervisor either spends a good portion of his time in commuting or lives off-campus near a center where student teaching is concentrated. The first of these alternatives is wasteful of time; the second divests the college supervisor of campus resources. Anyhow, he can have little influence upon the development of the trainee's teaching skills. He sees the trainee infrequently. Whatever formative influences play upon the trainee's skill development are certain to come from his supervising classroom teacher.

College personnel who are freed of the responsibility of supervising student teachers can be reallocated to the development and conduct of work in diagnostic and remedial procedures and techniques in the various subjects, the diagnosis and treatment of conduct problems and learning disabilities rooted in physiological dysfunctions and emotional disturbances. In addition, the staff will have time to introduce the trainees to some of the basic skills of instruction and classroom management through simulation and micro-teaching.

When the trainee has acquired basic knowledge in his teaching field and has been introduced to the basic elements of the foundations of education through protocols and systematic analysis of concepts and theories; when he has learned to identify common learning difficulties and disabilities and has been introduced to the more useful remedial materials and procedures; when he has acquired a modicum of experience in teaching through micro-teaching and simulation and has been awarded a bachelor's degree, he has learned about all a university can provide at the preservice level. Nevertheless, he is not yet a teacher; he is not prepared to assume responsibility for a classroom. The fledgling is ready to begin an internship.

The Role of the School

The public schools cannot perform the functions set forth above, for they have neither the facilities nor the personnel. The school, however, does have an important role to play in the preparation of the teacher. This role is to accept the products of teacher education institutions as interns and to assume responsibility for developing them into full-fledged teachers. The duty of the school is to provide practice in the skills of diagnosis and teaching under actual school conditions over a specified period. The length of the internship should be fixed by experience, but it is reasonable to suppose that experience will indicate a period of at least one year.

An intern should be a resident in training after graduation from a university. In fact, his certification as a teacher should be contingent upon the successful completion of an internship and on the recommendation of the authorities under whom the internship was served. Until then he should be certified as an intern on the recommendation of the university from which he graduated. Interns should not be used to reduce the instructional load of teachers nor the number of teachers in a system. The intern's remuneration should consist of an allowance sufficient to cover his living expenses as a single individual.

The protection of the intern is of signal importance. The experience of university authorities in the assignment and training of student teachers indicates that the intern must be protected against abuses, many of which are undoubtedly attributable to good intentions but nonetheless work to the detriment of the trainees. Some of these are noted here to indicate the sort of pitfalls that must be avoided as the school becomes responsible for interns. Principals have not infrequently selected supervising teachers, not because they were effective as teachers, but because it was hoped that they would themselves improve as they tried to train others. In other cases, student teachers have been assigned to relieve the burden of large classes. The intern is in the school to learn, and while he can be helpful, this is a byproduct and not the object of the internship. He should be assigned only to teachers who are known to be effective on the basis of objective data about the achievement and well-being of their pupils. He should never be assigned merely on the opinions of supervisors and principals.

The only agency that can safeguard the intern's interest is the state. The state, not the local educational agency, should certify the intern. It should also establish procedures for selecting the teachers from whom interns are to receive their training. In these matters state officials should be guided by criteria approved by the legitimate organizations of teachers. Furthermore, the intern program is financially a state responsibility, because the state has the resources and the interest in widespread school improvement necessary for the development of a statewide intern program. A local educational agency is not likely to assume responsibility for the upkeep of interns even were the agency financially able to do so. Such an agency would find it difficult to justify the expenditure of local tax dollars for the support of interns who are free to accept jobs outside the community or even outside the state. For this reason, and also because teachers need released time to work with interns, the state will find it necessary to allocate funds to local educational authorities specifically for intern programs. The programs should be periodically evaluated. This can best be done statewide since problems of sampling and design can be more easily handled by access to the total intern population. If the state is responsible for the program, it is thereby in position to provide for the evaluation.

The Deployment of School Personnel

To provide personnel for an intern program is to take on a task of major proportions. Although school systems have been engaged in the training of teachers for a long time, they are neither staffed nor organized for that purpose. They have looked to the universities for the design and administration of the student teaching programs and have never regarded teacher training as their responsibility. However, an effective intern program can be developed only if the state and the local school authorities give it high priority. This emphasis can be made a reality only by forming a competent staff to carry on the entire program. To do this will require not only the selection of competent teachers as trainers of interns but also the redirection of the supervisory staff. The supervisory function came into being many decades ago when teachers were not quite prepared in the knowledge and skills of teaching and in the subject matter of instruction. Today, with improved teacher competence, the need for supervision has become less and less. Nowadays, probably less than half of the supervisor's time is devoted to the improvement of instruction. Much of his time is spent in conferring with administrators and teachers, doing paper work, working with groups of parents, participating in group conferences, and traveling.[21] In fact, supervision has become an aspect of administration. The supervisor is becoming more involved in liaison activities between the administration and the teachers and community. The time is approaching when the deployment of the supervisory staff must be reconsidered in light of the need for a training program to smooth the transition of the intern from the college classroom to a full-fledged teacher. After the trainee has finished his internship and has been placed in a teaching position, he will still need consultant help for a year or two in adjusting to the burdens of teaching. It is the function of the school's supervisory staff to supply this assistance.

Summary

The impact of the foregoing discussion is that teacher education must do an about-face. First, it must emphasize diagnostic and treatment skills and knowledge at the undergraduate level to a greater extent than the skills and knowl-

[10] Walter R. Borg, "Protocols: Competency Based Teacher Education Modules," *Educational Technology,* Vol. XIII, Number 10, pp. 17–20. He has produced a series of four protocol packages on classroom management: Learner Accountability, Transitions, Group Alerting, and Withitness.

[11] A program of training in the techniques and procedures for development of protocol and training materials was initiated by the USOE in 1970. The program is in its fourth year, and a corps of individuals has become highly qualified developers of materials.

[12] Richard L. Turner and others, *A Specialty Catalog of Teaching Skills* (Albany, N.Y.: The State Education Department, Division of Teacher Education and Certification and Multi-state Consortium on Performance-Based Education, 1974).

[13] Jean Piaget, *The Psychology of Intelligence* (London: Routledge & Kegan, Paul), 1950; *Logic and Pyschology* (Manchester: Manchester University Press, 1953); Barbel Inholder and Jean Piaget, *The Growth of Logical Thinking* (London: Routledge & Kegan, Paul), 1958.

[14] Courtney B. Cazden and others (eds.), *Functions of Language in the Classroom* (New York: Teachers College Press, 1972).

[15] Vernon C. Hall and Ralph R. Turner, "The Validity of 'Different Language Explanation' for Poor Scholastic Performance by Black Students," *Review of Educational Research,* Winter, 1974, pp. 69–81.

[16] Robert L. Ebel (ed.), *Encyclopedia of Educational Research* (London: The Macmillan Company, 1969), p. 817.

[17] Borg, *"Protocols."* Additional materials on classroom management are being developed at Indiana University under the direction of David Gliessman and Gary Ingersoll.

[18] Turner, op. cit.

[19] Paul Olson and others (eds.), *The University Can't Train Teachers* (Lincoln, Neb.: Nebraska Curriculum Development Center, University of Nebraska, 1972).

[20] One of the best treatments of the deployment of staff is found in *The Power of Competency-Based Teacher Education,* edited by Benjamin Rosner (Boston, Mass.: Allyn and Bacon, 1972).

[21] Ebel, op. cit., p. 1397.

CHAPTER VIII

Training of
School Personnel

Efforts to improve school effectiveness in the last decade have assumed the competence of instructional and administrative personnel and have concentrated upon measures to release their abilities. This is the import of measures to decentralize the schools, to provide bonus payments, to create honorific titles, to differentiate the staff, and to introduce other innovations such as the voucher plan and performance contracting. Some critics have asserted that the school's chief defects are its inflexible bureaucracy, lack of community involvement, low teacher incentives, and lack of teacher dedication. Where these conditions have been ameliorated, the improvement in pupil achievement has been disappointing. While not denying the relevance of some of these conditions, the position taken here is that the ability of teachers to induce learning is the critical factor in shaping the school's influence on children and youth.

Inservice and Developmental Programs
The competence of school personnel is improved by two types of programs: inservice and developmental. Inservice

training is defined as any training of school personnel to
prepare them to satisfy a need of the school system. The
skills and concepts comprising the substance of the training
program are determined by deficiencies in the instructional,
administrative, and support services of the school. Developmental education, in contrast, consists of experiences and
studies to satisfy the personal needs of the school personnel.
Its character is determined not by the deficiencies of the
system, but by the interest of each individual in his own
personal and professional development and career advancement. The aim of the training and experience, not the content,
determines whether the program is inservice preparation. If
a study of the school shows that a deficiency in the instructional
program is one that might be remedied by new procedures
and techniques in teacher training, then the personnel responsible for inservice training should become proficient in
these developments. This would be required by the system
and would be inservice preparation. If the same persons decided
on their own to learn the new procedures and techniques
for career advancement, this training would be for developmental ends.

Inservice Training and the Needs of the System
An inservice program must be designed for the system.
The program must also be adapted to the needs of individuals
defined in terms of shortages in knowledge and skills as
determined in reference to the needs of the school. Individual
needs will be determined by self-analysis of one's teaching
behavior based on video-tapes and other forms of recording,
by diagnostic inventories of relevant subject matter and
pedagogical concepts and principles, and by conferences with
others including the director of the inservice program. The
findings of these analyses form the basis for deciding what
inservice work a teacher is to take. The policy of allowing
just any college course to count as inservice training should
be abandoned. In far too many cases, courses taken for the
master's degree are very little related to a school's deficiencies.

The needs of the school system are the crucial factors in deciding upon the needs of the personnel and thus the character of the inservice program. For this reason it is of signal importance that the school's research staff regularly identify the administrative, instructional, and curricular deficiencies of the system. Procedures must be established for involving the school personnel in the review and assessment of the deficiencies ascertained by the research department.

Deficiencies are always described in reference to goals. One of the indispensable goals of the school is the development of the ability in all children to read, write, and compute. Any pupil who does not realize this goal has reduced chances in life. Since one of the immediate and pressing goals of school reform is to raise the level of achievement in these fundamentals for all children and youth who are not now achieving at satisfactory levels, the first assessment of personnel should be made in terms of the knowledge and skills that will increase teacher ability to induce learning of these fundamental tools.

A second domain of the system's need is for curriculum adjustment. The thesis set forth in an earlier chapter is that the curriculum should be reshaped, particularly at the secondary level, to relate more directly to individual utilities. The selection and utilization of a subject matter with this orientation will require knowledge of social functions and of the relation of the disciplines to these functions. When such knowledge is available, it will be possible to assess teacher needs for knowledge and to design a program to provide it.

The belief that laymen and teachers can determine the needs of a school system is a fetish of the political mind. They can only criticize and weigh the relative importance of the deficiencies revealed by rigorous study. Assessment of the school's needs calls for research. As a general rule, each local school authority should maintain a research department that is constantly conducting studies to determine the needs of the system. The research staff should give particular attention to the areas of administration, curriculum, instruction, and pupil conduct. The staff should not only detect and describe particular deficiencies but should also propose priorities for consideration by the faculty and for action by the local school authority.

The research departments of many school systems are inadequately financed, poorly staffed, and required to devote their time to the collection of data to support administrative policies and decisions that have little bearing on the instructional program. The school is a system for delivering a product disciplined, among other things, in skills of learning and fundamental knowledge. Evaluating school efficiency in doing this job ought to be the primary concern of the research department. Only if this basic information is available can a needs assessment of a school system be made and a defensible program of inservice preparation be developed.

Essentials of Program Development

After the deficiencies of the system have been identified and personnel needs defined in reference to them, the school can undertake the task of developing measures to enable the personnel to acquire the knowledge and skills in which they are deficient. This task will involve the identification of the relevant knowledge and skills and the collection of appropriate materials of instruction and instruments of evaluation. It will also require a staff especially prepared to organize and conduct the training program.

A program cannot be developed by perfunctory efforts based upon common sense. If a number of the personnel need additional skills, then the skills that are either empirically known to be efficacious or are theoretically justified must be selected. The mere identification of skills by name is not sufficient. To say that one needs to know how to ask probing questions or to identify speech defects is not to identify the skills involved. Skills must be stated, and the indicators of the skill must be specified. For example, a teaching skill in elementary language arts can be stated as follows:

A. *Skill:*

The teacher identifies differences between speech patterns used in the classroom and those expected at the pupils' developmental level. Indicators:

1. Given a tape of pupil discourse from various age groups, let the teacher rate the utterances from youngest to oldest speaker. Criteria should take into account:
   a) accuracy of teacher's identification;
   b) attributes teacher uses in making his judgments (vocabulary, etc.).
2. Given a tape of discourse by a number of pupils from the same grade level, the teacher identifies the nature of speech deviations from the expected developmental level.
3. Given a classroom, let teacher perform 2. above.

B. *Skill:*

The teacher uses information gained in exercise of skill A. and identifies or prepares instructional objectives for individual learners. Indicators:

1. Given knowledge of a specific pupil's speech pattern and the expected speech behavior at that level, the teacher prepares an instructional objective for that learner.

C. *Skill:*

The teacher adjusts instructional techniques and materials in light of diagnosis in A.2. and objectives in B.1. above. Indicators:

1. Given pupil progress, the teacher decides what changes are required in materials and techniques.[1]

The foregoing represents the sort of analysis required by a systematic approach to training. If the basic skills and their indicators in teaching are known, it should be possible to determine the skills in which a particular teacher needs to gain proficiency, assuming that the needs of the system have been determined. As noted in the preceding chapter, Turner and his associates have made considerable progress toward developing a catalog of skills in various areas of instruction.[2]

The catalog lists skills, their indicators, and the context in which they can be identified and practiced. Such a catalog can be useful in shaping an inservice program to the needs of the system.

Teachers and administrators may need pedagogical knowledge as well as skills. The knowledge, for instance, may consist of such concepts as reinforcer, social role, withdrawal, and aggressiveness.[3] This sort of knowledge may entail no teaching skills; its use is simply to interpret the teacher's or administrator's perceptions and to enable them to anticipate certain pupil behavior in particular conditions or, in the case of developmental concepts, at given periods of development.

Since the beginning of university preparation of teachers and administrators, definitional knowledge has not been sufficient. Teachers and administrators often know a concept verbally but are unable to recognize the behavior to which it pertains in a given situation, for they cannot identify the behavioral attributes defined by the concept. Although useful in discussion and in shaping educational policies, verbal knowledge is useless in understanding observable behavior.

Shaping the inservice program to the needs of the school personnel for knowledge of pedagogical concepts and principles is not unlike that of shaping it to the need for skills. The chief question is: What are the knowledge deficiencies? An analysis of the system will indicate the basic concepts and principles that enable the personnel to operate efficiently. If teachers and administrators can interpret the behavior, objects, and events to which these concepts and principles pertain, their knowledge is adequate. If they cannot, it will be necessary to assemble materials to help them acquire the knowledge.

It should be pointed out that concepts are usually given names, like "reinforcer" and "social role." Often the name is taken as the concept as, for example, when one says "The concept of social role is important." "Social role" designates the concept. School and college personnel frequently use the names of concepts without understanding the reality they embrace. This is the case because definitions are often treated loosely and without means of portraying the indicators of the concept. Inservice training, like preservice training, should avoid this pitfall. It can do so if the materials of instruction incorporate the indicators of concepts and provide for their exemplification. The following example will lend concreteness to the sort of analysis to which concepts must be subjected if their meaning is to be clear: Suppose the concept of structuring is to be taught through the use of protocol materials. In order to develop a protocol the concept must be defined and its indicators clearly stated.

Definition:
  Structuring is a set of statements about the essential character of expected classroom activities or behaviors.

Indicators: The statements may
  1. pertain to immediate activities or future activities;
  2. emphasize the theme or topic to be discussed, either by describing its parameters or simply naming and announcing it;
  3. emphasize procedures to be followed by giving step-by-step directions;
  4. emphasize the criteria by which performance in ensuing activities will be evaluated;
  5. provide a transitional function, binding what has preceded to what is now to be undertaken. [4]

A film that depicts those indicators would constitute a protocol on structuring, and the protocol plus learning activities and evaluation materials would make up a package for learning the concept of structuring. The catalog of concepts from which the above example is taken contains other fundamental pedagogical concepts analyzed in the same way. It should be useful to those who are responsible for formulating inservice training programs as it provides ready access to the indicators of some of the more important concepts.

A study of the needs of the school system may show that teachers are deficient in the knowledge that pupils are expected to learn. Their knowledge can be deficient for at least three reasons: a change in the school's objectives; new knowledge that calls for a change in the content of instruction; or failure to acquire appropriate knowledge while in college. If part of the curriculum is to be oriented to basic social functions, as suggested in Chapter VI, new content would be added to the program of studies. Teachers would be deficient if they were unacquainted with the knowledge called for by these additions. An example of the influence of new knowledge is the updating of biology and physics in the 1960s. Workshops and summer institutes were established to modernize the teacher's knowledge in those fields. It is frequently claimed that the number of teachers who are deficient in systematized knowledge, especially at the elementary level, is larger than it should be for effective teaching. If this is the case, it can be attributed to the fact that the universities have been all too slow in designing programs in the disciplines to cope with the requirements of public school teaching. Regardless of the causes of the deficiencies in systematized knowledge, there is every reason to determine the needs of teachers for such knowledge when assessment of the school system so indicates.

The question of how skills, pedagogical concepts and principles, and academic knowledge are to be taught is one that can be answered in a variety of ways, depending upon local circumstances, facilities, and personnel. A few basic principles are being suggested rather than simply describing an archetype of instruction. All will agree that teachers learn in the same way as their pupils: The more concepts and principles can be made operational, the more likely they are to be learned and used; skills are learned by practice and reinforcement, rather than by talking about them. This means that laboratory-type materials must be used in a program to meet the needs of teachers. These materials take two forms: protocol materials and training materials. Protocols are audio or audiovisual materials, although they can sometimes be discursive, designed to show the indicators of concepts; training materials are designed to show how to do something or to give practice in doing it.[5]

Protocol materials are used to teach concepts, but they can also be used to teach principles. They are reproductions of behavior, either staged or candid, which show the attributes of a particular kind of behavior embraced by the concept. For example, a five- or ten-minute film that shows a teacher reinforcing her pupil's behavior can be used to teach the concept of reinforcement. Instead of merely giving a definition and one or two verbal examples, the attributes of reinforcing behavior can be pointed to in varying circumstances.[6] The film can be played over and over again as the learner, the teacher in this case, analyzes and studies the behavior.

This method is not unlike teaching students how to identify different kinds of trees by taking them to a forest where the trees' distinguishing attributes can be observed. One may ask why not take teachers to the classroom where they can learn to recognize the different kinds of behavior instead of relying on audiovisual materials. The answer is easily found. Unlike trees, behavior does not tarry; it vanishes as it happens. It can be discussed only as it exists in memory. Since individuals do not see the same aspect of behavior as it occurs and, in consequence, remember different things, efforts to use classroom observations to teach concepts rest on shifting grounds. Video-tapes, films, or tape recordings can be played over and over for repeated analysis and study. Protocols are almost indispensable in a program to help teachers to recognize various kinds of learning difficulties and disabilities as well as conduct problems and to acquire other pedagogical concepts and principles.

Training materials are used to enable the teacher to acquire the skills he needs. They consist of specifications of skills to be practiced, the conditions of the practice, and video recordings of the practice performances. The teacher can then observe his performance, analyze it, and, with assistance, ascertain the points at which he needs to improve.[7] In some cases, he may observe a film showing someone performing the skill as a model. He can then compare his own performance against the model. There are many variations of this general procedure. The materials can also provide for simulation in which the teacher is required to practice a number of skills in the same time frame. Finally, an indispensable requirement is that the teacher try out his skills in classroom situations to see whether or not he has reached a satisfactory level of performance. He may need to return again and again to the practice situation, if the classroom tryout is not satisfactory.

There can be no substitute for skillful performance in teaching. To raise teaching to a higher level of performance is to develop a program of systematic inservice training and to revise the university program of teacher preparation. Unless teachers have the ability to diagnose learning difficulties and disabilities and to remedy them, it is unlikely that the achievement levels in reading and computation, suggested in the chapter on achievement floors, can be reached. Were it not for the fact that few teachers possess diagnostic and coping skills in these fundamental areas of learning, the goals of school reform would be easier to achieve. It should be added immediately that the cause of these deficiencies is not attributable just to teachers but also to faulty training programs.

Local Responsibility for Inservice Training

Alleged decline of pupil achievement and efforts of some state governments to legislate competence of school personnel have increased concern over inservice training. One expression of this concern is the rise of teacher centers as an instrument for planning and carrying on inservice programs. In a few cases these centers have been fostered by state legislation and encouraged by federal authorities. These developments have given rise to tensions between the schools and the universities as the latter have long considered inservice training their obligation. Neither the universities nor the school systems can assume complete responsibility for the conduct of inservice programs. There are some 15,000 local school systems containing countless schools. The universities have neither the staff nor resources to survey and analyze the needs of those systems even if they were authorized to do so.

The import of the analysis set forth in the preceding section is that needs assessment is a responsibility of the local school system. Its own research staff is the proper agency to make the assessment and to work with inservice personnel, local and university, in setting up training programs to rectify the deficiencies indicated by research. Where the assessment undertaking requires services that cannot be supplied within the system, school authorities should turn to outside agencies such as universities for assistance. In any event, the responsibility for identifying the deficiencies in the schools and for working out measures to deal with them is a responsibility of the local school personnel and cannot be shifted to universities or other agencies.

While the local system is responsible for its own effectiveness, a successful long-term program of school improvement must be based on the cooperative endeavor of the local school authorities, state educational agencies, universities, and the educational arm of the federal government. The school's failures in one locality can and frequently do become social and economic liabilities in another. Although local in its control, the consequences of a school's program are national in scope. Ineffective schools are not ineffective only in Podunk or Central City but wherever their pupils go. They affect both individual and social utilities. The plight of Central City can be attributed partly to the debased schooling given to the minorities in the South, Southwest, and other parts of the country that supplied the original stock of the present-day ghettoes. State and federal involvement in inservice preparation is therefore ultimately justified by its benefits to the commonwealth. No less persuasive is the argument from the principle of equality; each pupil is entitled to be under the guidance of competent teachers no matter where he lives. Most local school systems are not financially able to provide adequate inservice training. Even if they were, a local school agency is not likely to assume complete financial responsibility for a long-range inservice program; it is not easy for local authorities to justify the expenditure of tax dollars for the support of an inservice program when teachers can readily move to other school districts.

The success of inservice programs hinges on the research staff of the local systems. If these staffs are made up of individuals who are technically competent and, equally important, competent in both the theoretical and practical aspects of education, the basics of school improvement are in place. The leaders of the staff must be thoroughly knowledgeable in the fundamentals of teaching, curriculum development, teacher training, and administrative procedures and techniques from the standpoints of both theory and practice.

A major hurdle in the path of inservice development is the lack of competent research personnel.* The development of such personnel is a responsibility of the universities. But they can develop a research training program only if there is demand for their products. Public schools are in dire financial straits and are unable to meet the demands for higher salaries and reduction of instructional loads. They cannot support an adequate research staff. The impasse can be broken, however, by federal and state grants to support research centers in local systems, first on a limited exploratory basis and then more extensively if the initial efforts are promising. The establishment of such centers must be safeguarded against the appointment of incompetent personnel. The leaders of the staff should be selected from among the best minds in psychology and pedagogy and among those only the ones who are thoroughly acquainted with public schools and the training of school personnel.

Who will provide the training in the inservice program? The selection and organization of the inservice staff cannot be determined apart from the exigencies of a particular school

*See Appendix A for an extensive exploration of the question of reforming the program for the preparation of research personnel.

system; however, a few observations should be made. The director of the inservice program should be thoroughly versed in the training of teachers. He should have a staff drawn from a number of sources. Among these are teachers whose pupils consistently achieve satisfactorily in fundamental learning abilities, reading and computational specialists in the system, and university instructors in such areas as learning difficulties and disabilities, audiovisual technology, and teacher training.

The involvement of the universities in an inservice program can be justified for a number of reasons. The subject matter deficiencies of the experienced teacher can be remedied by instruction in the disciplines provided by the universities. The newly acquired knowledge that comes from educational research can best be provided by colleges of education. College personnel can also be helpful in the development of materials and in the conduct of inservice training.

Each staff member has a particular role to play. When they are miscast the program will suffer. A university instructor in reading, for example, is not necessarily a skilled classroom teacher of reading. On the other hand, he knows how to diagnose and prescribe for stubborn cases. The classroom teacher may not know how to make a thorough diagnosis, but he does know how to follow the prescription in the classroom setting and can demonstrate the proper performance for the benefit of other teachers. The technologist is not only competent in media but also knows instructional theory and can facilitate the selection, development, and utilization of protocols, training materials, and other instructional devices. The entire aim should be to develop an inservice team that can raise the level of classroom performance.

To sum up, the development of inservice training programs is the responsibility of the local school system, but state and federal support is essential to the development of a training program based on assessment of the system's needs. A research staff is critical, for only research can establish the needs of the system. If the staff does its work well, the faculty

and administration will be able to decide priorities intelligently, and the training personnel will be more likely to devise
an effective program. Since the research staff is crucial, it
is essential that the universities develop programs to train
research personnel. But the universities can safely undertake
such programs only after federal and state governments have
pioneered in the development of research centers and the
demand for research personnel thereby created.

Specialization and Career Development

Inservice training is one thing; a university-based program
of personnel development is another. A teacher, administrator,
or staff member can engage in study for enjoyment or for
career advancement. This is a matter of personal decision
and does not necessarily contribute to improvement of job
performance. The individual may travel in summer, enroll
in university summer sessions, take extramural courses, or
engage in summer work or other activities. What is gained
from these experiences may result in better performance on
the job, but that is an accident of the experience unless the
purpose of the activity is to enhance one's ability in his job
as a teacher, administrator, counselor, or whatever. In any
event, this type of self-improvement is to be distinguished
from training indicated by the needs of the system.

In this sort of personnel development, colleges of education
have a unique function—to develop high-quality personnel.
The college's program should not be designed to upgrade
administrators and teachers. That is the task of inservice
programs. Rather, the college program should be planned to
prepare selected individuals for specialized functions at all
levels of education. Among these are positions in the various
disciplines of education in the colleges themselves (educational
psychology, counseling, history and philosophy of education,
educational sociology, educational economics, curriculum and
instruction, administration, special education, measurement
and evaluation) and positions in administration, instruction,
research, and other specialized functions in the schools.

The need for content specialists is just as great. Such a specialist must possess thorough knowledge in at least one discipline and must also understand its relationship to the social functions it serves. Few schools have as many as one or two teachers with the knowledge to challenge the apt pupil intellectually. It has become fashionable to talk about humanistic education. It is fantasy to expect such education to be fostered by teachers who have only slight knowledge of the intellectual traditions in philosophy, history, literature, arts, and religion and who lack the mental discipline that instructional control of such knowledge requires. By the same token, the humanistic aspects of the sciences, mathematics, and other subjects are likely to be neglected in the interest of achieving the prosaic, even though important, elements of these disciplines. The depth of knowledge in the disciplines possessed by specialists in the elementary school can be less than in the high school. But the claim that these specialists are necessary to assure an effective school at either level is not easy to refute.

Where are the various specialists, pedagogical and academic, to be prepared? Only the universities have the manpower and facilities to produce them. The programs to prepare each of these specialists should lead to advanced degrees. The degree should be a professional degree after the fashion of the doctorate in medicine and law. This means that the program, except for research workers, should require no dissertation and no other trappings of programs leading to research degrees. Instead of a thesis, a candidate for a degree should be required to demonstrate his mastery of the knowledge expected of him and the skills to apply it. If he is a specialist in learning problems, he should be required to demonstrate his ability to deal with them successfully. A content specialist should show that he can handle curriculum problems and organize and conduct instruction proficiently at different levels of comprehension.

The leadership in colleges of education suffers from profound confusion about the nature of education as a field of study.

At times education is held to be a professional field; at other times it is unwittingly conceived as a social science whose undergraduate major prepares one for further study leading to a graduate degree. In the latter case, the instructional program emphasizes cognitive information with little attention to the development of professional skills. This is evident not only in the undergraduate program but also in programs leading to advanced degrees where most courses are theoretical. At advanced levels, the student is evaluated by his performance on verbal tests and the quality of his doctoral thesis. If professional competence were the goal, the student would be given extended practice in the skills of the profession as well as preparation in theoretical work. And instead of verbal tests and a dissertation as evidence of his ability, he would be required to demonstrate that he can perform as a professional. Many doctoral graduates in education go into university positions where they engage in the preparation of teachers. Only a few, perhaps no more than 5 percent, ever do any research. Yet they are given no systematic preparation in the skills of teacher training. While the post-baccalaureate work of the teacher is largely professional, its financial support, like academic departments, is geared to student enrollments and the credit hours they generate. In the end, this practice precludes the development of quality professional preparation since it ties the education of all school personnel to the less expensive nonprofessional programs of the universities.

The universities alone cannot prepare specialists. While most of the program will be provided on campus where there is ready access to such resources as libraries, techniques laboratories, and curriculum materials, the schools are the setting in which the specialist must ultimately work. The program should therefore enlist the cooperation of the schools in providing cases for analysis, curriculum problems, and all sorts of practical situations. Since the number of specialists in training at a given time will always be small, the schools can provide an effective laboratory without disrupting their own program. Nor is that all. A few specialists are already in the schools, especially in the larger systems, and their involvement in campus instruction would maintain an intellectual liaison with the schools, a relationship that would tend to increase the reality component of the program.

Perhaps the most serious personnel deficiency is in school administration. All can agree that the level of competence among principals and superintendents continues to be at a low ebb. Unless administrative positions can be filled with individuals highly competent in pedagogical knowledge, the intellectual tradition, and human relations skills, and with a research orientation, it is likely that little progress can be made toward school improvement. Yet few colleges of education can boast of a quality program to develop administrative effectiveness. It is not unusual for a principal or a superintendent to complete the work for a doctor's degree with little change in his performance.

The inservice program should be clearly distinguished from the specialist program. The purpose of the inservice program is to induce concepts and skills to meet the needs of the system. It is to be carried on in the school system with the cooperation of the universities. The specialist program is university-based and involves the schools as a laboratory and a source of instructional assistance.

In summary, the proposition advanced in this chapter is that reform of the school is contingent upon improvement in the performance of its personnel and that such improvement is most likely to occur through a systematic program of training in which specific needs are identified and measures taken to meet them. If working conditions are improved and incentives increased, there is little likelihood that the achievement of pupils would thereby be enhanced unless personnel performance, especially that of principals and teachers, is improved at the same time. In order to improve performance, training programs must be changed. Upgrading of personnel should take place in the school system and should be based on an analysis of the deficiencies of the school's instructional program and the knowledge and skills needed to rectify these deficiencies. The inservice program is one that can be kept on target only by constant analysis of the system itself to determine its shortcomings, an analysis that can be made only by competent research workers. Beyond the inservice program lies the university program to prepare specialists to raise still further the level of competence of the school personnel. The aim of colleges of education, at advanced levels, should be to develop school personnel that is ever more capable of solving its own problems.

FOOTNOTES

[1] James D. Walden, "Teaching Skills in Elementary Language Arts" in *A Specialty Catalog of Teaching Skills,* by Richard L. Turner and others. op. cit.

[2] *Ibid.*

[3] B. Othanel Smith et al., *Teachers for the Real World* (Washington, D.C.: American Association of Colleges for Teacher Education, 1969), Chapter 4. See also Alice H. Hayden, (ed.), *Body of Knowledge Unique to the Profession of Education* (Washington, D.C.: Pi Lambda Theta, 1966).

[4] Bryce B. Hudgins and others, *A Catalogue of Concepts in the Pedagogical Domain of Teacher Education* (Albany, N.Y.: The State Education Department, Division of Teacher Education and Certification and Multi-state Consortium on Performance-Based Education, 1974).

[5] B. Othanel Smith, Donald E. Orlosky, and Jean Borg, *Handbook on the Development and Use of Protocol Materials for Teacher Education* (Chipley, Fla.: Panhandle Area Educational Cooperative, 1973). See also *A Catalog of Protocol Materials in Teacher Education* (Chipley, Fla.: Panhandle Area Educational Cooperative, 1973).

[6] B. Othanel Smith et al, op. cit., Chapter 5. See also Richard L. Turner, "Relationships Between 'Teachers for The Real World' and 'The Elementary Models,'" in *The Power of Competency-Based Teacher Education,* (ed.), Benjamin Rosner (Boston, Mass.: Allyn and Bacon, 1972), pp. 188-221. The psychology of observational learning is summarized by Alfred L. Baldwin in his paper, "Social Learning," in *Review of Research in Education,* (ed.) Fred N. Kerlinger (Itasca, Ill.: F. E. Peacock Publishers, 1973), pp. 34-57.

[7] Borg, *The Mini Course, A Microteaching Approach to Teacher Education,* op. cit. See also B. Othanel Smith, op. cit., Chapter 6.

CHAPTER IX

The Role of the
Building Principal

The principal receives more information about the total operation of the school than does any classroom teacher. He is closer to the realities of school operation than any member of the central administration. The principal is therefore a crucial figure in the improvement of the school, and his selection, training, and evaluation are critical issues in school reform; they must be in accord with the purposes of the schools.

The training program for principals would be easier to define if differences among their roles did not exist. Unfortunately, this is not the case. All principals do not have identical duties and problems. Wide variance in the size of school enrollments, diversity in the characteristics of students and faculty, differences in the quality of facilities and school equipment require different actions by different school principals. Other differences arise because of the level of schooling they administer or the organizational and educational pattern of a given location. Elementary school principals and high school principals face different responsibilities. The principal who directs a school that is organized around self-contained classrooms performs duties different from one whose school emphasizes team teaching and open classrooms. The tasks faced by today's principal require that he consider factors unknown to his counterpart of twenty or thirty years ago.

Whether his troubles are manifested in terms of a generation gap, racial unrest, student militancy, intra-staff polarization, school-community welfare, or some other aspect of a social system in upheaval, somehow we sense that these are all facets of one large interlocking rend in the fabric of the society and the school. Intuitively, we also sense that the most crucial of the principal's tasks in this type of society and this type of school is to pull centrifugal forces together so that his school can function effectively as an educational institution.[1]

No principal is sheltered from these problems.

Although there are wide differences in the tasks performed by different principals, many similarities are also apparent among the various principalships. In describing the training program for principals, the purpose here is to define the common elements in their preparation and to expect the characteristics of a given school to be accommodated by the principal's ingenuity. The competent principal should know that he must make decisions according to local circumstances. Before he can make those decisions properly he must acquire the competence to obtain appropriate information, to establish priorities, to act effectively on his decisions, and to make optimum use of the time and resources available. The formal training program can give the principal some help in local decision making, but the ability to lead a school must be gained from actual school experience.

Conditions Affecting the Principal's Role

Two major developments have altered the principal's role today from his role of twenty or thirty years ago. One is the tendency of the school systems' central administration to assume policy-making and administrative prerogatives previously handled by building principals. The other development is the more influential role assumed by teachers and their organizations.

The first of these developments, the shift to central control, originated to coordinate the schools within a system and to eliminate overlapping and conflicting procedures. Central purchasing, for example, can reduce costs through volume buying. A central administration can usually manage the total system's finances more economically than can individual building principals. In addition to purchasing, centralization has been developed to coordinate bus routes, select textbooks, regulate extra-class activities, and determine deadlines for reports from teachers and building principals. Although many of these provisions improve the efficiency of the schools' operations, today's principal spends much of his time responding to rules and regulations originating from the central administration.

Teachers frequently associate their principals with the central administration rather than with themselves and their concerns at the building level because of this trend to central control. The emphasis on central administration concerns was reported in the findings of a survey of elementary school principals completed in 1958 and replicated in 1968.[2] In the survey, 100 principals were asked to describe their actual and ideal time allotments in six categories including curriculum and instructional leadership and administrative responsibility. According to the two surveys, the time spent in curriculum and instructional leadership decreased during the decade, and the time spent on administrative responsibility increased. The data in this survey indicated that principals spent more than twice as much time as they preferred in attending to administrative matters, including central staff concerns. Today's principal wants to spend even more time than his counterpart of ten years ago on instructional leadership. The time spent in contrast to the preference expressed by principals is increasing. If the potential of school principals is to be realized, this trend must be reversed.

There is some difference of opinion regarding the principal's relationship to the central administration and his relationship to the school he administers. While principals may complain that they are burdened with central administrative demands, those in central administration often counter that principals do not use the freedom they now have. There is little merit in arguing the question of who is right. The productive solution is to clarify the work to be done and then establish the appropriate division of labor to assure attainment of mutually desirable ends. If the problem rests with the central administration, restrictions on the building principal should be removed to enable him to function professionally. If the principal lacks the knowledge, ingenuity, or confidence to manage his school, then additional training and different selection procedures for principals should be employed.

The second development affecting the principal's role is the knowledge gap and professional distance between the principal and the classroom teacher. Teachers become proficient through advanced training and are often equal or superior to the principal in pedagogical knowledge. They often know more about textbook selection, standardized tests, teaching materials, school development, and pupils than the principal. This contrast between the knowledge of the teacher and the knowledge of the principal can cause friction to arise if the principal fails to respect and learn how to use teacher knowledge to best advantage. The knowledge gap between principals and teachers evolves when principals fail to keep abreast of pedagogical developments and teachers gain in knowledge through additional training and experience. Unless the principal has current knowledge, he will weaken his intellectual base for administrative decisions and may revert to the authority implied in his position as justification for administering the school. The closing of this gap calls for present-day principals to undergo training to catch up with the current knowledge and continue their training to prevent dissonance between teachers and principals from arising. If the principal and teachers work as partners in coping with instructional problems, there is a lower probability that the two will be separated in instructional matters in the future. The principal's status in teacher organizations has also been weakened in recent years. Organizations such as the National Education Association consider principals eligible for membership, but local affiliates in increasing numbers have discouraged or disallowed membership for principals. The building level administrator is consequently dissociated from the classroom teachers not only intellectually but also professionally. The principal is "in the middle" between the central administration, teachers, and community, and the purpose he serves in the school can be negated by any of these factions. Yet the building principal is the person who represents the local school to the central administration and the community and makes crucial decisions about the school he administers. An improved approach is needed. To enable the principal to function effectively, the purpose he serves and the relationship he has with others must be appropriately defined.

The Principal as an Inquirer

A central consideration in defining the principal's work is the locus of authority in decision making. If the locus is imbedded in the position of authority in the hierarchy of school organization or the power to withold services, then those individuals who hold power over principals will control their decisions. Carrying this basis for decisions to its logical conclusion and assuming that people wish to seek autonomy or authority, the school system can become an agency in which the personnel in the structure are forced to compete for power to enable them to perform professionally. If the authority for decisions is imbedded in knowledge about schools rather than position or power, the school bureaucracy can be an agency in which information is sought as a basis for making decisions. In this latter position, the principal and every other professional in the system become seekers of information rather than subordinates to whomever holds a position of power. The preferred role for the principal is this latter role. He should be trained to seek information from teachers, central administration, community, pupils, and so forth. On the basis of that information, he can provide the leadership the school requires to organize and implement its responsibilities for schooling.

Within this role the principal is an inquiry-oriented professional whose task is to raise questions, identify problems, delineate issues, and bring the resources of the local school, the central administration, and the community to bear on the solution of such problems. He can make decisions and recommendations on the basis of evidence rather than on the basis of the position that he or anyone else may occupy in the organizational hierarchy of the school and community. The principal in this role can serve teachers, community, and the central administration to the advantage of all groups. The inquiry-oriented principal does not proceed without obtaining information to assist him. Inherent in this approach is the expectation that data will be collected and that research will be carried out to shed light on problems under investigation.

The entire burden for identifying problems and issues should not fall on the principal. He should be alert to concerns brought to his attention by teachers, parents, pupils, or others. The principal can ask the research division of the system to help assess the school, identify its problems, and assist the faculty in their search for solutions.

The research division is typically used to obtain data on enrollment projections, building needs, and fiscal questions and generally to serve the central administration in its policy-making responsibilities. One cannot belittle the importance of these decisions at the central administrative level, but it is a heavy loss to a faculty and principal if they cannot also have the research personnel at their disposal to solve local school problems. Elaboration on this approach requires more attention than can be given here, but in brief outline it would probably be necessary to divide the research division into two units: one to serve the central administration and the other the faculty and principal of each local school. To make use of such a research unit, principals must become competent in identifying questions about their schools, and the principal and the research staff must receive training in how to work with one another. The research staff in most school districts will not be trained to assist local schools with the identification and analysis of the problems that arise. They will need additional training to carry out their duties in helping the faculties of individual schools.

There must be limitations to the principal's responsibilities. For example, when disputes arise between teachers and the central administration on noninstructional matters, the principal should be allowed to maintain a position of neutrality. There may also be community programs that do not affect the school directly in which the principal should not be obligated to be involved. He may choose to participate in community activities as any citizen might, but his position as principal does not require that he engage in activities beyond the duties required of him as a school principal. These limits do not impose any restrictions on a principal or any other professional who chooses to engage in legitimate civic, political, or social activities.

Training programs for principals seem like a logical procedure to prepare principals for the complicated role they must fill, but training programs have not usually improved administrative performance. The training given and the work to be done have not been in agreement. One recent analysis of administrative effectiveness not only revealed that the number of courses completed in educational administration was correlated negatively to the exercise of professional leadership, but that administrative performance was unrelated to number of years spent in college, number of years devoted to graduate study, number of hours taken in undergraduate education courses, and number of hours in graduate education courses.[3] Training has even impeded development that was eventually needed to function successfully as a principal, according to this study. The relationship between the training program and the work of the principal must be examined.

The training program should be revised to enable future administrators to receive training that coincides with the responsibilities of their work.

In the determination of the role of the building principal the description of his duties must be flexible enough to accommodate the variety in his work, specific enough to determine when he is succeeding or failing, autonomous enough to permit important decisions, and restricted to realistic, feasible expectations. Inquiry-oriented principals can serve the purpose of school reform only if their inquiries are directed toward the proper goals. The proper goals are those that attend to the purpose of schools and particularly those that relate directly to the instructional program. The training that should enable principals to succeed and the description of their duties are provided in the remainder of this chapter.

An Administrative Model

The scope of administrative responsibility at the level of the individual principal is provided in Figure 1. It includes the factors that should be considered in the selection, training, and evaluation of principals. The model also provides categories of responsibility that a potential principal should consider before entering and completing a training program that will enable him to become a school administrator.

In Figure 1 the section with diagonal lines identifies the area in which the payload of the schools is to be delivered. This intersection represents the principal's effective, professional, competent interaction with the pupils and teachers in the building he administers. The primary purpose of administrative activity should be to improve the contacts that occur at this intersection. The remaining portion of the diagram includes areas of responsibility that are part of the support system for the school and are also vital responsibilities in the duties of the principal. The relationship and description of these categories encompasses the principal's work, for which training should be provided.

The model lists the three populations with whom the

Figure 1
A Model of the Principal's Responsibility

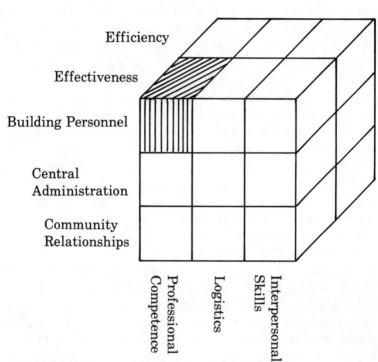

principal works—the community, the central administration, and the personnel in the school building. It includes the application of professional knowledge, logistical skills, and interpersonal abilities as the generic areas of competence needed for performing his duties. The third dimension in the model calls for the ability to distinguish between efficiency and effectiveness in administrative behavior.

If the principal's work is to be done well, it must be restricted to the feasible and important. The model's representation of the principal's work is a definition of the scope of his activities. The contention here is that the most responsible leadership in school administration will develop within a structured context. When the principal's role is limited to specified areas of responsibility, he becomes free to concentrate on appropriate tasks without the burden of extraneous concerns that detract from thoroughness in his work. The successful implementation of school reform requires of the principal more than superficial knowledge about the areas for which the schools are responsible. His responsibility to initiate and maintain useful changes in the schools can best be carried out within a defined role that has been clarified according to the purposes to be achieved. A broad and loose definition of administrative responsibilities can be disastrous; a narrow definition that is too restrictive can be equally harmful. The model defines a moderate viewpoint, and the principal should achieve a high level of competence within the restricted responsibilities he is expected to assume.

The principal may have ties and responsibilities with elements outside those listed in this model, but his work should not regularly be diverted to these other factors. When much of his time is spent on activities outside the model, he is not serving properly as a building principal. Other professional experiences have some value, but the principal should be cautious about commitments to tasks that fall outside the boundaries of the model.

The dimension in the model that lists the populations with whom he works includes the community, central administration, and building personnel. A community is usually defined as people with common interests living in a particular area. This definition does not suffice to define the school community. The attendance area from which pupils are drawn for a particular school is no longer limited to the area contiguous with the school. Pupils frequently attend schools some distances from their residences. The community is not a well-defined area or group of people who can be specified. For the purposes of defining the community for the principal, children who attend a given school and their parents comprise the school community with whom he should work. The central administration includes the school board, superintendent and his staff, and supervisors of the school district. The building personnel include teachers, paraprofessionals, clerks, custodians, pupils, and others such as visiting teachers, student teachers, the school nurse, and specialists and consultants who regularly come to the school.

It is important for the building principal to work with and understand the community, but this relationship should consume less time than he devotes to the personnel in the building he administers. Some would disagree with this emphasis and place more responsibility on the principal to work closely with the community.[4]

The principal's usual subordinate relationship to the central administration should be reduced. The building principal should have the autonomy and flexibility to respond to local school conditions without requiring continual approval from the central administration. The central administration should give the principal power to act on issues in his own school setting. This should strengthen the principal's hand and help unify the principal and teachers in the local setting. In addition, the principal should solicit information from the central administration and advise them on the procedures and help they can provide his school.

The primary work of the principal should be his work with the building personnel. The principal must serve as instructional leader if the school is to deliver the benefits that can come from organizing its resources. He serves in this capacity by monitoring total school progress and organizing the building personnel and resources to identify and analyze problems, to find solutions, and to compile resources needed to carry forth the program and to evaluate results. The principal is in a special position to carry out these duties. The mixture of teachers, pupils, facilities, materials, objectives, and unique characteristics of the school must be blended appropriately to optimize learning. The principal's chief task is to work constantly at keeping these components in the best relationships to each other. He should devote most of his energy to this leadership and coordinating function.

The second dimension in the model includes the categories of professional competence, logistics, and interpersonal relationships. The interpersonal relations category is important to maintain an effective school: No principal should ignore the feelings of teachers, pupils, parents, or others with whom he works. The willingness to listen to others and to respond appropriately to their requests is a vital element in the successful leadership of the school.[5] Those who are unable to relate to others with humane understanding are poor candidates for leadership positions in the schools. The development of a relationship that is characterized by the promotion of other's abilities is the crux of the interpersonal relations component of the building principal. The principal must help others to perform at their best.

The principal's logistical expertise refers to the managerial responsibilities required in his position. A school is a complex organization that should function smoothly enough to avoid the difficulties that come from disorganization. Pupils, facilities, and learning experiences must be managed with minimum confusion and conflict. The efficient organization of the school should not be confused with rigid mandates that create a restricted and tense atmosphere. The purpose of efficient organization is to enable everyone in the school to know what they can count on in regard to schedules, use of facilities, rules and regulations, and deployment of resources. After the principal has established plans that work, changes that disrupt those schedules should be undertaken only after obvious and major improvements are evident. The purpose in stressing caution in logistical administrative change is that the quality of schooling is not likely to improve merely through changes in the operating procedures of the school, but considerable time is often wasted discussing relatively insignificant changes. Obvious problems should be eliminated in school routines. Once these routines have been arranged and students and teachers are familiar with them, it is not worth developing minor gains in efficiency if the time expended detracts from more important matters involving the instructional program directly. After the principal has organized the school and it is functioning adequately, his energies should be spent on solving instructional problems rather than tuning the school to a finer organizational pitch.

The principal's professional knowledge is derived from the pedagogical learning in the foundations of teaching, his knowledge of the subjects taught in the school, his experience as a classroom teacher, and the information about the totality of the school program, which accrues to the office of the principal. Some of this information accumulates from the composite of individual teacher reports and information, and some of it comes at the request of the principal as he calls for crucial data required to make decisions. He should be able to select important topics of school-wide concern and relate his knowledge and data on those topics to the building personnel. The principal who has been a successful teacher and who has excelled in the acquisition of knowledge and in problem-solving ability can multiply his talents through the teachers with whom he works. The responsibility of the building principal to exert leadership in the educational program is one of his most demanding and trying tasks and should receive the bulk of his efforts.

This requirement that the principal exert instructional leadership throughout the school raises a question about the span of control that a principal can be expected to manage. The principal who administers a school with a large faculty usually faces a more difficult problem than one whose school has a small faculty. Some authorities hold that the principal can deal with only a few people who serve as leaders of segments of school personnel; others contend that it is possible for the principal to maintain individual contact with each teacher. Part of this issue is whether teachers should be separated from the principal by another layer of administrators or if the principal should maintain direct contact with each member of the faculty. The answer lies in the reality that the building principal is responsible for the total operation of the school; therefore, he must maintain contact with each teacher. Unless he can keep abreast of the instructional program in all sectors of the school operation, he will be unable to lead. Teachers are also professionals. This fact makes it easier for a principal to work with each teacher since teachers today require direct supervision less than administrative cooperation.

It is unrealistic to expect a principal to devote much time to visiting individual classrooms and supervising teachers. But there are better ways to obtain critical information that will enable him to remain well-informed about the entire school. To enable the principal to serve as the instructional leader, the goals of the school can be predetermined. The principal can obtain information on teacher and pupil progress toward those goals and utilize that information to maintain or improve the effectiveness of individual teachers. An appropriate system of information management allows him to be adequately informed to make appropriate decisions about the learning of pupils and the effectiveness of teachers. On the basis of the information he receives, the principal may then work with department chairmen, cluster leaders, or inservice directors to implement instructional leadership and changes, if they are needed.

The third dimension of the principal's responsibility is in the distinction between an effective and efficient administrator. The major difference between these two terms is that the efficient person can concentrate on getting things done right, and the effective person concentrates on getting the right things done. The two terms do not describe opposing behaviors because doing the right things well requires using the best way to go about it. But a principal is ill-equipped if his judgment does not enable him to distinguish between an efficient school and an effective school.

The routine tasks of the principal should be handled efficiently. These include such activities as maintaining attendance records, ordering supplies, collecting lunch money, and keeping the building clean. The principal who has organized these routine matters with a minimum of inconvenience to the least number of people is an efficient principal. He might also be an effective principal, but one cannot tell by observing his handling of routine school matters.

The contrast between efficient and effective solutions is most evident in the different questions a principal tries to answer. The efficient principal asks if he is doing things the right way. The effective principal questions his activities by asking, "What am I doing that really does not need to be done at all by me or anyone else?" "What am I doing that could be done better by someone else?" "What am I doing that wastes the time of others?"[6] The answers to these three questions should help the ineffective principal to locate areas for improvement and should reassure the effective principal.

Locating areas for improvement and learning how to behave more appropriately are not the same. After it is determined that a principal is engaged in ineffective behavior, it does not automatically follow that he will improve. If the duties to be performed are the only duties he knows how to perform, then he needs more than diagnosis of his weaknesses. He also needs training so he can improve his performance.

The Training Program

It is easier and more common to describe what is expected of the school principal than to specify a training program that will prepare him for his work. The responsibilities of the principal are often stated in general mandates such as "maintain healthy relationships among teacher," "give leadership to the instructional program," or "organize the resources of the school to improve the learning of pupils." These broad statements serve little purpose when a specific training program is required.

An effective training program develops from concrete plans. The recommendations presented in this section require specific experiences and call for cooperation between local schools and universities. If a principal is trained exclusively by the school system that intends to employ him, the school system will lack the depth, variety, and current knowledge required of a competent leader of professionals. If the universities have the sole responsibility for his training, the program will lack the reality that can come only from training in actual operating procedures. The combination of the two should supply the schools with building principals who are knowledgeable about the alternatives they have for managing schools and who are also able to relate their knowledge to the specific school where they work.

The trainee will be assigned to work with an experienced principal during part of the training program. The schools should not assume that any experienced principal is qualified to provide training. Principals who are regarded as potential supervisors of trainees should be trained in two additional aspects of their work. One aspect is the analysis of their own behavior to clarify the activities they perform that make them effective. The other part of the training is in learning how to transmit their ability to a trainee. School districts should organize an instructional program that would help experienced principals to become effective in working with prospective principals. Trainees should be assigned to principals who have undergone this training.

The training program includes five parts. The first part requires that the candidate for a principalship complete a period of successful teaching. The second part provides for limited administrative experience under the direction of an experienced principal. The major purpose of this phase is to enable the school system and the candidate to evaluate their decision to consider an administrative assignment. The third portion of the training is a university-based year of formal training. The fourth part of the training calls for a practicum as a practicing principal or as an assistant principal. The fifth part is a trial period that precedes final certification; it is called inservice because experienced and newly trained principals should both undergo this phase regularly. The newly trained administrator must successfully complete the inservice portion to receive a permanent certificate. The experienced administrator should perform adequately or else receive additional training and possible reassignment if he continues to function inadequately.

Teaching. The training of the building principal begins when he starts his first teaching assignment. At that early time in his professional career he may not plan to become a principal. Nevertheless, the principals who complete this program of preparation will be selected from classroom teachers. Part of the reason for this teaching requirement is that teachers respond overwhelmingly in favor of teaching experience as a prerequisite to serving as a principal. One survey of teacher's attitudes on this question revealed that 96 percent of the teachers felt that principals should be required to serve as teachers before becoming principals.[7] Nearly half of those who favored teaching experience felt that five or more years of experience should be required. If teachers feel that classroom experience is vital for a principal, it would be a tactical mistake to risk adverse teacher reaction by discounting teaching experience.

The requirement for classroom experience is also included because the building principal will work closely with classroom teachers. His credibility with teachers and his knowledge about their problems are both enhanced if he can use his experience in the classroom as one source of information in performing his administrative duties.

In addition to experience in classroom teaching, the quality of his teaching must also be considered before a teacher should be encouraged to pursue a principalship. The number of years of teaching experience required and the level of performance should be determined by the local personnel. Building principals should be primarily responsible for identifying teachers whose leadership qualities and teaching performance are outstanding. The school system should have a referral procedure whereby teachers who have been thus identified can be further reviewed for possible admission to the training program. Teachers nominated for administrative training should be free to remain in the classroom or to assume other positions where their ability can be utilized. The position of the building principal should not be the only assignment for productive use of superior teachers. Teachers who prefer to remain in the regular classroom should be permitted to do so; differentiated assignments might provide the means to utilize their abilities.

After a teacher consents to enter the training program, he should be given an opportunity to test this decision for himself and for those who have made the nomination. An exploratory experience in the school system can give the candidate the opportunity to evaluate the wisdom of the selection. This assignment is an opportunity for him to assess his own interest in becoming a principal and to evaluate how well he copes with typical administrative situations. This second phase is the exploration period.

Exploration. The trainee should be given a reduced teaching schedule and assigned to an experienced building principal during the exploration phase of his program. His exploratory period should be planned for an academic year. A systematic sequence of experiences and responsibilities should be organized to include at least one responsibility in each of the nine cells representing the divisions of work presented in the model. Wherever there is an intersection of two dimensions, a cell is enclosed within which an activity should be planned for the trainee to perform. This helps organize the exploratory experience. For example, the intersection of building personnel and professional competence is one cell that gives general limits to a set of experiences to be assigned to the trainee.

The trainee's work in each of the nine cells should be assessed in regard to how well he carries out his assignment and evaluated against the factors of efficiency and effectiveness. The trainee's responsibilities should be arranged to avoid disruption of the usual school program. In any school there is enough work to use additional help with the administrative duties. The trainee can supply some of that help while gaining the benefits that come from his exploratory year. To guide the principal in determining these experiences, a list of duties that might be assigned to a trainee in each of the cells should be provided. The responsibility for deciding the trainee experiences should rest with the building principal. The number of incidents the trainee handles must be limited to a sample since he cannot be overburdened with tasks that prevent him from attending to his teaching duties. The nine assignments are discussed next.

Building Personnel—Professional Competence. The activities for the trainee in this cell call for him to interact with the building personnel in the solution of an instructional problem or the maintenance or improvement of an existing instructional program. His professional competence in working with teachers can be displayed in a variety of ways. He might be assigned to provide assistance to beginning teachers. If a team teaching approach is used, he might be assigned to assist the team with its work. He might be asked to work with teachers who are having some difficulty with discipline in the classroom. He could be asked to assess the standardized testing program and recommend improvements in the program or in the use of the information obtained. The important consideration is that the trainee should have at least one assignment during his exploratory experience in which he helps improve instruction by applying his pedagogical knowledge.

Building Personnel—Logistics. The trainee could be asked to assess and recommend continuation or improvement of the school's logistical operation. This assignment might include teachers, pupils, or both. The teachers' duties might be examined for better ways to utilize teaching personnel. The trainee might be asked to examine all the duties building personnel assume and to determine if the best use of school personnel has been organized. He might be asked to review scheduling arrangements for pupils and for teachers. He could examine fire drill plans, lunchroom arrangements, bus routes, and pick-up and unloading stations. In the secondary school, he might study provisions for student parking and the regulations that govern student driving and suggest improvements. He might be asked to plan the teaching assignments for teachers, pupil's schedules, and the school facilities and review his recommendations with the principal.

Building Personnel—Interpersonal Skills. The purpose of his assignment in this cell should be to identify a problem involving interpersonal relationships and to plan its solution. The persons involved might be any combination of pupils, teachers, and other personnel in the building. Differences often arise within a school since many people with diverse backgrounds and responsibility must work together. The trainee can be given a sample of the variables at work in handling interpersonal relationships within the school setting.

Central Administration—Professional Competence. The central administration benefits from reports on the school's operation. The trainee might be asked to compile information about a program that was initiated and supported by the central administration and then submit a report to them. His report might concern the acceptance of a new textbook, the effectiveness of a new remedial program, or the use of audiovisual equipment. The central administration must ask questions if it is to serve the schools adequately. The trainee can learn how to gather information that either supplies the central administration with the information it needs or assists in analyses that might be repeated throughout the system for central administration use. The central administration could supply the trainee with assignments that would help in making decisions about the school system.

Central Administration—Logistics. The trainee should be responsible for examining at least one operating procedure entailing cooperation between the central administration and the local school. For instance, he might learn about the procedure for selecting new teachers. He might study the interviewing policies, assessment of personnel needs, factors that determine the appointment of a teacher to a given building, and the role of the building principal in the decision. The trainee might review a regulation that is in effect by studying its origin, public hearings, the intent of the regulation, its promulgation, and its consequences. The trainee could learn about the channels of communication and hierarchy of decision making with the activity he includes in this cell.

Central Administration—Interpersonal Skills. At least once during the year, the trainee should present a report or recommendation to the superintendent and his staff or to the board of education. His report should be based on potentially useful information he has obtained in his exploratory assignment. Although content should include useful substance, the trainee's ability to present his report with clarity and effectiveness is equally important. By issuing a report he can demonstrate his ability to communicate. The decision to continue beyond the exploration year to the next step in the training program should depend partly on the trainee's ability to cope with the questions and conditions imposed on him by his presentation. The presentation is an opportunity for the trainee and central staff to assess his potential in respect to poise, organizational talent, ability to articulate his presentation, and adroitness at thinking and talking through an issue with the superintendent or the board.

Community Relationships—Professional Competence. The trainee should meet with parents or other members of the community on at least one planned occasion. If the school is changing the program of studies, the trainee can be assigned the task of notifying parents of the new development. Some changes that may require explanation are: a new system of reporting grades, the addition of a new course or course sequence, a new organizational pattern, special instructional materials, developments in guidance and counseling of pupils, or any instructional program in which parental involvement is expected. In any of these topics the school may have established successful programs that ought to be made known to parents but have not been. The trainee could be asked to remedy the information gap between the school and the community by presenting an explanation to parents.

Community Relationships—Logistics. The trainee can assume responsibility for an event that calls for public attendance. The usual school events that attract the public provide a natural choice for this assignment. Most schools have an agenda of open houses, career days, school plays, musical performances, athletic events, honors assemblies, commencement exercises, or special programs. The trainee can be asked to take responsibility for managing one or more of these events. This experience should acquaint him with the array of tasks to be completed in planning a public event; it will also enable his building principal to assess his thoroughness and competence in planning events involving the community.

Community Relationships—Interpersonal Skills. The effectiveness of the trainee's interpersonal skills will be displayed in the process of carrying out his assignments in the two cells bounded by Community Relationships—Professional Competence and Community Relationships—Logistics. The trainee might be given the experience of handling an incident involving the community. He may be asked to respond to all complaints of a certain type from parents, i.e., any problem related to property damage by pupils between school and home or any incident involving parental objection to grades. A parent may wish to talk to someone at school about his child, and the trainee can be asked to handle the request. Some planned public exposure in areas that require him to employ effective interpersonal relations skills should be prescribed during his exploratory year.

Upon completion of the exploratory year, a review board should decide his potential as a future administrator by assessing the trainee's performance in each of the nine cells. Each experience should be evaluated on the basis of how effectively and how efficiently he carried out his tasks. In addition, the review board should have the judgment of the building principal, teachers with whom he has worked, and the central administration. If the review board approves the trainee, he can proceed to the instructional phase of the program.

Instruction. The instructional phase of the training program should be handled primarily by university personnel with cooperation from the local school. The period for instruction should be one academic year. The school system should share the cost of the training program by offering a leave of absence, continuation of fringe benefits, salary, and other support to enable the trainee to engage in the program without personal hardship.

One major emphasis in the university training must be assistance to trainees in serving as inquiry-oriented principals. Instruction in this approach should help trainees learn how to identify school issues and problems, to formulate hypotheses, and to organize and implement approaches to problem solving. Inherent in this approach is the importance of remaining objective until data have been collected and rejecting or accepting approaches on the basis of their results.

The university instruction should be responsible for relating the training program to the school system by individualizing the instruction of the trainees enrolled in the program. It is likely that a group of ten, twenty, or more trainees might enroll in the training program at the same time from several school systems. The research and study completed in the course of their training should include assignments related to their own school districts. If instruction is provided on such topics as scheduling procedures, lists of pupils, teachers, and facilities in the school the trainee knows best should be used rather than a hypothetical example. If the trainees share their information with one another, the unique problems and solutions of one school can become new information for other trainees.

The model provided in Figure 1 serves as a broad definition of the instructional program, but the instruction should not be compartmentalized into the separate cells that appear in the model. Knowledge, skills, and situations cut across the cells in the model; the instructional program should be organized to supply fundamental information that will afford assistance throughout the model rather than instruction restricted to any single cell. For example, when the topic of interpersonal skills is treated in the instructional program, it would be inappropriate to restrict it to one specific audience.

Interpersonal skills can be applied in all professional relationships. The role of the university is to help the prospective principal acquire knowledge to carry out his administrative duties. In many instances, the knowledge acquired by the principal will not be directly employed. The training of the school administrator in school law is a good example of this. A principal cannot expect to become an expert on school law. However, enough knowledge must be included in his training program to assure that he does not ignorantly blunder into legal difficulties. He can learn how to minimize the chances for litigation against him and the teachers in his school and how to acquire the help he may need if legal action arises.

The product of the training program should be a principal who possesses the foundation knowledge he needs to make administrative decisions and the pedagogical knowledge to relate to the teachers, and one who comprehends the significance of his decisions in administering an effective and efficient school. He should become sensitive to the complexity of his tasks and should gain some practice in making decisions that distinguish between the important and the unimportant. He must become a person who can relate the responsibilities of an individual school to the responsibilities of the central administration and perceive the individual school within the context of the total educational system, including state departments, federal government, and universities. He should learn to make decisions that appropriately divide his time and the time of those under his direction according to the tasks of highest priority.

Each university will vary its administrative instruction to utilize the talents of its own faculty to best advantage. At the same time, the university must meet its obligation to supply the trainees with the knowledge and inquiry skills that enable a principal to manage effectively and give productive leadership to the school. The trainee's experience in the exploratory phase should enable him to help plan his own training, and the university should adjust to his requests wherever possible.

Throughout the training program the university must consider how it will instruct trainees to respond rationally to school reform. Unless criteria are determined and taught to principals, they will be subject to the whims and impulses of those who promote change in any direction. If the universities support the emphasis in the model for training building principals, they will reinforce the expectation that schools must deliver instructional services to their pupils.

The principal is in a position to accept or reject requests for a change. The criterion he should employ is the value of the intended change toward the improvement of the instructional program of the school. He also must attend to the cells in the support system to avoid undue disruption and to obtain the help that will increase teachers' effectiveness. Whenever a recommended change is said to lead to appropriate ends, the principal should be prepared to investigate the claim and support it if it holds up. If a recommendation for change does not focus on the appropriate purpose of the school, the administrator should discourage the use of his or the faculty's time on that proposal, however popular it may be. If the universities can succeed in helping the building principal make critical decisions concerning the long-range consequences of reform, basing them on data and professional competence, then the university training program will serve its proper function.

Practicum. Each nominee who successfully completes the instructional period should be assigned to a one-year practicum. In the case of a trainee who is preparing for a high school principalship, the assignment should either place him in an acting principalship or in a position as an aide to a principal. A person preparing for a principalship in an elementary school might be assigned a school to administer by himself. In any event, the assignment should be adjusted according to the characteristics of the trainees and the schools. The striking contrast between the work of the principal in a relatively small elementary school in a trouble-free neighborhood and the work of the principal in a large inner-city school calls for a different rate of induction into full-time responsibility as a principal. The practicum should be tailored to the individual and his career goals.

The practicum should be under the direction of the local schools with a supervisory committee assigned to work with the trainee. One member of the supervisory committee should be a principal who has been trained to supervise administrative trainees and is an experienced administrator in the school district. Another member should be drawn from among principals with whom the trainees have served as aides. Where an acting principalship is assigned, an experienced and trained principal whose assignment is similar and whose proximity to the school is convenient should be asked to serve on the supervisory committee. The supervising principal should serve as a person to whom the trainee can turn for guidance. The practicum should not be a "sink or swim" assignment but one in which the trainee is given help with the tough problems he must learn to handle.

Still another member of the supervisory committee should be a member of the university faculty. The university member of the committee should serve as a resource in discussing and deciding solutions to problems that were included in the instruction phase. The university faculty member can offer his own assistance to the principal or serve as a contact to locate other members of the faculty who can supply particular help. In addition to the supervising principal, one member of the central administration should serve as a liaison between the central administration and the school. The assignment of a member of the central administration to this task forms a contact for the trainee with the central administration so that he can raise questions or make suggestions that are more appropriately handled by the central administration than by local school personnel.

The model should help organize the practicum just as in the exploratory phase, although the emphasis in the practicum may be different. In the exploratory phase the trainee sought experiences in each of the nine cells on the face of the model. If the activities of the school did not normally include activities in one of the cells during the exploratory period, an effort should be made to create an assignment that will include the experience. In the practicum the trainee should use the model to help him determine the priorities on which his effort should be exerted but there is no demand that he include experiences in each cell. The purpose of the model during the practicum is to select the major school objectives within the priorities of the local school and to seek the attainment of those objectives. If the major problem in a given school is logistical, the trainee may concentrate on improving organizational procedures. If the relationship between the community and the school is badly strained and interferes with school effectiveness, he may stress improving those relationships. The school goals during the practicum should be within the model but should be selected according to the specific situation in the local school.

Another difference between the exploratory phase and the practicum is that the trainee should work considerably more with the faculty as a whole during the practicum. The trainee should gain experience and receive help from the supervising principal in working with faculty committees, guidance counselors, and staffing problems. The trainees should learn to work with each element of the school within the context of the total school situation.

Upon completion of the practicum, the three supervisors should collaborate in evaluating the work of the trainee and make recommendations concerning his certification as a building principal. Upon the recommendation of the supervisory team and application by the trainee, a temporary certificate can be issued by the state authorizing the trainee to serve as a building principal at the level for which his training has prepared him. A review of his work after a period of three years should be required before full certification is granted.

Inservice Training of Principals

Principals, like teachers, should be regularly evaluated and provided with inservice training. To enable them to recognize and overcome their administrative difficulties is to remove one of the chief barriers to school improvement. It cannot be overemphasized that the inservice program should be based on the evaluation of their work. Usually the evaluation of principals is infrequent, subjective, and occurs only when trouble arises. The evaluation of the building principal should be periodic and based on a systematic procedure that has as its first goal the improvement of his performance.

Annual goals for the building principal can be established.[7] The goals should be tentatively set in a joint meeting with at least one member of the central administration, one peer principal, and two teachers. The goals should also be discussed and explained to the entire faculty, giving the teachers a voice in shaping the list. Through discussions with the teachers and with final agreement between the principal, central administration, and his peers, the goals for a school should be established. The building principal would then have a basis for priorities in his work and a means to evaluate his success at the end of the year. The model in Figure 1 provides the categories in which a principal should establish goals. In some categories the goal might be to maintain the status quo, as it is likely there are areas in which the school is functioning successfully. Disruption of adequately operating procedures and programs of the school is undesirable. Whatever the goals, the evidence required to demonstrate their attainment should be specified.

If the central administration finds that the building principal requires additional support or help in meeting goals, such help should be given. Other principals may have solved similar problems and might share their ways of handling them. The teachers should be a valuable asset in finding answers to some problems the principal encounters. If the goals are made public and feasible, the progress in the school can be measured against those goals. The assumption in this arrangement is that the central administration will encourage realistic but important goals and that the teachers will share a professional concern for meeting established goals for the school.

If a building principal fails to achieve his goals over a period of time, or if the goals he attempts rarely include instructional improvement at the building level, then the question of whether he should remain as a building principal must be raised. If he cannot achieve some goals within one year, the time might be extended, but goals should be met within reasonable time periods. Reassignment is one consideration for the building principal whose performance falls below acceptable levels over a period of time, because a principal might fail in one situation and succeed in another. The advantage in following this evaluation procedure is that goals are established so that the principal and the teachers know what they are setting out to accomplish each year. The evaluation of the principal can be based on performance rather than subjective ratings and judgment. The weaknesses in any principal can be identified and remedied, and the schools that lack effective leadership may receive different principals who are more likely to give improved leadership.

FOOTNOTES

[1] Daniel U. Levine, "The Principalship in Schools That Are Coming Apart," *NASSP Bulletin,* November, 1970, p. 25.

[2] Joseph Melton, "Role Perceptions of the Elementary School Principalship," *The National Elementary Principal,* February, 1971, pp. 40–43.

[3] Edwin M. Bridges and Melany E. Baehr, "The Future of Administrator Selection Procedures," *Notebook,* January, 1971.

[4] Frank C. Mayer, "The Role of the State Elementary School Principal's Association as Seen by a Superintendent," *The National Elementary Principal,* February, 1971, pp. 52–55. Cf. Harvey Goldman, "New Roles for Principals," *The Clearing House,* November, 1970, pp. 135–39.

[5] Monroe Pederson, "Effective and Ineffective Actions of the High School Principal," *Journal of Secondary Education,* October, 1970, pp. 260–64.

[6] Peter Drucker, *Drucker on Management* (London: Management Publications Limited, 1964).

[7] NEA Teacher Opinion Poll, "Should Teachers Evaluate Principals? Should Principals Have Teaching Experience?" *Today's Education*, April, 1971, p. 2.

CHAPTER X

Professional Competence

In the preceding chapters, ways to improve teacher competence were discussed. The primary purpose of this chapter is to explore the conditions necessary for the optimum exercise of that competence. The professional worker must enjoy a high degree of autonomy, because he has knowledge and skill to meet a need that the client cannot meet himself and because of the possibility that harm may come to the client because of interference. No matter how much professional competence an individual has, he can be thwarted in his efforts to render his services properly. No professional can pursue his work entirely free of limitations placed on him by the state, his clients, resources, and his ability. Nevertheless, no practitioner can ply his art with a censor looking over his shoulder. General conditions of work can be so incompatible with the use of professional knowledge that it becomes impossible for the practitioner to exercise his competence. These conditions are often found in a teacher's career.

The circumstances that affect the teacher's work can be

grouped into three categories. The first is the immediate working environment, the area where teaching takes place. The second is the school environment, which is made up of the components of the school's operation that lie beyond the classroom. The final category is the service environment or the domain outside the school; it is often loosely referred to as the community.

The Immediate Environment

The immediate environment is composed of the conditions that affect the teacher's performance as he interacts with pupils in the teaching situation. The identification of these conditions and the changes in them that can liberate the teacher is an important step toward school improvement. The first of these conditions is communication. There is much discussion today about the importance of communication in a school system; how it can be facilitated between the administrative staff and the teachers, between the school personnel and the community, between pupils and teachers and almost everyone except among teachers. The teacher is isolated, cut off from communication about professional matters with his peers and from practically all other sources of information about the problems that confront him.

Many schools have sought to remedy the teacher's dearth of information by establishing professional libraries in the building. The books are seldom used except as reference material for courses taken for credit toward a degree or increments on a salary scale. Teachers have little time to use the books. Anyhow, they contain little of practical substance. A teacher confronted by the difficulty of handling a particular problem of learning or conduct does not want textbook discussions of learning theories, personality aberrations, curriculum design, theories of method, or general ways of teaching different subject matters. He wants to know how to diagnose and treat the particular case. He needs details, not generalities.

It is frequently claimed that such practical knowledge does

not exist, that the handling of practical situations is too idiosyncratic to be shared with others. This claim appears to confuse idiosyncracy with eccentricity. Every profession enjoys differences in style, mannerism, and temperament among its members. Teaching is certainly no exception. There are established ways of dealing with different kinds of problems in every profession. While the practitioner will suffuse these ways with his own style and temperament, he will nevertheless adhere closely to the established mode. The point is so patent that it should go without saying, but the frequent repetition of the claim of idiosyncracy requires the point to be made again and again.

The solution of problems encountered in teaching involves diagnoses of difficulties, ways of using materials of instruction, ways of relating to the learner, teaching skills, and behavior reinforcement. The same can be said about problems of classroom management and control. The problems of misconduct can be classified, and their treatment can be described in useful terms. The practical knowledge and wisdom of the profession lie scattered among teachers and among schools waiting to be assembled and organized. Other professions have handbooks on problems and solutions. Teachers have curriculum guides that emphasize objectives and general procedures.[1] Unfortunately, they are long on objectives, short on means and materials, and blank on problems and how to deal with them.

Teachers need consultation on problems of learning and conduct where the difficulty is so complex that help is needed in deciding upon the nature of the problem itself. Sometimes these cases may be serious enough to require the participation of social workers, psychologists, or physicians. Certainly there are pupil difficulties rooted in physical conditions that only a physician can handle. Some schools hold staffing sessions on serious cases to decide whether to refer them or to continue to deal with them in the school. Such sessions usually deal with problems of conduct rather than specific learning difficulties. Opportunities for consultation among teachers who have confidence in each other is sorely needed if teachers are to exercise their competence in problem cases for which they individually have no satisfactory solution. The present arrangements for free periods does not make consultations possible. Teachers of the same area are typically not free at the same time, and teachers in the elementary school often have no free time at all.

The development of an effective arrangement for faculty communication will probably entail modifications in the system of self-contained classrooms, although such changes in themselves will not guarantee consultations. The ungraded classroom and team teaching promise to open channels of communication. Unfortunately, they can just as readily lead to an arrangement in which a head teacher manages a group of assistants with little or no consultation among the head teachers themselves. A number of plans for facilitating communication among teachers should be designed and tried out. At the high school level, time for planning and consultation as well as time for conferences with pupils can be provided by reducing the number of class periods per week now required for a unit of credit. The practice of five class periods per week is a convention without empirical support.[2] The institution of the open campus at the high school level now makes the transition to fewer class hours per unit of credit administratively feasible. Time alone is not sufficient, however. Teachers will need to become less inhibited and more knowledgeable about their own teaching problems, their successes and failures. This approach can be promoted by inservice training that emphasizes teaching problems, learning difficulties, and the knowledge and skill required to cope with them.

The second factor in the teacher's immediate environment that affects his interaction with pupils is the work load. Teachers do more than teach.* They also grade papers, keep

---

*Teachers rate noninstructional duties as the third most difficult problem they face. See National Education Association, "A Comparison of Teacher and Educational Leader Assessments of Teacher Needs," March, 1973.

records, issue texts, collect money, supervise hallways and lunch rooms, and perform a host of other duties.[3] Many of these duties should probably be shifted to teacher aides and clerical personnel. However, they are not the main feature of the work load; that feature is the teacher-pupil ratio. A popular theme among some authorities who take the research on class size at face value is that the number of pupils in a class has no bearing on achievement. Dozens of studies of class size support this claim.[4] They give no consistent evidence that the number of pupils in a class affects academic achievement. Nor is there research support for the view that large classes increase discipline problems, reduce pupil attention, or lower the quality of work habits.

While the findings of research are impressive, there are economic reasons for defending large classes. If thirty or forty pupils can be taught as effectively as fifteen or twenty at the same cost, larger classes are defensible. Furthermore, reduction of class size to any marked degree even in the face of shrinking enrollments would require extensive investment in new classrooms.

Turning to the other side of the argument, it is easy to agree with the critics who claim that the research is flawed. These critics emphasize the point that it is not class size *per se* but what the teacher does that makes a difference in achievement. If a teacher performs with fifteen pupils in the same way as he does with thirty, naturally there would be little difference in the amount of learning. This point is a crucial one, and researchers have met it by varying instructional procedures. The results continue to confirm the general proposition that class size is not an important variable. The trouble with the research is that the accuracy of its findings is indeterminate. No record of teacher performance was made and analyzed to decide whether the performance in small classes was, in fact, different from that in large classes. It is well known that what theories of method prescribe, or even what teachers say they do, is not the same as what is actually done. The research on class size, consequently, is suspect.

In the final analysis, the whole to-do about class size is not directly germane to the problems of creating the conditions for the exercise of teachers' competence. The question is not how many pupils can be taught at one time without reducing the norms of achievement. It is whether or not there are learning difficulties that can be handled only in small groups or by individual attention. In research on class size, the findings are reached by comparing the average achievement of small classes with the average of large classes. In both cases, there are low and high achievers with the rest spread out between. Pupils who need little instruction are not likely to be affected by class size. The poor achievers are the ones affected by lack of individual attention, which large classes deny. Some pupils in the experiments do well in either small or large classes, and others do well in neither. The teacher must ask why the latter do not learn. His competence is displayed in the diagnosis and treatment of the difficulties rather than in the achievement of the average and above-average performers. The problem is not one of class size, but rather of how to identify the low achievers and provide place, time, and materials for working with them until they succeed.

As a matter of fact, pupils who need little or no instruction can probably be taught in sections of 100 or more just as effectively as in groups of ten or less. The problem is with the pupils who must have the teacher's help. For teachers of these pupils the question is one of case load. How many problem cases can a teacher handle? The answer appears to depend upon the nature of the cases and the judgment of the teacher based upon experience with similar cases.

The third factor that directly affects the teacher's perform-ance is the amount and kind of materials and equipment available. A professional worker cannot do the job expected of him without proper tools and materials. No one is more able than he is to decide what these should be. If he does not know what materials and tools are required for the job, he is incompetent. To choose for the teacher the books, maps, apparatus, and other materials he is to use is to belittle his competence and to rob him of the opportunity to keep abreast of developments in his field. His decisions about materials must, of course, be based in part upon his estimate of his needs and in part upon the budgetary resources.

Teaching is not Mark Hopkins on one end of a log and a student on the other. It is not just a verbal exchange between two minds interested in the same pursuit. Rather, it is an interaction among individuals whose interests are often divergent and whose backgrounds are so different as to require much effort in the search for common ground; it is an interaction that must often begin with weak motivations and continue by searching for barriers to learning and the procedural and material means of overcoming them; it is an interaction bound by time and conditioned by the social and material atmosphere in which it is carried on. Yet the Mark Hopkins stereotype continues to shape the public mind as well as administrative planning of what is needed to initiate and sustain teacher-pupil activities.

The poverty of the classroom is matched only by the poverty of the most indigent pupils. The rooms are typically formal and forbidding. Most of all, they lack simple learning materials, a condition which a few schools have tried to remedy by providing enrichment or activity rooms in science and mathematics where pupils can go for a few hours of the day, or learning centers where the most autonomous pupils can go on certain days to engage in activities that should be available to all in regular classrooms.

Each classroom should be equipped with audiovisual apparatus as recommended by the teachers themselves. Each teacher must be allocated funds for instructional materials. How much should be allocated to each teacher for this purpose? The answer will probably vary with the grade level and the subject of instruction. An answer for the elementary teacher may be quite different from the one given for a high school teacher. For purposes of illustration consider the question from a general standpoint. Suppose one estimates the cost of a standard-sized classroom, or the equivalent space in an extended classroom, at $30,000; a teacher's annual salary at $12,000; and the life of the classroom as thirty years. The total cost of the space and the instruction for the duration of the classroom would be $390,000. If administrative costs were added, the total would exceed $400,000. What percent of that amount should be added for materials and equipment to enhance the teacher's effectiveness? That is a basic question, for the teacher's success hinges largely on its answer. Less than 10 percent of the cost of constructing a classroom and staffing that classroom would provide each teacher with $1,000 annually for these purposes.

The fourth factor to be considered in the immediate environment is the teacher's assignment. It would seem reasonable to assume that teachers are assigned to teach a subject or at a grade level for which they are prepared. This is often not the case. Either because an appropriate teacher is unavailable or because it is inconvenient to employ one, misassignment is not infrequent. A nationwide study sponsored by the National Education Association gives some hint of this misassignment of teachers.[5] A total of 1,035 returned questionnaires, or 69 percent of those sent out, described 677 cases of misassignment. Fifty-nine percent of the cases involved lack of subject matter competence.

If teachers are not qualified to teach in the areas to which they are assigned or if they feel themselves to be inferior to the task, the purpose of the school is likely to be defeated. The frustration of trying to keep ahead of the pupils in an unfamiliar subject is of no advantage to the pupils, and it plagues the teacher with the fear of failure. A competent teacher is rendered incompetent when forced to work in an area for which he is not prepared by training and interest.

The School Environment

The work of the teacher is affected not only by the conditions that directly influence his moment-to-moment behavior in the teaching situation but also by the more remote aspects of the school such as administrative policies and arrangements. Many of the policies and administrative practices that hamper the school personnel in efforts to improve the school originate in the central administration and the governing board. To increase the effectiveness of teachers, it is necessary to free the faculty of each school from the entanglements of the system. School personnel engaged in developing and maintaining a quality school must be in a flexible posture, able to make on-the-spot adjustments to unforeseen difficulties that always arise when programs, policies, and practices are being altered.

The school personnel must have a high degree of professional autonomy, but they must be held responsible for results. Their first goal is to show that every child can be raised to the achievement floor. The purpose of autonomy is not to encourage grandiose and sweeping changes for the sake of something different. Neither is it to allow the faculty and principal to impose a ready-made conception of an ideal education upon the pupils and their parents. The schools have suffered enough ill-conceived changes in recent history. They need no more displays of energy in pursuit of impossible aims. What is required is a hard-headed approach to school improvement, one that begins with the school as it is; studies its programs and operations; and makes only such changes as facts, ideas, experience, and hard thinking justify.

The faculty cannot act effectively in a data vacuum. The relationship of the school personnel and the school system's research staff is crucial. The faculty and principal should use the research staff in defining needs. They must formulate the questions for which they need data; they must formulate programs and practices to be tested with the help of the research center. It may turn out that wholesale change is unnecessary; that only a few modifications in teacher performance, materials, and arrangements for teaching and for referral of obstinate cases for further diagnosis and instruction will suffice. To jump to the conclusion that some new pedagogical formula is necessary because intended outcomes do not occur or because the state of affairs does not match one's hopes, is a habit of the romantic mind. It is not the professional's approach to a social, economic, or educational malcondition.

Because the personnel must respond not only to internal conditions but also to external stresses and strains, they must have maximum freedom to utilize their competence, to recommend candidates for faculty and administrative positions, to make their own budget estimates, to use their funds flexibly, and to make any decisions that promise to resolve the difficulties they encounter.[6] A feature of the administrative arrangements that tends to preclude the exercise of these functions is the hierarchy within the school building as well as in the total system. A hierarchy is a necessary feature of any group organized to achieve specified ends; it is not something that can be abandoned at will. In the simplest school situation, as in the one-room school, the teacher is both principal and teacher in one. This is a simple two-step hierarchy—board, teacher, pupils. In a larger school with several teachers, the functions of teaching and managing are separate, creating a three-step hierarchy—board, principal, teachers, pupils. As the system grows, additional steps are added until finally there emerges the complex superstructure of the large school system. This superstructure, including both line and staff, came into existence at a time when the university preparation of teachers was in its infancy and teachers were ill-prepared. Whatever the explanation for the creation of the supervisory staff, it is clear that it was based on the supposition of incompetent teachers who needed direction on the job.

Teachers and principals agree that one of the most debilitating influences on school personnel is the organization of the school system into levels of responsibility governed by rigid rules and decisions made at the upper echelons. This system robs a faculty of the responsibility of formulating its own programs, determining the conditions of its efficiency and accountability to its patrons. Superintendents and their staffs object to this claim and point to conditions that free teachers and principals to take initiative and deal with their problems constructively. Two sets of facts militate against the superintendents' objections. The perception of teachers and principals does not correspond to that of the central administration. Since his actions are determined by the way the individual sees things, not the way others say they are, the perspectives of the administration count for little with the personnel at the school level. The perspective of the faculty constitutes its reality. It is also evident from research that almost a third of the faculty's time is consumed in tending to extraneous chores in order to maintain hierarchial functions and other noninstructional activities.[7] Furthermore, the bureaucratic mechanism separates teachers from the upper echelons; the superintendent seldom has contacts with teachers. The impersonal administrative structure, its power flowing from the top and little direct feedback rising from the bottom, breeds subordination and dependency and maintains a system of rewards that support it. The principal, caught up in this system, tends to interpret the rules and regulations to support a do-nothing policy.

The difficulty does not stem from bad intentions. The upper levels of administration wish to be helpful rather than to cause ineffectiveness. The source of the trouble is a built-in conflict of authority. At least two kinds of authority reside in the system: administrative authority and knowledge authority, sometimes referred to as expert authority.[8] The first is ultimately rooted in some interpretation of legal enactments, board policies, or delegated powers. Knowledge authority, on the other hand, comes either from research or professional wisdom or both and is typically specialized. The authority of a teacher of reading covers a different domain from the authority of a teacher of arithmetic, although they both have some common knowledge that cloaks them with authority broader than their respective specialities. If the exercise of administrative authority conflicts with the exercise of knowledge authority and the former is allowed to take precedence over the latter, the competence of the teacher will be neutralized. These conflicts are often interpreted in terms of loyalty to the administration, thereby putting the teacher in an embarrassing situation in which he must either surrender his professional integrity or run the risk of becoming *persona non grata.*

The tendency for administrative authority to influence the work of the classroom is related to the reward system. Teachers protect themselves against administrative controls through manipulation of pay by salary schedules; they match the power of school management with their own collective power. Salary schedules and collective negotiations leave little incentive for initiative exercised for economic gain, but efforts to depart from this system are typically met with stiff resistance by teachers themselves. This is apparently attributable to the belief that merit increases will amplify the power in administrative hands and thereby further reduce the autonomy of the teacher. Were the teacher's autonomy more secure, merit differentials could be more palatable, although the question of how merit is to be determined would still deter serious consideration of the matter.

Despite the widespread appeal of merit pay among laymen, the fact is that some research evidence indicates that material incentive is not the driving force it is popularly believed to be. Two sets of conditions can positively influence teachers. The first of these consists of environmental factors such as administrative arrangements, working conditions, status, security, and salary. The second set is composed of the factors that give rise to growth and feelings of accomplishment on the job. Among these are evidence of achievement, recognition, responsibility, and the challenge of the work itself.[9]

Job satisfaction is more often related to the second set of conditions. One study reported that of all factors contributing to extreme job satisfaction, 81 percent involved growth, accomplishment, and responsibility; only 19 percent pertained to the conditions of work such as status, security, and pay.[10] Of all factors contributing to extreme job dissatisfaction, 69 percent belonged to the latter and only 31 percent to the former.

There is no evidence that either causally or correlatively links teachers' receipt of material increments with higher pupil achievement in either rural or inner-city schools. Furthermore, if increased promotional latitude is related to increased pupil performance, it has yet to be persuasively demonstrated. Nor has it been shown that "Teacher of the Year" awards or other pat-on-the-back approaches have been useful.[11]

It stands to reason that factors that impede work or motivate it do not do so in the abstract but are themselves conditioned in their effects by the kind of organizational structure in which they function. Furthermore, properties of organizational structure vary in their effects according to the sort of tasks to be performed. Where the work is functionally rationalized, as on an assembly line, a tightly structured organization is more effective than a loosely structured one. Where the processes of work are flexible and contingent upon the problems to be dealt with, as in a classroom, a loosely structured organization is more conducive to effective work.[12]

Teaching requires flexibility of performance. It cannot be reduced to a routine in a tightly ordered system without circumventing the very motivational factors—responsibility, challenge, accomplishment, and growth—that evoke the best the teacher has to give. School improvement requires the reconstruction of the internal administrative structure and mode of operation, if motivational factors are to be enhanced.

Perhaps no question is more important in the management of professionals than this relation between administrative and specialized authority. There are two tendencies in a hierarchy: One is loyalty to the system; the other is loyalty to specialized knowledge and skill. While a highly competent faculty will feel some commitment to the hierarchy in which they work, they are more likely to perceive loyalty in terms of commitment to the use of their knowledge and skill than to the views and decisions of administrative personnel. There is no ready answer to the question of how conflicts of authority can best be handled, but it is clear that an answer is of primary importance in any plan of school improvement.

It is not feasible to set forth an administrative structure and operating procedures compatible with the exercise of professional competence. The matter requires far more care than can be given to it here. It is feasible, however, to suggest some conditions that a suitable structure and system of procedures would satisfy. They are as follows:

1. A school with its faculty is the functional unit of a school system. The most general guiding principle must be to create an administrative system conducive to the exercise of initiative and competence of the faculty of each school.

2. The internal organization and administrative policies of the school must be decided by the faculty, including the principal.

3. The responsibility for the school's program, its successes and failures, must be placed upon the faculty. If a faculty is to have professional autonomy, it must be responsible to its clients no less than to the public. It cannot hide behind the administration when the school is attacked and expect to enjoy the freedom to which a professional is entitled.

4. No rules, plan, or course of action affecting the curriculum, instruction, or conditions of work may be introduced in a school without deliberate approval of the faculty.

5. Criticisms and complaints about the school's program, its rules and regulations, or anything affecting the school's patrons should be received by a designated member of the personnel. These objections must be immediately followed up, analyzed, and organized for periodic presentation to the faculty or an appropriate faculty committee for action.

6. Provision must be made by the research center of the school system in collaboration with the faculty for periodic evaluation of the school to determine its strengths and weaknesses and to determine clients' attitudes toward the school. The results of these evaluations should be reported to the

faculty and the central administration for their information and for such action as may be indicated.

7. The principal is the guiding head of the faculty. He must be such because of his knowledge and skill and not because of his position. His appointment by the board of education must be made on recommendation of a committee consisting of representatives from the school's faculty and representatives of the faculty of at least one other school. Outside representatives are essential in order to broaden the perspectives of the committee and to prevent a faculty from succumbing to its own weaknesses and fears.

8. Except in instructional issues between the faculty and the central administration, the principal should be neutral.

9. The annual budget of the school should be prepared by the principal within broad guidelines given by the central administration and with the advice and consent of the faculty. It should be the principal's responsibility to negotiate the budget with the central administration.

The fundamental purpose of this list of conditions is to place the instructional program and procedures under the authority of the professionals who carry on the formal process of schooling and direct semiprofessionals or nonprofessionals who work with them. In other respects, such as keeping records and preparing reports, each professional is subject to the requirements of the hierarchy.

The Service Area and the School

Schools today are situated in a great variety of districts. One of these is a basic administrative district, which is under the control of a single board and an administrative corps. There are a number of variations on this basic pattern. Sometimes it includes elementary or secondary schools only. It is often coterminous with a county or a city. The standard pattern of school control is the administrative district. This kind of district is to be distinguished from an attendance district, which is a geographic area served by a particular school. A number of attendance areas may be found in a given administrative district. In the agrarian society of seventy-five years ago, the administrative district typically had the same boundaries as the attendance district. School consolidation and urbanization have reduced the number of governing districts and increased the number of attendance areas within districts. An important effect of these changes is to separate the governance of the school from the people whose children attend the school. The busing of pupils to achieve integration has dispersed the school's clients and removed them still further from the center of school control.

This separation has become the basis of a new struggle to reshape the control of the public school. The struggle was implicit in the community school movement of the 1930s and '40s, which involved the formation of community councils through which school personnel and laymen together could plan school policies and programs.[13] Not only did numerous councils become functional but also state and regional conferences on the relation between school and community were occasionally held throughout the nation. This movement attempted to make the local unit of school control and management coincide with what was conceived to be a natural sociological community similar to the village. As this union of community and school control was effected, the school was to become the center of education for the entire community, helping to be the focal point for the renewal of community life.[14]

The ideology of the community school movement of forty years ago came from the classical theory of liberal democracy and was epitomized by the slogan: "Whoever is affected by a policy should participate in shaping it." This ideology is too complex to be spelled out here. One of its essential points is that participation in political processes results in self-development, protection of one's interest, renewal of leadership, and a sense of community. Furthermore, it was believed that social and personal conflicts can best be resolved through participation. Debate among those holding conflicting opinions, according to this view, is sublimated physical combat, a constructive way to deal with differences about facts, values, and interests involved in the formation of policies and programs. The actual outcomes were typically viewed as less important than engagement in the process. This ideology still lives in the minds of those who emphasize the importance of process in teaching and administration as well as in plans of school reform.

The question of power is overlooked in this view of the political and social process. Reason and reasonableness are contingent on the distribution of power. The repository of overwhelming power can act arbitrarily and typically does. This is the hard fact that the community school movement of the last few decades either ignored or did not see. It did not recognize that the people of poverty, including a broad section of the major minorities, were outside the school councils and without a voice in deliberations about policies and programs. Except for this neglected aspect of the political and social formula, the community school movement is today essentially the same as it was at its inception four decades ago.

The powerless—the impoverished and the minorities—are now engaged in a struggle for power. Among them are some who still adhere to the old political and social formula. Also among them are some who see the community and the school as a rallying point in their struggle for power. They see the outcome not merely as a means of enabling individuals to improve themselves but as a new order of things in which power is to be more equitably distributed.

The proposition that members of the school community should participate in the development of the school program raises a fundamental question. How much control of the agencies that produce goods and services should the consumer have? In the last century, the relation between these agencies and the consumer was closer than it is today. Commercial and industrial establishments were small and approximated the conditions for competitive price competition. Monopolies and oligopolies were few, and professionalization and special-

ization of services were in their infancy. Under these conditions, the consumer often exercised direct influence upon
producing and service agencies. A large proportion of the
population lived on farms or in small towns. Eighty percent
owned the means of their own livelihood. As self-sufficient
members of society, they were relatively free to bargain for
goods and services. Medical service is a striking case. A
hundred years ago physicians treated patients in their homes.
Physicians carried drugs in medicine cases. Prescriptions to
be filled by pharmacists were unknown in many parts of
the country. Operations were performed in the home under
the watchful eye of family spokesmen who often interfered
with the surgeon's procedures, telling him what should be
done to reduce the patient's suffering and to safeguard his
life. The minister was frequently called upon to reconcile
the family so that the surgeon could proceed with the operation.

The control exercised by the consumer today is greatly
reduced and in many cases virtually eliminated. This has
been brought about by three sets of conditions.[15] One is the
public support of certain services. Among agencies providing
these services are public schools, state universities, state
hospitals, and public health and welfare offices. Since the
consumer pays little or nothing directly for these services,
he cannot withhold compensation if they are not satisfactory.
Of course, the individual contributes to the support of these
services by paying taxes, and he can show his displeasure
by voting against tax increases. However, this expression of
dissatisfaction amounts to little unless it is expressed by a
majority and the tax in question is for a specific service,
as in the case of local school taxes.

A second set of conditions is the growth of large corporate
enterprises and their tendency toward monopolization. Although the individual pays for the goods and services these
entities make available, his influence on them is trifling.
They are often the only agencies that provide the desired
goods or services. If one wishes to purchase insurance, send
a telegram, or place his savings in a bank, he finds that

the conditions he must meet and the benefits he is to receive are already specified. He can either accept them or forgo the services. If he turns to other banks or insurance companies, the individual encounters the same codes; as for telegrams, it is Western Union or nothing. Whether one thinks of automobiles, newspapers, mass media, movies, books, or whatever, the story is similar. The agencies responsible for them are mostly indifferent to individual consumers.

The third set of factors leading to the separation of consumers from the agencies producing goods and services is the specialization and professionalization of services. Forty years ago Whitehead called attention to the professionalization of modern society as one of its chief characteristics. The growth of professionalism is attributable to the multiplication of knowledge. One craft after another is developing theoretical underpinnings that increase foresight and improve skills and techniques. These professionalize the crafts and raise them progressively beyond the layman's comprehension and ability. If the profession is incorporated into a bureaucracy and its services publicly supported, its members are removed from pressures generated by the client's refusal to pay for the services. Even outside the hierarchy, the professional is relatively free of the client's pressure. The theoretical status of his professional knowledge and skill makes it risky for the layman to demand a significant role in shaping the services to be rendered. The professional typically knows what is better for the client than he knows himself.

The specialization of services, like their professionalization, reduces the influence of the consumer. The complexity of household equipment and vehicles of transportation and communication makes it necessary that the owner call upon service enterprises for repair. Anyone who has attempted to secure the services of a plumber, electrician, or auto mechanic has learned that his bargaining powers are slim, and efforts to participate in the service adds nothing to its quality. Such efforts may even terminate the service altogether.

The loss of direct influence by the mass of individual

consumers is driving them to political action as the most likely means of redressing grievances that they cannot correct individually and directly. The ever-increasing number of voluntary organizations to promote one cause after another is striking evidence of the consumer's discontent. The fact that organized efforts often represent minorities should not be taken to mean that the drift toward collective social action is limited to those who have been deliberately discriminated against. The trend includes the masses who are caught up in a network of institutions, agencies, and enterprises that affect them vitally and over which they have no direct control.

Organized efforts of parents to participate in the development and operation of school programs and to circumvent the educational bureaucracy by alternative schools and voucher schemes are to be understood in the context of the consumer's increasing debilitation. Frequently a parent feels that principals and teachers are more concerned about maintaining policies and rules than about the benefit of his child. Some adjustments that parents insist upon cannot be made because they are not justifiable from a professional standpoint. Some are not feasible because of the school's limited resources. Still others are incompatible with school policies and rules and can be made only by inviting disapproval from upper echelons. Regardless of the reasons, failure to meet parents' requests for adjustment is likely to be perceived as the workings of an impersonal and inflexible system.[16]

The production of goods and services by large social entities will characterize modern society as far into the future as anyone can see. Attempts to break them into small independent units will fail, and efforts to circumvent them will result in less effective bureaucratic structures or in others like the ones they are designed to replace. This much is entailed by the accelerated production of theoretical knowledge in all domains of endeavor and its translation into applied sciences. The question is not how to escape a world of bureaucracies and large-scale operations. This cannot be done; the clock cannot be turned back. With respect to the school, the question is: How can the consumer participate without reducing the effectiveness of the professional?

School personnel have always been confronted by citizens and social groups who make little or no distinction between decisions and policies that are the function of the profession and those which are partly the function of the public. One of the persistent complaints of the school's critics is that the professionals have appropriated to themselves all questions of policy, programs, and decisions. This is a bogus claim, for it is an established fact that few school boards, if any, have ever abrogated their power. They certainly exercise controls over school personnel by fiscal as well as educational, social, and administrative policies and regulations. It is equally true that one pressure group after another has forced teachers and principals to acquiesce in their demands about how to teach, what to teach, what to teach for, and even what to include in tests. The movement to involve the community has at no time ever really faced this issue of professional autonomy. Instead it beclouded the whole issue with the community council whose relationships with the legally constituted school board and the school personnel were never spelled out in workable terms.

No school policy, program, practice, or decision should be considered to be out of bounds of public scrutiny and criticism. The question is not whether parents and other laymen should be involved in the work of the school, but rather in what matters they should participate. It must be decided what aspects of school work are best assigned to the school personnel and what are best assigned to public deliberation. If the school program is failing to prepare some pupils in basic learning so that they are denied jobs because of the quality of their schooling, their parents and indeed the polity are obligated to see that corrections are made in the school program. If the policies and practices of the school discriminate against pupils because of their poverty or their social and ethnic affiliations, the offended parties and citizens generally are obligated to bring about a reckoning in the school. If the school program provides for the college-bound pupil but does not provide equally well for the pupil who must enter a labor union, the political and social forces outside the school should bring about a change in school policies and programs. These are examples of matters in which active lay participation is legitimate.

The design of programs for the correction of such deficiencies is not a task the layman is equipped to perform. He may know what he wants but not how to obtain it. Neither does he know what tasks and skills are to be performed by the teacher, counselor, or other school personnel. These are domains the laymen enters at the risk of thwarting his own hopes. If he does, he is certain to learn, probably too late, that he has made a grievous mistake.

The layman cannot exercise control over the teacher's performance without reducing its quality and destroying the conditions under which his competence can be effectively utilized. While the autonomy of the teacher must be safeguarded, parents and the general public must have evidence that the school's purpose is being realized; that the achievement floor is being attained; and that rules, materials of instruction, and procedures are being persistently purged of biases against the impoverished, the minorities, and women. They must have evidence that the program is adjusted to each and every pupil, that the criteria of the utility of schooling are being met.

Lay participation is a variegated phenomenon, and a general pattern for it can be laid down but arbitrarily. But two principles seem to hold: that an attendance area includes all the people who should share directly in shaping a school's policies; and that classroom teachers should not be distracted from their primary responsibility to teach by over-involvement with parents and other laymen. These principles are rejected by some authorities. The first principle is opposed on the ground that it leads to localism and provincialism. The principle does run the risk of releasing the influence of the narrowness of life and experience that persists in many areas.

However, the criticism overlooks the extent to which the mass media and geographic mobility have broadened local perspectives and interests. Neither does this criticism recognize the influence of court decisions, state and federal regulations and programs, and legislative enactments upon local groups concerned with public education.

The critics of the second principle claim that teachers are already too isolated; that they know too little about their pupils' parents; and that they are dwarfed as persons because they are too narrowly identified with social and political activities. These are persuasive points. Naturally parents should know teachers just as they should know anyone else who significantly affects the life of their children. Likewise, the teacher can perhaps better identify with the pupil given knowledge of his parents. Such knowledge is unlikely to be translated into teaching performance because the connection between the two is tenuous. Were this not the case, learning in small towns would be more conspicuous. Knowledge of parents and their homes does not constitute teaching skill, nor does it yield information that the teacher can use in locating the pupil's stumbling blocks.

The more extended argument for the involvement of teachers with their pupils' parents stems from the claim that school achievement for children of the poor can be improved only by improving their home life. If the truth of this claim is ever shown conclusively, the fact would in no way indicate that the classroom teacher should be the one to improve the home. The teacher's energies would be absorbed in the task of teaching even if all pupils were reasonably apt.

Moreover, the notion that the teacher would be more effective if he were constantly engaged in community activities is suspect. It is not easy to stand against this claim. No one can argue convincingly against expanding everyone's experience and knowledge, whether they are teachers, carpenters, or architects. The question does not focus there but rather on whether such participation pays off in teaching effectiveness.

Hidden behind the notion of social involvement is a picture of the ideal teacher as a well-rounded person with antennae turned in all directions and fully attuned to what is going on in the world about him. This is an unrealizable hope, for few individuals have the energy or the inclination to be so involved. In any case, there is little reason to suppose that such involvement would pay off in increased pupil achievement. The teacher's energy is finite, and teaching is a taxing enterprise. To know each pupil's learning difficulties, to prescribe how to deal with them, and to follow through on the prescriptions is in itself almost a superhuman task. It is a task too often poorly performed and probably accounts for more failures to learn than any other set of conditions. The teacher must be a professional devoted to the job of teaching. Perhaps few ideas can be more threatening to a teacher than the widespread view that since the school is related to everything, the teacher must be actively involved in everything.

Modes of Lay Participation

Social and political pressures for the participation of laymen in the development of school policies and programs raise three questions: What is the purpose of the participation? How is the legitimacy of the participants established? What is the mode of participation?

The purpose will vary with the position and viewpoint of the person. Some will settle for a simple political objective such as the development of positive attitudes toward the school or public support for a permutation; others will refer to the doctrine that participation is good in itself; still others will say that the purpose is to restore the school to the people by delivering it from the professionals and the politicians. The overriding purpose, however, is to improve the school. This purpose is not understood in the same way by everyone, for "improve" is not a neutral term. The expression "improve the school" must be defined by references to public criteria. By "improve" is here meant that the school is moving toward a curriculum broad enough to cover the needs and capacities of any and all pupils in fundamental and advanced learning; that all discrimination against pupils and personnel because of race, sex, religion, or social status is being eliminated; that every pupil's achievement in basic knowledge is approaching the minimum floor; and that the utilities of schooling are moving toward maximum. Lay participation is not necessarily motivated by such a purpose; in fact, it may and often does impede movement toward these ends.

The legitimacy of participants is a fundamental matter. To whom are they accountable? The body politic is represented by the board of education. It can be said that the membership is often weighted with professional and commercial interests, that minority groups are typically not represented. This claim is supported by convincing evidence. The conclusion drawn by many is that since individuals do not ordinarily rise above specialized orientations, boards of education do not represent a synthesized perspective of the body politic. This conclusion is probably true. Nevertheless, a school board is legitimate. It is legally established; its members are duly elected, and they must stand accountable at subsequent elections.

In what sense are school councils or advisory boards legitimate? The proponents of councils can reply that the question is not relevant because councils do not take official action but rather advise the principal and faculty. The matter is not so simple. To act on advice of the council is likely to court the displeasure of the board. If the council's advice is presented to the board as a proposal and the board disapproves it, a conflict can arise if the council presses its concerns. Conflicts and political struggles between advisory groups and school boards have arisen in the past and can do so again. In such cases, the question of legitimacy is fundamental.

Any constituted body can be legitimate if it is sanctioned by law. If school councils are established by state legislation, they are legitimate. Conflicts between the council and local boards may still occur, but the status of the council cannot be questioned. If the functions of the council are specified in the legislation, the probability of conflicts is thereby reduced. Again, a council can be legitimate if it is sanctioned by custom; the sentiments and traditions of the people support it. This form of legitimacy is more fundamental and secure than that created by legislative fiat. Legislation that runs counter to mores and sentiments is likely to suffer an uncertain tenure. Few school councils, if any, are sustained by the sentiments and mores of the community, and only a small number enjoy legal status.

Granted that the body politic has an interest in its schools, in what ways can it be involved? The three modes of involvement now being used in one form or another are the cooptative, feedback, and shaping modes. In the cooptative mode a number of laymen are selected as an advisory body typically referred to as a council. The council speaks for itself since it has no constituency to which it must answer and from which it gains information.

The existence of school councils is attributable to the separation of administrative units and attendance areas and to the "eclipse of the community," as Dewey put it. The administration of the school system, as pointed out earlier, covers a number of attendance areas. This has resulted in the divorce of parents from officials who set the policies and programs of the schools their children attend. By creating councils, school officials hope to bridge the gaps thus created, to restore the sort of confidence and working relationship with parents that was possible in the old-fashioned community.

The cooptative mode suffers from the fact that the sense of community has been lost. In many localities, especially in urban regions, the people no longer reflect a body of common experience and wisdom upon which school personnel can draw. Instead, the shrinking body of common beliefs and activities is overlaid with specialized experience, narrow perspectives, interests and motives. There is a widespread lack of identification with any nucleus of beliefs and activities by which the business of the body politic is conducted. This has resulted, among other things, from division of labor, specialization of knowledge, differentiations of interests and association, urbanization, and bureaucratization.

What could be more reasonable than the belief that by bringing together members of this fragmented community a new synthesis to support school improvement would emerge? But why should one expect that council members will rise above their own narrow outlooks any more than board members? Is it because they are freed from the pressure of decisions and actions that constantly weigh heavily upon board members? Is it because they are presumed to have more ability and greater knowledge of civic affairs? Is it because they are deemed to be less selfish? Or is it precisely because they are the spokesman of narrow points of view and are willing to press their claims? All one can say now is that these queries beg for concrete and practical answers grounded in social reality as well as theory.

Feedback is another mode. In this type of involvement, the body politic is considered to be a reservoir of feelings and opinions about almost every aspect of the school: its offerings, level of achievement, homework, help on personal problems, treatment of pupils, discipline, financial demands on parents, cleanliness, lunch arrangements, information, school taxes, and a host of other things.[17] Through questionnaires this reservoir can be tapped. The information gained thereby can be organized and presented to the school's patrons for discussion and suggestions for improvement.

This is a flexible mode of involvement. It commits the principal and the faculty to no particular unit of the body politic as does the school council. The group of participants can be small or large and can contain this or that segment of the population. The data from the questionnaires help to define the topics for extensive exploration, and they indicate the matters about which the public is dissatisfied. Furthermore, the risk of conflict with the school board is reduced to a minimum because there is no formally constituted body that persists from problem to problem to take issue with the local school authority.

The third mode of involvement is shaping. It is designed to form favorable public attitudes toward the school. It seeks no information but only presents information to the public on the programs and procedures of the school and the school's effectiveness. The information may be presented through brochures, films, and public meetings. This mode calls for little public activity or involvement with the school personnel. These modes are not mutually exclusive. Indeed, all three are employed by some school systems. If used with care they can all be helpful to the school personnel. The main point to keep in mind, however, is that involvement of laymen in the consideration of school problems is not the same thing as school improvement. Just because participants are satisfied with their involvement, or citizens are pleased with the outcomes, the school is not necessarily effective as judged by the achievement of its pupils or its individual and social dividends.

FOOTNOTES

[1] A few handbooks of classroom practices have appeared. Most of them have dealt primarily with problems in special education and reading. A recent one is Philip H. Mann and Patricia A. Suiter, *Handbook in Diagnostic Teaching* (Boston, Mass.: Allyn and Bacon, 1974). However, these are short on treatments.

[2] B. Othanel Smith and others, *Fundamentals of Curriculum Development* (New York: Harcourt Brace & World, 1956), pp. 217–18.

[3] Ellis A. Hagstrom, "The Teacher's Day," *Elementary School Journal*, 62: 422–31. See also Malcom M. Provus, *Time to Teach: Action Report* (Washington, D.C.: National Education Association, 1966).

[4] For a brief review of the literature, see *Encyclopedia of Educational Research*, Fourth Edition, 1969, pp. 141–146. See also Ian Templeton, "Class Size," *Educational Management Review Series*, Educational Resources Information Center, No. 8, August, 1972.

[5] Elaine J. Chisholm, "The Working Environment of Teachers" in *Summer Institute on the Improvement and Reform of American Education*, DHEW Publication No. (OE) 74-12008 (Washington, D.C.: Department of Health, Education, and Welfare, 1974), pp. 239f.

[6] Some of these rights have been won in the last two decades through collective negotiations. See Myron Lieberman and Michael H. Moskow, *Collective Negotiations for Teachers* (Chicago, Ill.: Rand McNally, 1966). See also *Summer Institute on the Improvement and Reform of American Education* op. cit.

[7] For a summary of studies see *Encyclopedia of Educational Research*, (ed.) Robert L. Ebel 4th ed. (Toronto: Macmillan Company, 1969), pp. 154f.

[8] Amitai Etzioni, *Modern Organizations* (Englewood Cliffs, N.J.: Prentice-Hall, 1964), p. 54. See Kenneth D. Benne, *A Concept of Authority* (New York: Bureau of Publications, Teacher College, 1943); and Peter M. Blau, *The Organization of Academic Work* (New York: Wiley-Interscience, 1973).

[9] Frederick Herzberg, "One More Time: How Do You Motivate Employees?" *Harvard Business Review*, January–February, 1968.

[10] Ibid. See also *Summer Institute on the Improvement and Reform of American Education*. op. cit., p. 80f.

[11] Larry Barrett and Roslynd McClendon, "School Personnel and the Problems of Incentives," in *Summer Institute on the Improvement and Reform of American Education*, op. cit., p. 82.

[12] John J. Morse and Jay W. Lorsch, "Beyond Theory Y," *Harvard Business Review*, May–June, 1970.

[13] Herbert M. Hamlin, *Agricultural Education In Community Schools* (Danville, Ill.: Interstate Publishing Company, 1949); see also Helen Storen, *Laymen Help Plan the Curriculum* (Washington, D.C.: Association for Supervision and Curriculum Development, 1946).

[14] Maurice F. Seay and Harold F. Clarke, *The School Curriculum and Economic Improvement*, Bulletin of the Bureau of School Services, Vol. XIII, No. 1 (Lexington, Ky.: University of Kentucky, 1940). For an extensive review of the school in relation to social problems see "The Community School," Part II of *The Fifty-Second Yearbook of the National Society for the Study of Education* (Chicago, Ill.: University of Chicago Press, 1953).

[15] The conditions are adapted from Etzioni, *Modern Organizations*.

[16] Mario D. Fantini, *Public Schools of Choice* (New York: Simon and Schuster, 1973).

[17] Harold C. Hand, *What People Think About Their Schools* (New York: World Book Company, 1948); see also James A. Conway, Robert E. Jennings, and Mike M. Milstein, *Understanding Communities* (Englewood Cliffs, N.J.: Prentice-Hall, 1974).

CHAPTER XI

Money for Reform

The fundamental issue concerning school finance is whether society's investment in schooling is a justifiable deployment of the nation's fiscal resources. If the schools fail to contribute to social and private economic benefits, the justification for their existence must rest on noneconomic returns. The case for school support on the basis of nonfiscal results might be sufficient to continue school support, but the argument favoring public support is strengthened if economic benefits are also obtained.* The first section of this chapter provides a discussion of the yield from investments in schooling. The next issue discussed concerns adequacy and equity in raising and disbursing funds. Inherent in this second issue is the

---

*Social and personal benefits for economic institutions are only a portion of the potential benefits of schooling. Returns from schooling that accrue to the individual and the society in the political, expressive-integrative, and kinship institutions also should be analyzed and evaluated. The state of research on economic returns is less than perfect, but it is considerably advanced when compared with the study of dividends from schooling in these other areas. Plans should be made and implemented that would determine the contribution of schooling to other institutions in society. Meanwhile, the economic return from schooling is one area in which a relationship between schooling and benefits can be described.

assumption that present taxing and spending patterns can and should be altered. The final section of this chapter describes the federal role in school finance.

Economic Returns from Schooling

A discussion of the economic returns from investment in education is provided because the economic benefits are part of the rationale for school support. Those who make decisions to fund the school enterprise, those who pay the bills, and those who attend schools would like reasonable assurance that their decisions and efforts are justified and that investments in school will yield a satisfactory return. This emphasis on economic returns concerns itself principally with the premise that,

> . . . education represents a stock of resources just as surely as does land, industrial plants, or oil wells for education does have the ability to generate future satisfaction and future income. The economic value of education as a form of capital is a function of the income stream it is able to generate. When education is viewed as a form of capital, decisions with respect to education, whether made by a student, by his family, or by public or private agencies, are viewed as investment decisions and are based on the relative rates of return available to alternative investment opportunities.[1]

Obtaining a return for investment in schooling is an economic fact of life, and part of the national or individual motivation for supporting schools is to receive economic benefits.

Economic returns from education include social returns and private returns. The difference between social and private returns is critical to understand the value of investments in schooling. Social returns are benefits to society; private returns are benefits to the individual's well-being and his personal income. The relationship of schooling and private returns has typically been the basis on which returns for schooling have been evaluated. The issue should be divided into two parts for analysis: the investment's return to society and its return to the individual. If the schools contribute to the society's economic strength, continued fiscal support of the schools can be defended on economic grounds. Support of the schools is not likely to endure if society fails to benefit from schooling. If schools also contribute to private economic gain, the case for school support is strengthened further. Schools should plan to contribute to individual returns, but failure of the schools to satisfy the private expectations of some of the populace is not a sufficient basis on which to withdraw support. Many factors beyond the control of the school contribute to the eventual success or failure of individuals. It must be emphasized, however, that favorable social returns are today becoming a necessary part of the justification of financial support of the schools. Favorable private returns are an additional benefit.

When taxes are expended for enterprises the public views as unnecessary or counter-productive, public support for those enterprises will decrease and eventually be withdrawn. The legal basis for public fiscal support of schools was established over one hundred years ago, but legal support alone is a weak basis on which to rely. The best basis for maintaining support is evidence that the nation as well as the individual benefits from schooling. Unless the case for benefits is convincing, financial support for schools backed by legislation and court rulings will probably disappear. Law alone will not sustain school support.

The task of equating fiscal returns with schooling is extremely complex. An investigator must decide if he will base rates of return on historical information, which may not predict future consequences, or on future earnings, which may be affected by unforeseen variables. Studies on economic returns have not been uniform in selecting the variables and purposes of their separate investigations.

One approach has been to calculate the private investment in schooling for a given level of completion and then compute increased earnings as a private return on the initial investment. Under this approach, if a college degree costs $20,000 and the annual increased income for obtaining the degree is $3,000, then the return for the investment is 15 percent. Another example of calculating the social return is to contrast the taxes paid by those who achieve varying levels of schooling. If the average high school graduate paid $1,250 annually in taxes and the average elementary school graduate paid $1,000 annually, then the additional $250 is an increase of 25 percent paid into the government's coffers as a social return from schooling. However, if the additional amount paid is adjusted by the additional expenditure for supporting secondary schools, the percent of return is reduced. If an individual bears the cost of his secondary schooling in a private school, then the return to society should not be discounted by the cost for additional schooling.

An additional point to consider is that some individuals have accumulated wealth because of factors other than their school attendance. They may have inherited their money, or they may have gained it by overcoming deficiencies in their schooling or by taking advantage of the opportunities that came their way. Also, if an industry finds that its profits increase when it hires according to schooling levels and augments its personnel with on-the-job training, then private and social returns occur, and the effects of schooling alone on these returns is confounded by mixing schooling and pre- and post-employment training in the calculations.

Because of the measurement and research problems of determining fiscal returns, the evidence derived from these different considerations must be regarded as approximations. However, the percentages of return are high enough and consistently positive enough to suggest that when a nation chooses to invest in its resources, some of that investment should be in the schooling of its people.

Common sense suggests that schooling is beneficial to society. Those who occupy positions of leadership in the social and private institutions are typically those with high levels of school attainment. Comparisons between products and services of today with those of decades ago makes the contribution of knowledge to living conditions self-evident. The

knowledge required to improve transportation, communication, medical treatment, and research activities and to
reduce time and effort in the labor force are related by evidence
or inference to the educational system's contribution to the
society. Other factors illustrating public support include the
public's defense of compulsory attendance laws, the willingness of laymen to serve on boards of education with little
or no compensation, and the voices of protest that oppose
the closing of school when teacher strikes or financial shortages cause a reduction of the school year. All of these reactions
add to a general position of public support of the schools.

Although these examples may be persuasive, more substantial evidence must be reported to support the argument that
schooling is a deserving recipient of the nation's fiscal support.
Economists have begun to conduct studies on economic returns
to education, and their findings are reassuring. The reason
economists are now selecting schooling as a variable in the
evaluation of economic growth is given in *Returns to Education*.

> Concern for education by economists started about fifteen years
> ago when empirical investigations in the United States revealed
> that output was growing much faster than inputs as conventionally
> measured. The part of the growth of output unaccounted for by
> conventional inputs come to be known as the "residual" or the
> "coefficient of our ignorance." Original explanations of the residu-
> al such as "technical change" or "shifts of the production function"
> were of little help analytically. How could a country shift its
> production function or induce technical change so as to achieve
> a higher level of output?
>
> This led researchers to try to open the black box of technical
> change and reduce the unexplained residual. The main initial
> development was the quantification of the increase in the quality
> of labour inputs and this led to the creation of a new field in
> economics known as the "economics of human capital", or more
> narrowly, the "economics of education". Since then there has
> been almost 180° shift of emphasis in development planning,
> the emphasis changing from physical to human capital as the
> major source of growth.

Once education has been seen as an investment, the next question was: what is the monetary pay-off from this investment? For, if the objective is an efficient allocation of resources between different uses, the yield on investment in men has to be compared with that on investment in other forms of capital. Suppose, for the moment, that the returns to investment in human capital can be satisfactorily measured. Then, if the returns to investment in a particular educational level are higher than the returns to physical capital, we would conclude that there is under-investment at this level of education. Conversely, if the returns to human capital are lower than the returns to physical capital, then investment in the second form of capital should be given priority. Therefore, at the centre of any discussion of optimal resource allocation lies the concept of a profitability measure of investment in education.[2]

In one analysis of returns from education, the yield from investment in schools in over thirty countries was studied. Using the residual approach, it was reported that social returns for education resulted in an average of 19.4 percent increase in economic return for primary education, 13.4 percent for secondary education, and 11.3 percent for higher education.[3]

Another investigation was conducted using data for nine western nations for the period 1950–62. It was found that education accounted for 40–50 percent of annual growth income.[4] If this analysis is correct, then the utilization of knowledge as a national resource is nearly equal to the use of all other factors that influence the economy. These relationships exist at the national, regional, and state levels. For example, Japan is currently investing a higher percent of its gross national product in education than any other nation (about 12.5 percent) and is also enjoying an impressive economic and industrial boom.[5] India is suffering from poverty and economic inadequacy, and its investment in schools as a proportion of total wealth is one of the smallest of any highly populated nation in the world (about 2.4 percent).[6]

In the United States a comparison of the ten states with the lowest per capita income to the ten states with the highest per capita income reflects the lower investment per capita in schools provided by states whose personal income is also quite low. The amount of per capita expenditure for education in the ten poorer states averages $176.95, while the ten wealthiest states average $219.26.[7]

It would be presumptuous to attribute the economic condition of a nation or state solely to the investment made in its schools. The argument could be posed in the reverse that only those areas that have succeeded in developing an industrial complex that generates wealth can afford the luxury of investing heavily in schools. Whichever basis one chooses to examine the relationship between schooling and national wealth or schooling and social returns, the fact is that low investment in schooling and poor economic conditions go together.

That investment in schools yields social returns is supported by the above studies. No nation that wishes to develop or maintain its strength can disregard an investment in the schooling of its youth. Studies that have investigated and dramatized the relation between schooling and economic return serve as an appropriate reminder that youth are valued subjects for cultivation.

In respect to private returns, the average personal income of those who attain higher levels of schooling is greater than the average personal income of those who complete lower levels of schooling. A recent example typifies the evidence that has been reported. In 1970, the Bureau of the Census reported that in 1968 males 25 years of age or older who had not completed elementary school could expect to earn $196,000 during their lifetime; high school graduates could expect to earn $350,000; and those who completed four years or more of college could expect to earn an average of $586,000.[8] Personal income based on years of schooling consistently reveals the same pattern as reported in these figures. Those who attain higher levels of education also earn more income. In the study cited earlier reporting social returns for thirty nations, private rates of return using the residual procedure were also given. This study showed the primary school and secondary school rates of return to be 23.7 and 16.3 percent, respectively, while the private rates of return for the university level was 17.5 percent.[9] To illustrate the magnitude of these latter returns, if one placed $1,000 in an account at age 20 and his money compounded at the average rate reported in this study, by age 60 the account would exceed $1 million and would be considered a sound investment by almost any standard financiers might apply.

Despite the generalization that investment in schooling yields a fair social and private return, further analysis shows that private economic returns include exceptions. A hint of the discrepancies in private returns is revealed in a list of conclusions reported on the consequences to individuals for investments in schooling. An analysis of the returns to population subgroups was undertaken to examine the possibility that racial, ethnic, and sex biases may affect the returns that different people derive from schooling. The findings in this report provided evidence that investments in schooling do yield a favorable return, but the rate of return was inconsistent across such variables as race, sex, and geographical region.

1. For the private domestic economy in the United States, the annual rate of return for all schooling was estimated to be between 10 and 15 percent before personal taxes.
2. An annual rate of return for investment in elementary education was estimated at 35 percent or higher.
3. An annual rate of return on investment in high school education for white males was estimated at 25 percent; estimated rates of return to members of minority groups ranged downward to near zero for southern rural black males.
4. An annual rate of return on investment to improve the quality of elementary and secondary schooling was estimated in the neighborhood of 25 percent.
5. An annual rate of return on investment in college education of approximately 15 percent before personal taxes was estimated for white males; estimated rates

of return ranged downward from 15 percent for rural males, women, and nonwhites.

6. An annual rate of return on investment in graduate education of about 15 percent was estimated when stipends awarded graduate students are treated as earnings.[10]

This suggests that the rate of private return is not automatic; variance among groups does exist. The discrepancies in economic returns on investments in schools result in a social and private loss of human potential. The loss to society is expressed in the following statement.

> Education like most forms of capital, pays dividends only when it is used. Unemployment reduces the return on educational capital. Not only is a considerable amount of educational capital idle during times of high unemployment but also the skills of workers tend to deteriorate when they are idle. This underlines the importance of maintaining a high level of employment for failure to do so not only substantially reduces the rate of returns from investment in educational capital but causes depreciation of the educational capital itself.[11]

The schools are dependent on society to remedy the ills that waste human talent. Society depends on the schools to supply people whose abilities and knowledge will be useful to the individual and to the society. This objective cannot be met unless adequate resources are provided. The next section includes a discussion of current practices of raising funds and the consequences of present procedures of providing fiscal support for the schools.

Adequacy and Equity in School Finance

The maintenance of financial support for the schools is one of the society's most complex problems. Part of the complexity is due to the massive size of the school enterprise and the range of responsibilities the schools have assumed. Fiscal decisions are also complex because of the variety of taxes, different tax bases, and possible formulas for collecting revenues. Taxation policies must account for a wide range of factors at the local, state, and federal levels to ensure equity in the collection of revenue. The discrepancies in need for money in different urban, rural, and suburban locations contribute heavily to the difficulty of distributing the money equitably. The entire issue is further clouded by the task of establishing priorities for spending within the school enterprise: i.e., teacher training, materials, facilities, reductions in pupil-teacher ratios, higher salaries, teacher-aides, etc. These fiscal issues have dominated the educational scene since public schools first began, and today is no exception.

The question of how to raise and distribute funds for schools was addressed prior to 1930 by such stalwarts as Elwood Cubberley, Paul Mort, George Strayer, Henry Morrison, and Harlan Updegraff. Their early work has been updated in more recent studies published in 1971 by the National Educational Finance Project (NEFP). The topics in the more recent work of NEFP are similar to those in earlier works, and many of the circumstances previously described in school finance are still vital issues today. For example, Cubberley stated in 1905 that the excessive burden of communities, born in large part for the common good, should be equalized by the state.[12] NEFP reported that, "we believe that the educational opportunity of every individual should be a function of the total taxable wealth of the state and not limited primarily to the taxing ability in the local school district."[13] The intention of these two statements, issued sixty-five years apart, is similar. They both urge that a broader base than the local level be utilized to support the schools. The major difference between the recommendations advocated early in the century and the present recommendations is that the state level of taxing was previously viewed as the savior of the local communities; today the state and federal levels of government are viewed as partners in solving fiscal problems.

The school system of the United States is a massive enterprise whose magnitude requires large amounts of money. In 1970, the elementary and secondary enrollments in public schools, private schools, and higher institutions totaled 59 million. These students were taught by about 3 million teachers. This vast sytem was supported by an annual expenditure of over $73 billion, which exceeded the combined revenues reported by General Motors, American Telephone and Telegraph, Standard Oil of New Jersey, and the Ford Motor Company.[14] Since the turn of the century, enrollments have increased rapidly, requiring the construction of additional facilities. Between 1958 and 1968, 701,000 classrooms were constructed and 180,000 antiquated classrooms were abandoned; the net increase made 1,764,500 rooms available for instruction. The building program during this ten-year period reduced the class size from an average of 27.7 pupils in 1958 to 25.5 in 1968. Between 1900 and 1970, the elementary school enrollment increased from 16 million to nearly 37 million pupils. Enrollment in secondary schools increased from about 700,000 pupils to nearly 15 million pupils, and higher education enrollment increased from 238,000 to over 7.5 million pupils.

During this century the general population increased in size two and two-thirds times; secondary enrollment increased twenty times, and higher education enrollment increased to twenty-eight times the enrollment of seventy years earlier. In 1900, fewer than 100,000 students completed high school; in 1970 nearly 3 million students finished high school. The development of the schools during this century has included a substantial reduction in illiteracy, an increase in the length of the school term, improvement in pupil attendance, an increase in the percent of the population enrolled in public elementary and secondary schools, and the highest percent enrollment of the total population in schools of any major nation in the world. This growth of the schools is evidence that the American people's confidence in the schools has generated massive support for them.[14]

Like any major enterprise, the educational system also has its faults, and the growth and status of its parts are uneven. There are problems and circumstances that cannot be dismissed. Some of these problems can be found in the fiscal policies and financial circumstances of today's school. Despite the increased school construction during the 1960s, when school doors opened a scant five years ago, 317,000 pupils in twenty states were attending school on shortened sessions; the need for classrooms had still not been fully met. The large cities are in dire financial straits according to reports issued in 1971. Chicago reported a deficit of $94 million, and New York a deficit of $76 million. Portland eliminated twenty instructional days to meet its budget. Projections for the future assumed serious deficits for most of the major cities, including Baltimore, Detroit, Los Angeles, Cleveland, Philadelphia, and San Francisco. The period since 1971 has seen little improvement in the financial circumstances of the nation's cities. [15]

The problems in school finance are more pervasive than the deficits reported in the urban centers of the country, although urban problems are a serious part of the total difficulty. The relationship of local, state, and federal funds, the discrepancies throughout the nation concerning the ability to raise funds, and the disproportionate expenses in different locales are crucial features of the problem. Approximately 52 percent of the financial support for schools derives from local taxes, and 97 to 98 percent of the local support comes from property taxes. [16] The property owner is paying for half the cost of elementary and secondary schools. If all property owners were assessed by the same standards, if all people owned property commensurate with their earnings, if all were taxed at the same rate, if all money were distributed equally according to average daily membership and adjusted to the cost of living in each area, then each pupil would receive equivalent financial backing from property tax sources. Obviously, these circumstances do not exist and never will. Thus, half the support of the schools comes from an arrangement that cannot be equalized. In addition to being raised locally, money is also spent locally. Communities differ drastically in their financial requirements because of the ratio of school children to property owners, assessed valuation of property, tax rates, and general tax burdens for other services required at the local level.

No two states finance their schools in exactly the same way, and each state utilizes both state and local tax sources, with the exception of Hawaii, which uses a state system of raising revenue for the schools. Since property taxes at the local level are so important in nearly all states, the local differences in ability to support schools becomes critical. Reports of variation in ability to raise revenue range from a district that had $1 million assessed valuation per pupil to a district that had $110 per pupil, or a ratio of about 10,000 to 1. Within one county in Illinois, the difference in financial ability in two different school districts is 150 to 1. In six northeastern states, the differences in financial ability between the tenth and ninetieth percentile in each state were calculated. The ability-to-pay ratio showed a low of 1.8 to 1 for Rhode Island and a high of 7 to 1 for Maine when local taxing capability was measured. Even when the extremes were discarded, the discrepancy in the ability to support schools was pronounced. The situation among states is similar to the circumstances among local school districts. The ten lower economic states average an investment of 7.72 percent of their per capita income in education while the ten states with the highest per capita income invest an average of only 5.86 percent. The poorer states impose taxes that collect a higher percent of their fiscal resources and still bring in a lower amount per pupil.[17]

The solution to this problem is for each state to give varying amounts to the local community and for the federal purse to be applied according to varying needs of the states. Precedents for this solution have been set, and a few examples illustrate the flexibility that is currently employed. Local support varies from 14 percent of the revenue per child in New Mexico to 88 percent provided at the local level in New Hampshire; the balance comes from state and federal sources in each case. State revenues range from a low of 4 percent in New Hampshire to a high of 70 percent in Delaware. Federal

revenue ranges from 21 percent in Alabama and New Mexico
to 1 percent in Vermont and Wyoming. Across the nation,
40.7 percent of the revenue comes from state sources and
about 7 percent comes from federal sources.[18] Despite these
flexible arrangements, a problem still exists because the
amount of money from the federal level is a small percent
of the amount needed; the burden of the local taxpayer is
not sufficiently relieved. The National Education Association
has recognized this weakness in fiscal support of public
education. The association passed a continuing resolution in
its 1973 annual meeting that the "Federal share of financing
public education must be at least one-third of the total cost."[19]
The situation facing those who make fiscal decisions about
the schools is epitomized in the statement issued by a task
force that investigated and made recommendations about
fiscal responsibilities for the schools.

> In a nation dedicated to the open society, to upward mobility
> for all citizens, we regularly distribute educational services in
> greater quantity and quality to pupils who live in the wealthiest
> and most advantaged suburban communities, and bestow consid-
> erably inferior education on children in the poorest school districts
> and in many of the older, deteriorating central cities.
>
> In a society which has become increasingly mobile and migra-
> tory, where our economy is indisputably national in character,
> we continue to treat education as a predominantly local function,
> raising the bulk of revenues for the schools from local tax sources
> through inefficient local tax collection mechanisms.
>
> In a federal system that has given the most democratic and
> dynamic revenue resource—the graduated income tax—to the
> national government, we rely upon it for only 7 percent of school
> funds typically turning to less elastic and more regressive state
> and local levies for fully 93 percent of all public school costs.
>
> In a country where for more than fifty years a consistent goal
> of educational policy has been "equalization" in financing public
> schools, communities rich in property tax base characteristically
> tax themselves at lower rates yet realize far greater yields per
> pupil than do less favored districts which tax themselves harder
> yet raise less proportionately and absolutely for their schools.[20]

Criticisms of funding practices have been made periodically for the last seventy years. The failure to establish a fiscal policy that will raise sufficient funds without putting an undue burden upon the local taxpayer continues to be a major theme in school finance. The plea for more funds to carry out research and supply enough general support to avoid the huge deficits incurred by most major cities in recent times is a recurrent demand. Public confidence in the schools has been high as reported in national polls,[21] but public reluctance to support bond issues for more expenditures is well-known. The defeat of proposals in local communities to raise school funds is most likely a consequence of overburdened taxpayers, impoverished adults in some segments of the nation's cities and rural areas, and the high cost of living, rather than opposition to schools. Nevertheless, schools are hurt by the general protest of local taxpayers at the ballot box. The realities of the fiscal potential of the nation and the priorities of the schools must be blended with other community services to develop a fiscal policy in support of the schools.

The Necessity of Federal Support

A shift away from local taxes toward state and federal support is the best direction for current fiscal policies to take. The increased support from federal and state levels should allow as much local choice as possible. The federal government can provide money for local schools without tying unwarranted strings to federal dollars.

Increased federal assistance is justifiable today because the population is now highly mobile and people travel across state lines in large numbers to take up new residences. The nation as well as the state and the local community have a large stake in the characteristics of people moving from one location to another. A state can no longer view its future workers and citizens as those who are born within its boundaries. Each state can expect its adult population to include many whose early years were spent in other locations. Thus each state, as well as the nation at large, is affected by inadequate educational opportunities. If a given state is unable to support its schools adequately, the state suffers from those who remain in the state, and other states suffer from those who leave. The nation loses in both instances, and the individuals are hampered throughout their life wherever they are.

Schooling cannot be the total solution to this problem. But it is probable that an increase in the levels of school achievement may help reduce the number of nonproductive members of society. A higher level of schooling attained by a larger portion of the nation stands as good a chance of solving the problems of both individuals and the nation as any other enterprise, since knowledge accounts for nearly half the gain that comes from the various economic enterprises of the nation.[22]

The role of the federal government in school finance should be increased. It should include at least four responsibilities. One responsibility should be to contribute more substantially to the equalization of educational support for each pupil. A second concern should be to provide emergency assistance to school districts whose circumstances require added resources. A disproportionate number of students requiring special instruction, the sudden influx of students into selected areas, or a strike that paralyzes the fiscal resources of a community are examples of emergencies that require immediate help. A third federal government function is to support cooperative arrangements among states to enable them to share and profit from one another's experiences in improving their schools. Organizations such as the National Commission of the States, Council of the Great City Schools, the Multi-State Consortium, and the program of National Assessment of Educational Progress are only a few examples of cooperative arrangements that cross state lines. The entire nation can benefit from activities that are not bound by the individual states, and federal participation is a useful resource to stimulate and maintain these shared efforts. The fourth role is to support experimental efforts and research to further the knowledge base and improve the use of funds. The establishment of pilot schools in real settings provides the best test of new approaches to school improvement. Pilot programs can eliminate the waste that occurs when programs are attempted on a full scale without a trial period. They can test the estimates of budget, time, and effort involved in implementing reforms, and they can also provide information about the feasibility and effectiveness of reform. The funds to initiate change through pilots should come from the federal level. The role of the local school district in pilots is to provide personnel, facilities, and public and professional commitment to carry out the pilot studies. The federal responsibility should be to provide technical assistance and to guarantee that fiscal support is maintained. Neither state nor local agencies can afford to divert sufficient funds from their budgets to sustain experimental studies and research.

Summary

The nation benefits from investment in schools, as do individuals. Firm data on this claim are impossible to obtain because of the confounding variables, but the evidence strongly suggests that schooling does pay off. On these two bases—individual and national benefits—fiscal support for the schools is a legitimate use of national resources.

The inequities in raising financial support for schools and the contrasts in educational costs in different regions and areas of the country result in uneven fiscal support. These discrepancies are revealed in the financial deficits that confront large cities, and the low-level pupil support in rural areas especially in the southeastern section of the country.

The consequences of inadequate schooling are not borne merely by pupils who reside in areas of weak financial support. This highly mobile nation, in which 20 percent of the population changes its place of residence every year, suffers from poor preparation of youth regardless of where they attend school.

The uneven distribution of natural resources throughout the nation leads to an uneven distribution of wealth. Equalization of support for a national program such as the system of schools, the interstate highway system, or national conservation requires coordination and support at the national level. In the case of schools, the state and local levels must retain a strong role in carrying out this work, but they cannot be expected to provide a fair opportunity for all youth without adequate financial help. Unless basic fiscal policies are changed, the results from research and pilots will be of no benefit. The basic financial need must be met, or nothing else can count.

FOOTNOTES

[1] *Alternative Programs for Financing Education,* Vol. 5 (Gainesville, Fla: National Educational Finance Project, 1971), p. 20.

[2] Psacharopoulos, *Returns to Education* op. cit., pp. 1–2.

[3] Ibid., p. 5.

[4] *Alternative Programs for Financing Education,* op. cit., p. 27.

[5] Morris Hath, (ed.), *Family '72 Almanac* (New York: New York Times Co., 1972), p. 728.

[6] Ibid., p. 715.

[7] Ibid., *passim.*

[8] W. Vance Grant and C. George Lind, *Digest of Educational Statistics* (Washington, D.C.: Office of Education, U.S. Department of Health, Education, and Welfare, 1973), p. 21.

[9] Psacharopoulos, op. cit., p. 5.

[10] *Alternative Programs for Financing Education,* op. cit., p. 25.

[11] Ibid., p. 21.

[12] Elwood P. Cubberly, *School Funds and their Apportionment* (New York: Teachers College, Columbia University, 1905).

[13] *Alternative Programs for Financing Education,* op. cit., p. 1.

[14] *Digest of Educational Statistics* (Washington, D.C.: Office of Education, U.S. Department of Health, Education, and Welfare, 1970) and *The New York Times Almanac.*

[15] Ibid., p. 51.

[16]Unpublished Data on Local School Systems Budgets, National Education Association, Research Division, 1971 (typewritten reports).

[17] *Status and Impact of Educational Finance Programs,* op. cit., p. 50.

[18]Ibid., pp. 49–119.

[19]Ibid., p. 59.

[20]Walter W. Heller, "The National Economic Setting for Education," *Today's Education,* November–December, 1973, p. 66.

[21]Joel S. Berke, Alan K. Campbell, and Robert Goettel, *Financing Equal Educational Opportunity* (Berkeley, Calif.: McCutchan Publishing Corporation, 1972), pp. 1–2.

[22]"Kappans Answer Gallup Questions," *Phi Delta Kappan,* September, 1971, pp. 35–36.

CHAPTER XII

Minimum Levels
of Achievement

This chapter describes an approach to the minimum levels of achievement advocated in Chapter V. Schools can be asked to raise pupils' achievement above minimum floors, but it will require more than a request and good intentions to achieve this goal. Until the elements necessary to attain minimum floors are identified and installed, the possibility of exceeding those floors is speculative. The approach recommended here is to establish sites to test the effectiveness of the recommendations for reform.[1] Advocates of school reform have an obligation to describe the practical operations entailed in carrying out their proposals. By specifying the changes that are likely to occur and predicting the implications for those who implement change, a reformer's recommendations can be judged according to practical as well as theoretical considerations. This description of pilots provides the practical plans and probable consequences of reorganizing schools and training personnel to enable pupils to exceed the minimum levels of achievement.

Outline of the Pilot

A national program of pilot sites should be initiated, including three to ten schools at each site. The schools should be contiguous, and the sites should include elementary schools, junior high schools whose pupils come from the elementary schools, and high schools whose pupils have completed the junior high schools. Sites could be chosen in any school district, but most of them should be located in urban and rural settings where pupil achievement has consistently been low.[2] A small number of sites should be established initially so that large sums of money will not be released until there is empirical justification for doing so.[3] This pilot is based on the following principles:

1. The best measure of teacher effectiveness is pupil learning that is attributable to the teacher.

2. Knowledge about effective teaching behavior should be derived from an analysis of the behavior of teachers whose pupils achieve especially well.

3. Attainment of minimum achievement floors by pupils should be a requirement in the pilot.

4. No ceiling should be placed on any pupil with respect to his potential or opportunity to achieve.

5. Effective teachers should be utilized in the inservice programs for training less effective teachers.

Figure 2.
Timetable for Pilot Sites

Year	Phase	Purpose
1	I	Planning and preparation to evaluate teachers and pupils
2	II	Evaluation of pupils and teachers; selec-
3		tion of teachers for special assignment
4	III	Training of educational personnel
5		Continued training of personnel; evalua-
6		tion of pupils and teachers; comparison
7	IV	with Phase II; dissemination of results

6. Inservice teacher training should take place primarily in settings that include pupils in typical school circumstances.

7. University personnel are most effective in the inservice program when they serve as researchers and resource personnel.

8. Knowledge about the morale, interpersonal relationships and attitudes of those affected by the pilot should be based on the report of a monitor whose record of decisions and their impact is made available to decision makers in the pilot.[4]

9. Responsibility for preservice teacher training should be shared by college personnel and local school personnel with the major role assumed by the college.

10. Responsibility for inservice teacher training should be shared by local school personnel and college personnel with the major role assumed by the local school.

This plan calls for selected school systems to commit resources to implement reform according to the above principles. Some variance in the details may be necessary to suit local circumstances, but these principles should be followed unless experience disproves their viability.

One of the most important considerations in planning pilots is the selection of evaluation criteria. Pupil achievement should be the dominant factor measured to assess effectiveness. Even though teachers express enthusiasm for a new approach, parents contend they like it, and administrators report a more efficient school with higher morale, all of these reactions combined are not sufficient evidence of an approach's effectiveness. The endorsement of these groups is a desirable concomitant; it is not possible to operate effective schools without support from teachers, parents, and administrators. However, the chief concern is that pupil achievement improve.

Although this pilot is a seven-year plan, improvement in schools could begin within the first two or three years. It may be found that the seven-year period may need to be extended to obtain dependable data. The pilot is divided into four phases. Phase I is devoted to planning and requires one academic year. Phase II requires two years and calls for implementing the plans made in Phase I. Phase III lasts one year and concentrates on inservice training. Phase IV lasts for three years, continues the training, and includes evaluation of the schools and decisions about revision of the plan. During Phase IV, development should continue, and the program should be disseminated throughout the school system, employing elements that have proven to be successful. Figure 2 outlines this timetable for each site.

Management of the Pilot

The management of the pilot should be shared by a director and a steering committee that includes teachers, community representatives, principals, and personnel such as university faculty and consultants. The suggested composition of the steering committee for seven schools is illustrated in Figure 3.

The director has the responsibility to coordinate and lead the schools in the pilot site. He should be chosen from the personnel in the school district to avoid the delays that often arise when a newcomer must learn the characteristics of a given school system before he can function effectively. The director will receive some of his training before the pilot

Figure 3
Suggested Composition of Steering Committee

Category	Number
Elementary School Teachers	4
Junior High School Teachers	2
Senior High School Teachers	2
Elementary School Administrators	4
Junior High School Administrators	2
High School Administrators	2
Lay Representatives	3–4
University and R & D Lab Personnel	2–3
Others	3–4
Total	**24–27**

begins. His training will give him information to initiate the pilot and will be provided by a national steering committee.* In addition to the initial training he receives, he will participate in periodic training sessions throughout the duration of the pilot. Each school district should choose its director with special care to assure the best possible leadership.

The teachers chosen for the steering committee should be selected by their peers. Each pilot school should be represented on the committee. The director should meet with the local teacher organization and establish an acceptable procedure for selecting the teachers who will serve on the steering committee.

The role of the pilot school principals requires that the school district arrange for administrators in schools who can promote the purposes of the plan. The selection and evaluation of principals must be based on the objectives of reform and each principal's willingness to serve in the schools. They must be acceptable to the classroom teachers and to the central administration to engender the highest level of trust and confidence among the teachers, principals, and central administration. The principal must be free to make decisions in the best interest of the plan without requiring approval from the central administration. His actions should be based on the recommendation of the director and the steering committee with whom the director will work.

Community members who represent a cross-section of the community's major concerns should be invited to serve on the steering committee. Organized community interests should be identified, and nominees from each interest group should be made. The major community agencies should be represented. One task the director must face is to determine the method of selecting community representation. He should do this in consultation with teachers and administrators.

University personnel should have research capability, and their work should include close ties with the public schools.

*See recommendations in Chapter XIII.

Faculty with specialized knowledge in the fundamental learnings and faculty with research ability should be especially useful members of the steering committee. Staff from educational laboratories and research and development centers should also be members of the steering committee if these facilities are nearby.

Replacement or rotation of members might be arranged if special problems arise, but the steering committee should plan to remain intact for the duration of the pilot. The professional members of the steering committee should be given released time; meetings should be held during school hours. Service on the committee should not impose an added burden on those who are selected to serve. Sufficient financial support to employ regular substitute help should be included. Payment should also be provided to the community representatives who serve on the steering committee to compensate them for their time and effort. University personnel who serve on the steering committee should be released part-time from their normal duties to serve. The members of the steering committee should not be handicapped either by loss of income or by extra work.

The topic of pupil achievement is emphasized in this chapter, but the techniques recommended to carry out this task also illustrate the procedure the pilot director should utilize in working with the steering committee on other topics. Usually the director will meet only with the members of the steering committee needed to conduct business. All members of the steering committee should be informed of meetings and allowed to attend. When an issue involving a specific topic is under discussion, the members of the steering committee whose responsibility is remote should not be required to attend. In the illustration provided in this chapter, the subcommittee of the steering committee will be referred to as the pupil achievement committee and will consist of no more than twelve to fourteen members of the steering committee. Figure 4 portrays this organization of the steering committee.

Membership of the pupil achievement committee includes

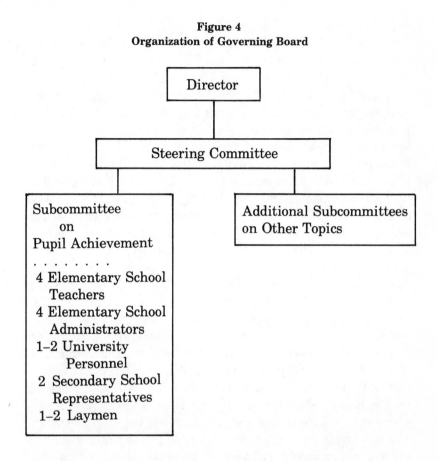

Figure 4
Organization of Governing Board

teacher representatives from each of the elementary schools, elementary school principals, secondary school representatives from the university, personnel from R and D centers or laboratories, and lay representatives whose interests and background would prove helpful to the committee.

The Pilot Operation

A student population of about 600 students in each of four elementary schools, 1,200 in each of two junior high schools and 2,400 in one high school is assumed for this illustration. For illustrative purposes, these figures serve to provide a basic context for discussion. Each of the four elementary schools will employ about twenty-five teachers; the two junior high schools will each have about fifty teachers; and the high school will be staffed by a teaching faculty of about 100.

Most of the burden for elevating pupil achievement in the fundamentals falls on the elementary schools. Although total responsibility is not placed on the elementary schools, they are most critical in raising the level of pupil achievement. Secondary school teachers are usually not trained adequately in helping students overcome basic difficulties. If the elementary schools can succeed in raising all pupils to the level of achievement where their learning can be applied to the acquisition of more knowledge, the program of studies and teacher assignments in the secondary schools can be altered extensively without the risk of students leaving school before they acquire the fundamentals. The secondary schools are not exempt from all responsibility for remediating learning difficulties. Secondary schools must also monitor the achievement of pupils and attend to their learning difficulties. However, the number of pupils they instruct in fundamentals should be drastically reduced by better instruction in the elementary schools. The teachers who remediate basic learning problems for secondary pupils should be drawn from among elementary school teachers who are trained to give appropriate instruction or from special teachers in the secondary schools whose preparation has been in teaching the fundamental subjects to secondary pupils.

The general tasks in this pilot are: to identify those teachers from among the 100 elementary teachers who are most effective; to provide for them to analyze their own teaching methods and receive instruction on how to teach other teachers; to utilize this new ability to improve the performance of other teachers, and to help improve the performance of pupils and beginning and student teachers.

Phase I. During Phase I of the pilot the 100 elementary school teachers should be assembled and instructed in the basic elements of the pilot. After the pilot has been explained, the teachers should select representatives to the steering committee who will serve during the operation of the pilot. The selection should include representation from all the schools in the pilot site.

The pupil achievement committee should establish criteria to measure pupil performance and to evaluate teacher effectiveness. The director of the pilot should inform the committee about the implementation of minimum floors and describe the pupil testing that will be conducted to determine the status of the pupils in the elementary schools. The minimum floors are critical to the overall success of the schools. The tests of minimum floors should be administered during the second year of the pilot at grades three through twelve to obtain baseline data on all pupils and during the remaining years of the pilot at the third-, seventh-, and tenth-grade levels. Testing of the minimum floors should continue beyond the duration of the pilot to determine the effects on pupils taught in the pilot as they enter and progress through school. Seven years may not be enough time to alter a school's usual practices and assess results, but an effort should be made to find answers within seven years because of the urgency and importance of this task. Additional years may be needed, however. The successful parts of the program established in the pilot period will also be continued as the method of operation for the entire school district. Follow-up of students will be continued with appropriate modifications as a regular part of the school program. The establishment of minimum floors and the testing of pupils to determine their success in meeting floors gives continual evaluation to the part of school reform that is designed to teach pupils the fundamental learnings.

The pupils will also be evaluated with other standardized tests and measures at each grade level in the elementary school. The pupil achievement committee has the responsibility of evaluating the existing testing program and supplementing it with additions or deletions that measure attainments the school regards as important. The committee must guard against the establishment of requirements in which high performance by pupils becomes so important that tensions between teachers and pupils are destructive. The pupil achievement committee may choose to develop additional measures for evaluating teacher performance and include pupil ratings, subjective observations, teacher interviews, or unobtrusive measures. The major concern is that the committee must define the effective teacher and then devise methods to measure him according to the criteria they establish. Those teachers who are especially successful in teaching low-achieving pupils should be identified. The performance of all pupils in fundamental areas must be one factor in the selection of the most effective teachers, but the effectiveness of teachers should not be judged exclusively on pupil achievement. Some teachers may have a preponderance of pupils whose barriers to learning are beyond the control of the teacher and may thus appear to be less effective than they actually are. Other teachers may employ tactics that induce learning but also produce damaging side effects. A teacher who abuses pupils may be able to bring about high achievement, but the concomitant learning is not desirable. Teachers who fail to bring pupils up to minimum levels of achievement should not be rated as superior teachers regardless of how popular they may be. Effective teaching and individual personality characteristics of teachers are different and should not be equated. Teachers who do bring about high performance are not necessarily superior teachers. The committee must decide the measures to be employed in locating teachers whose combination of high-performance pupils and acceptable methods qualifies them for rating as superior.

The criterion-referenced testing at the third-, seventh-, and tenth-grade levels will identify students who need special help in overcoming deficiencies in their learning according to minimum levels of achievement. The additional pupil evaluations at intervening grade levels will help identify teachers whose performance is superior. The evaluations of pupil performance and teacher effectiveness provide an opportunity for the pupil achievement committee to gather critical information about the relationship between teacher performance and pupil learning.

The first-phase planning will require one year. It should be reported to the steering committee and to the teachers. The essential features of the report will be a clarification of the assessment of pupil performance in achieving minimum floors, a description of the measures to identify the most effective teachers in the elementary schools, and a plan to assess pupil performance and teacher effectiveness.

Phase II. Phase II will require two years for completion and will consist primarily of implementing the testing and evaluation system developed during Phase I. During Phase II, pupil achievement will be determined on norm-referenced standardized tests and on criterion-referenced tests of minimum achievement floors. The pupil achievement committee will determine teacher effectiveness from information about pupil performance, supplementing that information with other measures of teacher effectiveness agreed upon during the planning in Phase I.

Data collection during Phase II should provide information on which to base judgments and make decisions about the activities in Phase III. During the second semester of the second year of Phase II, the most effective teachers should be identified. Three teachers from each grade level should be chosen so that eighteen teachers are selected from the original group of 100. During the latter part of Phase II, these eighteen teachers should begin preparation for a differentiated assignment during Phase III. Their assignment during Phase III will be to work as supervisors and instructors in inservice training, to work with pupils whose achievement is low, and to assist beginning teachers and student teachers assigned to the pilot site.

After the most effective teachers have been identified, the foundation for Phase III should be initiated. This foundation requires the collection of information on the performance of the effective teachers. The information should include the

performance of their pupils and the other factors employed
by the pupil achievement committee in selecting these teachers. Information on their teaching performance should be
obtained, including audio- and video-tapes of classes taught,
records and plans developed by the teachers, and any other
information that will enable the teachers to analyze their
own behavior. An accurate and comprehensive documentation
of the behavior of the selected teachers should be collected.

Phase III. Phase III will begin in the summer preceding
the fourth year of the pilot. During the summer the selected
teachers will receive instruction in three major areas. One
area will include instruction that will enable them to analyze
and interpret their own teaching behavior. The teachers should
be able to describe their actions, their reasons for those actions,
and the reasons their behavior was productive. They should
also be able to distinguish between effective and ineffective
behavior they may have demonstrated according to the type
of material being taught, to characterize the students being
taught, and to describe their own strengths and weaknesses.
As a consequence of this instruction, they should understand
how to analyze teaching and how to identify the characteristics
of teacher behavior that are productive.

The second area of their instruction is to learn how to
instruct others in effective methods. They should receive
instruction in the use of materials that may assist them in
helping inservice and preservice teachers. Instruction should
be provided on the use and availability of protocol materials,
training materials, mini-courses, and simulation materials.
Diagnostic and communication abilities should be improved
by the study of micro-teaching, observation techniques, and
improvement in the precision of language. Although the
selected teachers have a repertoire of skills and knowledge
about pupil instructional materials, additional materials
should be made available to them to expand their basis for
working with teachers and pupils.

The third part of their instruction will be to receive and
analyze the test data that have been gathered on pupils during

Phase II. These data should provide the selected teachers with information about the pupils and teachers in the pilot schools and should enable them to analyze the major strengths and weaknesses of individual teachers and the characteristics of individual pupils. As the teachers complete their training during the summer, they should begin the school year during Phase III equipped with knowledge about their own teaching behavior, techniques for helping other teachers improve their performance, and descriptive information about the teachers and pupils in the pilot schools.

A summer is not sufficient time to instruct these teachers adequately in all the knowledge they will require. Only a beginning can be made in the summer. Much can be learned about the effective methods of working with teachers in the classroom during the academic year. Their training should continue on a regular basis throughout the school year. During Phase III, the cadre of selected teachers will be divided into three groups. One group will consist of those assigned to work with the other classroom teachers at their grade level. Another group will be assigned the task of working with the pupils who are having the most difficult learning problems. The third group will work with beginning teachers, student teachers, interns, and college personnel in the preservice training program.

Figure 5 portrays the deployment of these teachers. The teachers in group A who are assigned to give individual help to students with learning problems should be released from a regular classroom assignment. All pupils whose level of achievement is below the minimum floors should receive concentrated help from these teachers. The teachers on this assignment will work in the four different elementary schools and will help students who are listed by the regular classroom teacher as pupils who require additional assistance. These teachers can give tutorial or small group instruction to pupils, confer with the teacher whose major responsibility is to give inservice training, and advise the steering committee on progress of the pupils in the pilot site.

Figure 5
Deployment of Teachers

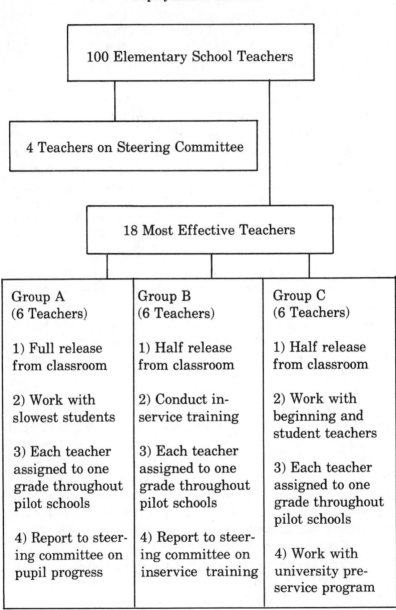

100 Elementary School Teachers

4 Teachers on Steering Committee

18 Most Effective Teachers

Group A (6 Teachers)	Group B (6 Teachers)	Group C (6 Teachers)
1) Full release from classroom	1) Half release from classroom	1) Half release from classroom
2) Work with slowest students	2) Conduct in-service training	2) Work with beginning and student teachers
3) Each teacher assigned to one grade throughout pilot schools	3) Each teacher assigned to one grade throughout pilot schools	3) Each teacher assigned to one grade throughout pilot schools
4) Report to steering committee on pupil progress	4) Report to steering committee on inservice training	4) Work with university pre-service program

The other two groups of selected teachers should each teach one-half day for part of their assignment. Group B teachers would be assigned to work with the other teachers at their grade levels and to help them to become more effective teachers. Each of these teachers would be in charge of the inservice training of approximately ten to twelve teachers at a single grade level throughout the pilot site. The assignment of the teachers in Group C is to help in the induction of the inexperienced or beginning teacher. All student teaching or other assignments of preservice trainees should be under the general direction of these teachers. University personnel should be advised by these teachers about preservice programs of preparation. This deployment of personnel would supply the pilot site with personnel who are prepared to assist the slow-learning pupils in the system, to assist teachers whose performance should be improved, to assist beginning of inexperienced teachers, and to influence preservice preparation. The arrangements in planning should include employment of additional teachers at each grade level to free enough time for the responsibilities of the selected teachers to be fulfilled.

The major activity during the one year of Phase III is the intensive inservice training for beginning and experienced teachers, the delivery of special assistance to pupils who require additional help, and alliances with student teachers and university personnel. The academic year included in Phase III should provide intensive help to improve the effectiveness of all teachers and to supply all pupils with improved instructional services.

Phase IV. The instructional assistance provided in Phase III should be continued during Phase IV. Assignment of teachers selected to deliver additional assistance might be rotated to allow for variety in their assignments and to supply help for different people who may not have benefited adequately from the work in Phase III. A primary responsibility in Phase IV is to collect data on pupil achievement and contrast the level of attainment with the performance of pupils during the previous years of the pilot. Comparative data on pupil achievement before and after Phase III will provide a partial basis for evaluation of the pilot. Many of the activities of Phase III will be continued during Phase IV. The additional responsibilities of evaluating the pilot and making decisions about its modification and continuation will become a critical element in Phase IV. If the pilots have been conducted carefully and good records have been maintained, knowledge about effective teaching behavior should be generated. The uses of this knowledge include continuous inservice training in the pilot site as personnel turnover occurs, and the application of this knowledge throughout the school district by shifting participants in the pilot to new assignments elsewhere in the district.

Variations on the four phases described in this pilot can be employed at the different pilot sites throughout the country. This description of the pilot supplies an illustration of how to implement the principles and recommendations advocated for school reform with emphasis on raising pupil achievement. The elevation of all pupils to minimum levels of achievement will not occur unless a concerted effort to apply resources and improve teacher performance is promoted. The above illustration focuses attention on improved achievement and gives a plan of action for directors of pilots to follow.

Other Considerations

Teachers should be protected from the conflict between trying to teach pupils who may not be ready to achieve at the prescribed minimum level and a mandate to elevate those pupils to a given level of performance. This problem can be handled best by delaying regular school activities until pupils display readiness to benefit from the usual instruction. Demands on pupils beyond their readiness to progress should be avoided. The school's tendency to admit pupils according to chronological age sometimes enters pupils whose background and maturity place them at a disadvantage, which remains a deficit throughout their school career. These pupils are likely to lag behind their peers in achievement.

During the first few weeks after the pupil's entry into first grade, teachers can assess his readiness to begin school. Tests and teacher judgment can identify the pupils who are predicted to perform at the lower levels of achievement. Rather than prematurely forcing these pupils into the usual system of schooling and taxing the teachers and pupils with unnecessarily demanding and frustrating expectations, these pupils should be provided with appropriate preparatory experiences. It is better for pupils to be delayed several months in the regular school program and then benefit from the school's offerings than to be saddled with academic failure or borderline achievement throughout their schooling. Although schools cannot control the events during the preschool years that may impede pupil development, schools can control the early school experiences for each pupil. Schools might continue to admit most pupils at the same chronological age as they do now but deny admission to those who are obviously too young and too immature to profit from the school program.

The differentiated instruction required to accomodate the individual readiness of entering pupils should receive support in the form of training materials and adult personnel (teachers, teacher aides, teacher assistants, specialists, and individualized instruction). The gains that come from this additional support, initial screening, and specialized instruction should yield multiple returns to the pupils, schools, and adult community. Failure to provide for those who are not ready for first grade dooms many of those pupils to twelve years of schooling at the low end of their class and poor preparation for functioning in school or society. The assertion that pupil readiness must be assured in the early stages of schooling makes the recommendation that minimum floors be established and implemented a reasonable possibility. The recommendation that pupils be screened at school entry should help teachers to elevate pupil achievement by guaranteeing better "raw material" to teach. The selection, screening, and special instruction of entering pupils is fundamental to their development and success in meeting minimum levels of achievement.

The directors of pilots should investigate and utilize technological advancements to strengthen the operation of the pilot.
It is inconceivable that any serious effort at school reform
can proceed without utilizing technological developments. It
is also difficult to prescribe the best utilization of technology
in school reform. Pilots provide the chance to systematically
develop and appraise the use of technology in developing
communication and information processing systems. Those
who plan and implement pilots have an obligation to the
remainder of the educational community to employ technology
and to determine the ways in which schools might be managed
and evaluated more effectively and efficiently. Because of
the successful use and potential of technology in today's world,
the schools must question their adequacy when they fail to
employ the available technology used in other sectors of the
society.

Judgment and discretion must temper the use of technology.
A dysfunctional nightmare of paperwork and data processing
can develop. However, the computer can be used as a mechanical clerk; it can collect, process, store, analyze, and present
information; it can analyze data against an expected distribution; it can restore a process to preset conditions; and it can
help in decisions about the proper course of action to take.
These uses of technology remain relatively untapped by the
schools. This lack should be investigated in pilot studies to
test the applicability, cost, and effects of improving schools.

Summary

There are pitfalls in the installation of a pilot that alters
the roles of teachers as much as this one does. Sufficient
incentives and guarantees must be offered to assure the
cooperation and effort needed to fully test the pilot and to
derive all possible knowledge from its installation. The role
of the central administration in local schools is reduced in
this pilot; the freedoms required may not be easily granted
by the administration. If autonomy for the steering committee
and sufficient supporting administrative personnel to work

with the pilot are not provided, the chances for success are heavily reduced. Teachers may not wish to compete with one another for the classification of superior teachers; morale problems might arise. Controversies are likely to emerge over the measures employed to evaluate and classify teachers. Cooperation among universities, local schools, and the state department of education concerning credit, degrees, and certification may not be easily obtained. These problems and many others can be identified in the implementation of the pilot. However, if educators subscribe to reform that builds on the potential resources in the schools, this example offers one solution.

Local schools could make many changes in the details of the pilot without losing the thrust of its intent. The basic principles presented at the outset of this chapter are more important than are the details listed. Any changes in principles should be carefully considered before discarding or altering them. These principles are the basic foundations of the pilot and should be included in the local plan.

Reform will not take place unless teachers are provided with conditions and training to improve their teaching, administrators are willing to assume new and cooperative roles, and the consequences of change are analyzed and studied. It is not possible for changes to be implemented unless some risks are taken by educational personnel. This approach is no exception, but it does provide some possible answers.

FOOTNOTES

[1] "Pilot Efforts and Policy" in *Windows to the Bureaucracy*. (Washington, D.C.: National Advisory Council on Education Professions Development, 1971), p. A–14.

[2] *National Assessment of Educational Progress*, Vol. 1 Report on Science; Vol. 2 Report on Reading; Vol. 6 Report on Citizenship; Vol. 8 Report on Writing (Denver, Colo.: Education Commission of the States, 1970–1972), *passim*.

[3] Bryce Hudgins, "Pilot Studies, Evaluation, and Transferability" in *Summer Institute on the Improvement and Reform of American Education*, op. cit., p. 239f.

[4] Donald M. Medley, "The Language of Teacher Behavior: Communicating the Results of Structured Observations to Teachers" *Journal of Teacher Education*, Vol. 22, Summer, 1971, pp. 157–65.

[5] Peter Drucker, *Drucker on Management*, op. cit., pp. 43–58.

CHAPTER XIII

Installation of Reform

The preceding chapters provide a discussion of topics considered essential to school improvement. Implicit in this discussion are changes in curricula, training programs for school personnel, administrative and organizational practices, conditions for utilizing professional competence, and fiscal policy. This chapter provides recommendations that lead to the implementation of these changes.

Basic Premises

These recommendations are made within the context of the existing system of schools. They are based on the premise that changes should be made by building on the school system's achievements rather than by ignoring the progress that has been made. The accomplishments of the schools are substantial, and there is little justification for promoting school improvement that ignores the existing strengths of the schools. Recommendations are without merit unless they solve a specific problem or improve an ineffective practice. This means that when recommendations are attached to the problems they are intended to solve, the relationship between difficulties and intended solutions should be established. Each recommendation listed in this chapter is linked to a problem that is perceived to be sufficiently serious to require alteration of present practice or a change in procedures. When a problem is stated it does not mean that there are no instances in which the schools are meeting that difficulty, but rather that the recommendations should be implemented on a larger scale than is presently the case. Recommendations are stated to encourage improvements to become common practice throughout all schools.

A discussion of the recommendation is provided for each of the problems cited. No final decision concerning these recommendations can be made until after the changes have been installed and then evaluated over a period of time. The results are not likely to be completely satisfactory. However, installation of changes in the schools will allow for further improvements to be made on an empirical basis. Until changes are identified, described, implemented, and evaluated, it is not possible to proceed on the basis of the effectiveness of any changes. The actual consequences should provide a data base from which additional improvements can be developed or that will verify the practicality or effectiveness of the change.

The recommendations that follow are organized around a format that includes 1) a statement of the problem to be solved, 2) a list of recommendations, and 3) a discussion of the recommendation.

Synoptic Proposals

This section contains a list of the recommendations that originate from the analysis and discussion of the schools presented in the preceding chapters. The order in which the problems and recommendations are presented has no special significance; all recommendations are considered important. Some changes may have a greater cumulative effect on each other, and others may be dependent on a sequence of changes. For example, changes that improve the conditions for the deliverance of professional competence will not greatly affect the performance of the schools unless the teachers are adequately trained or receive training to deliver an improved service. Improved training and improved conditions must both take place for either to be optimally successful. Other instances of interdependence will become apparent as the list of recommendations is presented and discussed.

Problem: The separation between the youth and adult society is extreme, and adult influence on socialization needs to be strengthened.

Recommendations:

1. All youth should participate in the adult world of work in order to become aware of adult roles and responsibilities.

2. Youth activities in the world of work should vary to include involvement in all four of the social institutions: kinship, political, economic, and expressive-integrative.

3. The schools should arrange for adults who work in society's institutions to assist in the schools as planners, teachers, and coordinators of youth-adult experiences.

4. Schools should reorder their priorities to increase the involvement of youth with adults but should not increase their current load by adding these additional duties to all of the tasks that are being handled by the schools. Current school responsibilities that are inappropriate for that institution should be reduced.

5. Several approaches with varying degrees of school involvement should be implemented on a trial basis to include youth's activities with adults, but the responsibility for schooling must remain the unique and principal function of the schools.

6. Additional time for pupils to engage in adult relationships can be provided by reducing the school's requirements to fundamental learnings, installation of mini-courses, and scheduling pupil time in school and in the adult community cooperatively with the pupil, school, and adult agency.

Discussion: The combined resources of the school and society should be organized and brought to bear on the task of preparing the young to participate fully in society. The abrupt change from dependence to independence experienced when youth leave the formal schooling process and take their place in the adult world should be softened by a gradual induction into the roles expected and required of them. This transition can begin early in the lives of all youth and can include exposure to the agencies that provide the cohesion any society requires to maintain and improve itself. These agencies include the familial, political, economic, and expressive-integrative institutions. Anyone who fails to grasp a functional understanding of the contribution these agencies make to society and the role of those who work within these institutions is poorly prepared to fend for himself. These recommendations are made in order to broaden youth's perspective about the society in which they are expected to survive. They are not made to exploit the young, as was done in the sweat shops at the turn of the century, or to prepare them for particular occupational choices. The recommendations are made for all youth to ensure that they become sensitive to the institutions that constitute the very essence of society. If the society in its many facets is an integral part of the lives of the young, then entry into adulthood will not be an entry into an alien world, but the normal extension of a process that has been initiated and shared by the schools and the multiple forces within society that shape and prepare its young.

Problem: Some youth complete their schooling but lack the fundamental knowledge required to function in society.

Recommendations:

1. A minimum achievement floor should be established in the fundamental learnings. All youth should receive instruction that will elevate them at least to the minimum level.

2. The content of the minimum floor should include all basic learning required for minimum functioning in the adult society.

3. The content of the minimum floor should include all requirements for the pupil to continue to learn the content in the remainder of the school program.

4. Pupils entering school should be evaluated to determine their ability to progress toward attainment of minimum levels of achievement with regular instruction. If special instruction is indicated, it should begin as early as possible to prevent pupils from lagging behind in achievement. The aim is to avoid creating insurmountable problems for the pupils and the schools in satisfying minimum levels of achievement.

5. The standards for minimum levels of achievement should be applied initially in the elementary school grades. Plans should be made to guarantee that all pupils achieve the minimum prior to the legal age for leaving school.

Discussion: The democratic system of government depends on the ability of a literate populace to express its opinion effectively at the ballot box. The basic tenets of democracy hold that the worth of the individual is of paramount importance. The economic system is dependent on responsible leadership and competent workmanship in the conversion of raw materials into salable goods in the competitive marketplace. Other illustrations of the activities that are crucial to the success of this society can be added to the list, but these three are examples in which the fundamental knowledge of the people is prerequisite to holding the society intact and providing for its proper growth. An ignorant populace can be misled by political acts more easily than a populace that reads, reasons, and reacts rationally. The worth of the individual can be maintained best if individuals have knowledge with which they can protect their rights and develop their potential. The extinction of ignorance is essential to the achievement of this goal. Economic institutions cannot grow or even survive without able leadership and supportive employees who have the ability to produce the nation's resources and to consume the products wisely.

Whenever an individual enters adult life without the fundamental knowledge that enables him to function in that society, the individual and the society are both harmed by his deficiencies. Remediation of this problem can be provided by establishing the relationship between minimum knowledge and functional behavior and then guaranteeing that all youth meet or exceed those minima before they leave the formal system of schools. Some may object to this recommendation with the argument that it is not feasible; such objections miss the point. The point is that society and individuals suffer from those who lack fundamental knowledge and that the problem is so severe that it must be overcome. Extensive time and resources must be employed to enable all individuals to participate effectively in society, but the goal cannot be regarded as impossible until every effort has been exhausted to reach it. There is no reason to delay initiation of the effort. The training of personnel, the fiscal support, and the research and evaluation techniques required to solve this problem still need further development, but enough is known to begin.

Problem: The present school curriculum is too narrow and restricts development. Requirements are retained that have little proven personal or social utility.

Recommendations:

1. The requirements in school curricula should be reduced to the essentials needed to reach the minimum floors in fundamental learnings.

2. After a student has achieved the fundamentals in the minimum levels of achievement, the remainder of his schooling should be elective.

3. The curriculum should include linear knowledge that will provide for some students to pursue a concentrated field of study, systematically, in depth, over a period of time.

4. The curriculum should include topics that will allow students to study a segment of knowledge or introductory knowledge within a short period of time.

5. General college requirements should be waived and replaced with requirements for particular fields of study.

a. The general studies portion of college study should be within the grasp of anyone who meets the minimum levels of achievement and has the motivation to attend and to work at the college level.

b. College enrollees in programs that lead to professional

positions or specialized work should meet prerequisites that are necessary for advanced learning in their chosen field and that include learning that exceeds the minimum levels of achievement required for all.

6. The twelve areas of systematic knowledge should serve as a guide for curriculum planning. All twelve areas should be included within the program of studies in every school district.

7. The traditional arrangement of offering subjects for an entire semester should be discarded and replaced with a system that offers a wide range of courses for various and flexible periods of time.

8. Mini-courses on a specific topic that may last only a few weeks should be commonplace.

Discussion: One of the drawbacks to the usual program of studies in today's schools is that it is bound to tradition and is responsive to a society that no longer exists. Previously, pupils who prepared for college enrollment found an appropriate curriculum that was tied to college admission requirements; others left school and entered society by learning on the job. The role of the school must be altered to serve contemporary needs. Today's curriculum should meet four demands. It should guarantee that all pupils reach a minimum level of achievement in fundamental learnings. It should relate the school's curriculum to the adult society such that youth, adults, and the world of work are not separate segments of society. The third requirement should be to open up the curriculum to include all major functions of society in a form that enables the pupils to acquire functional knowledge about their role in society and the ways in which the society can serve them. The fourth requirement should be to expand the school's elective curriculum to incorporate all the fields of systematized knowledge.

The expansion of the curriculum should provide two different services to all pupils. One service should be to offer sufficient work in a specific field to enable students to study a given interest or to prepare for a particular vocational outlet in depth. The other service is to make available a wide range of course offerings to those students who wish to obtain broad knowledge about many areas of learning but who have little reason to specialize in any particular field of study. This recommendation does not mean that every school district must expand its curriculum to include a thousand or more different courses. It means that the areas of systematized knowledge should all be represented in the curriculum. The extensiveness of that representation is a function of many factors including local characteristics, size of the school districts, qualifications of the personnel, and facilities.

Problem: School personnel are inadequately prepared to cope with difficult learning problems.

Recommendations:

1. Vicarious learning and discussions about teaching should be replaced with training that requires teachers to acquire diagnostic ability in classification of learning problems and the skills and knowledge to remediate those problems.

2. Study of actual behavior in films (or some other mediated form) and in the classroom should become the major thrust of preservice teacher preparation programs.

3. Materials that are used in preservice teacher preparation programs should be founded in research and developed through a sequence from initial planning through field testing to provide reasonable guarantees that the materials will be effective.

4. Preservice training should include instruction in theoretical knowledge through the use of protocol materials and the development of skills through the use of training materials that require performance from the trainees.

5. Training of beginning teachers should be facilitated by assigning these teachers to a reduced teaching load, providing them with competent supervisory assistance, evaluating their performance in order to help them improve, and determining if they should receive permanent certification after a reasonable trial period.

6. Experienced teachers should participate in inservice

programs where the school district supports their development according to the local needs, remedies their deficiencies in knowledge or skills, and offers them new knowledge from research and new methods to solve pupils' learning problems.

7. Materials utilized in the preservice program should also be incorporated in the inservice program as refresher materials or as additional materials that could not be included in the short time available for preparing teachers to enter the profession.

8. Each school district should give high priority to inservice training programs by supplying resources and leadership that will organize and implement a systematic plan of inservice training. This plan should address itself to solving the learning difficulties identified by the school's research staff.

Discussion: The heart of school improvement lies in the classroom performance of the professional personnel. The work of the teacher is complex and sophisticated and cannot be acquired in a few courses at the preservice level and a "survival" approach on the job. As the schools respond to the challenge to teach all pupils, teachers will require additional periodic training to obtain the ability to cope with the difficult learning problems that they are expected to solve. The educational researchers who identify improved approaches to the solution of learning problems and the classroom practitioner must be linked. This linkage can be provided through materials that reflect research findings in much the same way that research in any field leads to the development of products utilized by the practitioner to improve his work. The teachers application of an approach in the classroom is considerably more complex than the application of research findings in most other fields because of the dynamic human elements involved. Nevertheless, the relationship between theory and practice does exist; the schools have an obligation to create a training program in which preservice, beginning, and experienced teachers are systematically provided with the benefits of this research. Theorists must translate their findings into a usable form for others. The mediation of this process entails cooperation and leadership from all agencies engaged in the training of personnel. This includes the state and federal governments (which underwrite programs of research, development, materials production, and training of personnel) and colleges, universities, and local school districts (which work directly with teaching personnel).

Problem: Many of today's school principals are diverted from their primary function of giving leadership to the educational program of the schools by demands from the central administration, community, and other agencies. Principals often lack training to give leadership to the educational program of the schools. Both of these problems should be solved by clarifying the responsibility of the principal for the schooling of pupils and then providing a pre- and inservice training program that will equip principals to carry forth their appropriate duties.

Recommendations:

1. The duties of school principals should be realistically defined and should include the improvement of instruction as a primary responsibility.

2. The principal's first obligation should be to the pupils and teachers in the local school. The central administration should promote this relationship in its own policies and operations.

3. The training program for principals should be heavily laden with practical trial experiences to make the training congruent with the eventual duties of the principal and to determine the potential and compatability of the prospective principal with the administrative role before he assumes the duties of a principalship.

4. Potential school principals should be chosen from among those who have succeeded as classroom teachers.

5. School principals should be expected to achieve goals established jointly by the central administration and local school personnel. This procedure should include maximum autonomy for the local school to meet its goals through shared effort by the principal and the teachers in the local school.

6. The responsibility for training school principals should be shared by the local school district and the universities with the major responsibility placed on the local school district.

7. Principals should be trained to ask critical questions and to obtain research assistance in collecting data for help in finding the best answers to those questions.

8. All principals should be evaluated in respect to the goals of the school and provided with inservice training to remedy their weaknesses and to supply them with new information that is helpful to improve their effectiveness.

9. Principals whose schools do not function satisfactorily over a period of time should be reassigned or replaced to eliminate situations in which teachers and pupils suffer from inadequate school leadership.

Discussion: The unique role assumed by the schools in the society requires that they focus on the reduction of ignorance. All other functions sometimes ascribed to the schools are either shared by other agencies or exclusively the responsibility of other agencies. Some of these other functions include the teaching of values, the development of ethical behavior, or the selection of an occupation for one's work. The school shares some responsibility to be a positive force in the cultivation of desirable behavior in these areas but the schools are not alone in this effort. If the schools fail to help youth develop values, morals, or make appropriate educational choices there are other agencies that may fill this void or may even do much better than the schools, but the responsibility to provide each generation with fundamental and basic knowledge is the unique responsibility of the schools. If the schools fail to meet this obligation, there is no other agency or institution established to accomplish this end. A school that strays from its unique purpose and fails to educate its pupils is failing the pupils and society that supports the school. The building principal must protect the schools from intrusions that prevent the schools from fulfilling their purpose. The keystone of school improvement rests on the individual school level. The building principal is the most important single factor in determining the effectiveness of each school. Building principals can fulfill their roles if they are trained in how to carry out their work, if they are provided conditions that permit them to function well, and if they can work with the other professionals in the school to meet legitimate goals for their particular pupils. This set of circumstances calls for a clear definition of the role of the principal, pre- and inservice training that is tied to the work of the principal, autonomy to apply professional leadership and expertise, and reliance on knowledge embedded in all the professionals in the school system. The recommendations listed here on the preparation, assignment, and evaluation of principals are consistent with the purposes of the schools and should provide systematic and comprehensive training programs to improve the effectiveness of school principals.

Problem: The schools are not adequately staffed to handle the content of short courses on practical topics required for full participation in society.

Recommendations:

1. A thorough analysis must be made of social functions; the essential knowledge must then be selected in order to establish a program of mini-courses.

2. Teacher preparation should include practical work experience in order to help classroom teachers relate the content of their specialties to the realities of society.

3. Lay teachers who are engaged in important areas of community work should be utilized.

4. The professional and lay teachers should engage in shared planning and instructional activities in order to benefit from each other's knowledge.

5. Appropriate materials for each mini-course should be developed and edited to assure their readability at the achievement floor.

Discussion: The selection of topics and successful establishment of short courses to supplement the school program requires four developments: curriculum revision, materials development, flexible scheduling, and personnel training. A discussion of each topic gives general direction to the tasks that need to be done.

The analysis of social functions and the knowledge needed to understand them will require the work of a group of specialists in each area of knowledge. These specialists should be scholars who can divorce themselves from the trappings of their specialized knowledge and who are able to see and appreciate the concerns of laymen as workers, consumers, citizens, and "philosophers." They must also be able and willing to listen to persons of various occupations about what they do and what youth need to know in order to behave intelligently in society.

When analysis of social functions is completed, it will be necessary to prepare learning materials for each proposed mini-course. The preparation of these materials will require the work of specialists and teachers. Editors and reading specialists will be needed to review the materials to judge their acceptability in content and the level of reading difficulty.

Any program of schooling is controlled by structures that limit what can be accomplished. The structure of the daily schedule, the system of credits and examinations, and the allotment of time are typical examples. Perhaps the most important of these is the pattern of time distribution. The present timetable calls for early childhood, kindergarten, elementary, and secondary schooling in an unbroken sequence. This is not conducive to the development of a program of socialization in the adult community. The amount of time in the yearly schedule for each course is also fixed, typically requiring 16 to 18 weeks. The content is packaged accordingly regardless of whether the arrangement is useful to the consumer. This way of distributing time leads to inflexibility and must be altered.

The schools are ill-prepared to handle the content of mini-courses. Many teachers have little understanding of the new subject matter of these courses and little experience with the institutions and agencies serving the social functions.

Provisions must be made to remedy this deficiency in teacher preparation. It may also be necessary to use members of the adult community to teach some of the courses. For example, short courses in useful aspects of management, law, national defense, public order and protection, community planning, local government, landscaping, show business, and communication can be conducted by lay teachers who are actively engaged in such areas of work. They can bring a reality born of first-hand experience into each course, relating the subject directly to what the pupil as a citizen and worker would find most useful. A corps of lay teachers would bring youth into close association with a broad array of adults who are involved in important community work.

Teacher selection and preparation should be given as much attention as planning the program of mini-courses. School authorities will find it necessary to establish procedures for selecting persons whose qualifications appear to be promising. It will probably be desirable to seek the aid of organized groups in labor, business, industry, and the professions in selecting and soliciting laymen as teachers. The magnitude of the task will undoubtedly require a personnel staff assigned to this responsibility. Lay teachers must be sensitive to youth's orientation and concerns as they become involved in adult life. They must be able to eliminate the jargon of their specialties and to emphasize the most useful aspects of their subjects. They must have human relations skills and be able to conduct a discussion without losing pupil involvement. They must possess techniques of teaching such as questioning and diagnosing the points at which pupils have trouble in understanding what is being said. This will require that laymen be given preparation before they enter the classroom and that they be given help throughout their initial teaching experience.

Problem: Some youth attend no school or attend so few days each year they enter their adult years as illiterates. Whether these youth come from homes where adult lethargy toward school exists or simply leave school before acquiring minimum knowledge, they remain victims of the nation's failure to enroll all youth in school.

Recommendations:

1. A systematic accounting system should be employed that would identify each person under the compulsory school attendance age and record his school status.

2. Any youth who cannot be located in the schools should be traced, and provisions for his schooling should be made.

3. The accounting system should be organized to supply the adult community with projections of the numbers and characteristics of each age level of youth who will enter the adult society.

4. Care must be exercised in the establishment of a comprehensive accounting system to avoid infringement upon individual privacy and choice or to create an impression of controlling or limiting mobility and occupational decisions of individuals or families by a centralized agency.

Discussion: Each year some youth fail to enroll in school even though laws and regulations require their attendance. Pupils leave school before they have acquired fundamental knowledge. These youth may lack the parental guidance or adult support necessary to help them enter or remain in school. Help should be provided for them, but unless they can be found it will be impossible to give assistance. The first step is to establish a method of identifying all the youth of the nation. The enormity of this task is recognized, but an inventory of youth and their whereabouts is the only way to begin to solve this problem. The accounting system should call for minimal information and should require that data be collected according to guidelines that simplify the procedure as much as possible. A codification system that could designate each youth and the school he attends should be sufficient. A computerized system should be created that would list youth who do not appear on school rolls and then refer these students to the local school board. The local system would then have the task of contacting the person and arranging for his schooling to be started or continued.

Problem: Financial support for schools is inadequate in amount and is inequitably distributed.

Recommendations:

1. Schools should analyze the utilization of fiscal resources and determine if existing funds are being used effectively. This analysis should include an examination of the function of all personnel, the use of aides, and the possibility that administrative and supervisory staffs can be reduced in size.

2. Financial support to schools should be adequate to strengthen the scope and quality of basic research, applied research, and materials development.

3. Fiscal support should be adequate to pay salaries, provide year-round employment for teachers, and supply the schools with adequate facilities, equipment, and supplies.

4. The federal role in supporting the schools should be increased substantially to relieve property owners and those who live in states with limited income or wealth. The actual amount provided by the federal government is indeterminate at the present, but perhaps federal support should reach one-third of the total invested in schools.

5. Financial support should be highest where learning difficulties are most severe and where local and state fiscal support is most difficult to obtain.

Discussion: The problems in school finance have been well-publicized since the beginning of public support of the schools. In recent times the principles advocated by early reformers in school finance have been initiated. The role of the federal government has begun to increase, although unpredictably. This support should continue to be increased, stabilized, and distributed where the greatest shortages now exist.

Equalization formulas have been in effect to share the financial burden between state and local governments according to the ability of the local district to support its schools; further relief at the local level is needed. States have recognized that local school districts are not uniformly capable of supporting an adequate school program. The efforts to increase state support and decrease the responsibility of the local district should also be continued. Another trend is to increase support where special learning problems exist in order to offset the disadvantages faced by some youth as they try to obtain a level of schooling that will increase their chances at a productive life. The tendency has been to distribute these funds on the basis of poverty rather than on the basis of where the greatest learning difficulties exist. Low income and low achievement do tend to be concentrated in the same areas, but the assignment of funds on this basis does not assure that additional investments in schools are applied where they are most needed.

New formulas for the distribution of money must be developed; the usual ADA or ADM must be replaced by an awareness of the nature of the teachers' work and the fiscal support required to complete that work with pupils who have various learning requirements.

Problem: The knowledge base that provides for the improvement of instruction is thin and lacks the validation necessary to proceed with school improvement as confidently as would be desirable.

Recommendations:

1. Longitudinal research studies should be undertaken to find dependable answers to questions about the relationship between teacher training, teacher performance, and pupil learning.

2. Doctoral programs to train specialists in research should be supported.

3. Research should be carried on in the classrooms of the nation, where the variables of teacher training, pupil potential, and different kinds of learning are analyzed in settings that will increase confidence in the results of research.

Discussion: The complaint is often heard that teacher training is weakened by lack of knowledge about the relationship between teacher performance and pupil learning. The argument is extended to state that the effects of training on the teacher are negligible and that teachers discard the knowledge provided by their training when they enter the classroom. Although these statements may be partially true, they are not totally accurate. Certain teacher abilities, such as clarity in communication and good organization, have been shown to be related to increased pupil achievement. It has also been found that teachers can be trained to raise questions properly or to interpret standardized test scores and that the training is retained over a period of time. The shortage in these relationships is in the scope, depth, and variety of factors that have been examined in experimental studies. Sufficient support is needed to increase the knowledge on which teacher training programs can be established. Each year of delay in beginning this task prolongs the current situation in which teachers are prepared with inadequate theoretical knowledge and pupils and teachers struggle for the best way to interact with one another and the materials they employ in order to obtain the knowledge the schools should provide.

Problem: The organization, administration, and assignment of professional personnel does not capitalize adequately on their abilities, nor does it provide for career development and career variation.

Recommendations:

1. Classroom teachers should be provided with a caseload that reflects the difficulty of their assignment rather than a class load based on pupil-teacher ratios.

2. Teachers should participate fully in leadership in the instructional program, since their daily experience with learning problems gives them an advantage over most administrators, who are not as closely allied with pupils in the instructional process.

3. Sufficient personnel should be employed to enable classroom teachers to retain their teaching responsibilities and also have time to meet with one another and the school administration to plan, organize, and improve instruction.

4. Beginning teachers should have the benefit of supervisory assistance, favorable teaching assignments, and a systematic approach to induction into teaching.

5. Experienced teachers who are especially effective should have differentiated assignments throughout their careers in which their unique abilities can be applied to pupils, other teachers, administrators, and college personnel. This arrangement will permit them to be rejuvenated through differentiated assignments and inservice training supported by the school district.

Discussion: The literature is replete with recommendations to individualize instruction for pupils, but little is said about individualizing the careers of classroom teachers to develop their potential to its fullest. The teaching profession could be made more effective and more attractive if each member of the profession could depend on opportunities in which superior performance would lead to positions that employ his ability to instruct pupils, evaluate instructional materials, develop and improve teacher procedures, successfully induct others into teaching, and still retain his position as a teacher.

The usual division of labor is too rigid to permit the flexibility of assignments that would render the best service to pupils and provide the most appealing opportunities to teachers. For example, an experienced teacher may work in the classroom part of the day and help four or five beginning teachers during the rest of the day. A teacher in the elementary school may be assigned to instruct the forty students who are having the greatest difficulty in reading by meeting with them in groups of five at a time for his total load. It is likely that these assignments will contribute to the improvement of pupil learning as fully as the load carried by the teacher who instructs the average twenty-five pupils in eight subjects throughout the day. Deviations such as these from the usual classroom assignment are rare, however. Variations on differentiating the assignments of teachers are limited only by the ingenuity of those who plan teacher assignments. The chief controlling factor in defining teacher roles should be school effectiveness as measured by pupil achievement. There are many ways for teachers to work in the school. The variety that could lead to more effective schools and more professional and satisfied teachers should be thoroughly explored and implemented.

Problem: The conditions for the utilization of professional competence are marginal or in some cases damaging to the promotion of professional performance by many teachers.

Recommendations:

1. Teachers should be trained until they have the knowledge, abilities, and skills to cope with the problems they are asked to solve, and they should be assigned duties commensurate with their training.

2. Teachers should be provided with the freedom granted any professional to perform his duties without the interference that comes from excessive supervision or assignment to nonprofessional activities such as completion of reports, supervision of hallways, lunchrooms, and pupil transportation, or burdensome clerical chores that could be handled better by specialists trained in performing such duties.

3. The facilities and equipment required for teachers to function adequately should be provided.

4. Teachers should be given a load that is realistic in terms of number of pupils, severity of their learning problems, and level of achievement expected of the pupils under their direction.

5. Teachers should be full-time employees in their profession rather than being unemployed for part of the year. A system of leaves, sabbaticals, and paid vacations should exist for teachers just as it does in other fields of work.

6. Teachers' compensation should be elevated to a level that rewards the years of training they are asked to complete to enter the profession, the level of performance expected of them in their work, and the significance of their contribution to society.

Discussion: Many conscientious teachers work from early morning to late afternoon in their classrooms and continue to work another several hours in the evening in their homes. They have little opportunity during the day to attend to the planning, grading, and reporting that are required in their work. In addition to this heavy work load, they must often obtain additional training on their own time at their own expense. Often the training they receive is not as directly tied to their responsibilities as it needs to be. When the burdens of answering to administrators, the public, and other critics are added to an inadequate salary, it should be apparent to even the most naive that the life of a teacher will be sought and accepted only by the most dedicated. No profession should have to rely on such a high level of commitment to hold its membership.

If the slate could be wiped clean and the role of the teacher defined in terms of the ideal arrangement, it would probably include the following: 1) Teachers would be adequately trained and properly assigned to be able to succeed. 2) Teachers would be supplied with workloads that are realistic and would serve society by elevating all pupils to a functional level of achievement. 3) Teachers' responsibilities would include teaching, selecting instructional materials, evaluating pupils, organizing instruction, learning about and applying improved methods, and participating in the development of improved schooling. 4) Teachers would receive compensation on a year-round basis and would spend a portion of the time when youth are not in school attending to curriculum planning, materials selection, community interaction, and continued training that is essential to the improvement of the school's performance. This list is not exhaustive, but it does illustrate a different attitude than currently exists in which teachers are worked heavily during nine or ten months of the year and then laid off for two or three months to shift for themselves until school begins anew. It may be that some teachers prefer to work for a portion of the year, and differentiated assignments can be arranged for this purpose, but the maintenance of a profession employed part-time with low compensation and overwork is not a satisfactory arrangement. In the present circumstances, teachers suffer, pupils lose, and society receives less than it could from the schools. It is difficult to see any major advantage to the perpetuation of an arrangement that has all of these drawbacks.

Problem: The schools have limited experience in arranging for youth to obtain work experience in the major institutions of society. Several plans need to be tried to determine the best approach to providing such activities.

Recommendations:

1. One form of trial unit should be entirely divorced from the control of the local educational agency. It should be designed, operated, and managed by a local youth council whose members are drawn from agencies representing a broad range of social functions—mass media, hauling services, local government, health services, farms, manufacturing, etc.

2. One plan should be tried in which the program of socialization would be under the control of a subsidiary agency of the local board of education. Its members would include the local board and individuals selected from the community.

3. Another plan should implement the program of socialization through work as a function of the school. The superintendent and his staff, including the teachers, would have the responsibility for developing and implementing the program.

Discussion: Each plan should be tried in sufficient and varied locations to constitute a fair trial. Each plan may have its own strength and weaknesses. Some of the characteristics of each plan can be discussed.

The plan that is entirely divorced from control of the local educational agency can be coordinated with the instructional program. The administration, operation, and support of the two programs should be separate. The adult community becomes entirely responsible for this aspect of the assimilation of its youth; there must be no way for the youth council to shift the burden of socialization to the teaching profession. The council and its staff would be responsible for finding ways for youth to participate with adults and agencies responsible for performing the varied functions of the community. They would also supervise the socializing experiences of the youth and the selection and performance of their work. The youth council should be created by the state and supported by both federal and state funds. The daily schedules of the school and work can be matched to provide time for both programs. The instructional program can be correlated with social functions to provide the youth with learning experiences appropriate to their work.

In the plan utilizing a subsidiary agency of the board of education, the members of the agency would include those on the local board and individuals selected from the community. The subsidiary agency would constitute a youth council and would be directly responsible to the local board of education. It would be financed by funds allocated either by the state or the federal government. The subsidiary would have the power to appoint a director and a staff to conduct the program. The director would be responsible to the youth council rather than to the superintendent of schools. The staff of the council would develop and implement the program without depending upon school personnel. The basic difference between this plan and the preceding one is that all the public instruments of socialization are under the control of a single authority.

The plan requiring the school to assume responsibility for socialization raises all the objections in Chapter II about the residual function of the schools. Since it can be claimed that the school personnel can do the job if the school is given the same amount of financial support as that allocated to the other plan, it is recommended that some trials be implemented to test this hypothesis. The automatic daily contacts of school personnel with youth constitute an advantage for a school-based program. The coordination of school activities with work experiences should come under the direction of a person who establishes a cooperative working relationship with the building principal and the teachers but who is responsible to the superintendent. This plan would require that teachers be trained in the responsibilities assumed by adults in the various fields of work. Those teachers who possess the necessary work experience should be assigned to help with the work program at the outset. As more teachers become qualified, they should be included in the program. After the program has been under way, the closer involvement of educational personnel with the world of work should also enrich the teacher's background and enable him to perform better in instructing pupils in knowledge and skills that meet criteria external to the school.

Problem: Coordination of a major reform movement is required to guarantee that optimal use of resources and consistent development of research and improvement is carried forth.

Recommendations:

1. A national coordinating board should be established and charged with the responsibility of providing leadership in the development of school reform through a program of pilot studies.

2. Representation on the board should include those whose knowledge or position provides an essential component in carrying out school reform.

3. The coordinating board should employ expert help for task forces that would carry out particular functions such as the establishment of tests of minimum achievement, the training of directors of pilot sites, or preparation of personnel who will organize work experiences at the local level.

4. The coordinating board should have direct responsibility to pilot sites and indirect responsibility to other school districts for disseminating information obtained in pilot studies.

5. The coordinating board would have the responsibility of working with the agencies that fund the schools and advising them on progress and priorities for support.

6. The primary funding of the coordinating board should come from the federal government in order to give adequate support and neutrality to the board in its dealings with any particular site or state.

Discussion: Previous experience with coordinating boards reveals that it is possible to exert national leadership in a national program by establishing a group of competent people who assist in making decisions and supplying technical assistance to individual projects. The prototype of this board can be found in the Leadership Training Institutes (LTI) created by the Bureau of Educational Personnel Development of the United States Office of Education. On the basis of the experience of the LTIs, it is realistic to recommend that a relatively small panel of fifteen to twenty people, each representing an area of knowledge or a position of significance in the school enterprise, should serve as a central agency that would oversee the development of school reform. The board would be expected to employ study groups and task forces to carry out special assignments such as the development of tests of minimum achievement or the training of pilot site directors. The board would monitor progress and advise other schools about developments in the pilot program. The board would apply the best that is known to the improvement of schools and identify unfinished tasks that require additional investigation. Through the work of the governing board, the practical application of ideas in pilot schools, sufficient financial support to underwrite the effort, and analysis of the results, the knowledge and experience required to elevate the performance of the nation's schools have a good chance of being developed. Once this evidence has been acquired, the chances of improving the schools and raising everyone to a functional level in today's society could become more than wishful thinking.

Summary

The schools include personnel, buildings, materials, programs of study, and a stable position in the American society. Their full potential is yet to be realized. Optimum performance calls for a redirection of purpose, an infusion of resources, and complementary ties with society's other institutions.

The aims of the schools must extend beyond the classroom into the society, and they must provide achievement for all pupils regardless of place of birth, economic circumstances, or racial or ethnic characteristics. A lessor goal limits the potential of society and its people.

The resources to be developed include more knowledge about learning and the process of instruction. Resources include personnel who are recipients of increased knowledge and are trained in the application of more effective approaches. Resources also include sufficient financial support to enable professionals to work under desirable conditions with enough supplies to achieve realistic goals.

The relationship of the schools with society's other institutions requires a mutual effort that may need to be initiated by the schools but must be carried forward by the adults and the out-of-school institutions they represent. The collaborative effort should ease or eliminate friction between youth and adults, should assure the growth of the society, and should enhance everyone's lives in the economic, political, kinship, and expressive-integrative institutions of this specialized, bureaucratic, industrialized society.

The investment required in time, ideas, energy, and fiscal resources should be viewed in the context of the society's total commitment of all its potential. The symbiotic relationship between youth and the society cannot be ignored without imperiling society itself. Society must be maintained and restored by the coming generation since all adults who live today will someday expire, and those who represent the future generations will become its adult members. The coming generation has a large stake in the socialization they receive from the adults. It is important that both segments come to recognize this fact and that the school, the formal institution charged with transmitting systematized knowledge, view itself as the agency primarily responsible for generating a program that arises out of the society and returns to enrich it.

APPENDIX A

Reform of Educational Research
Bryce B. Hudgins
Washington University

The focus of this paper is on the questions of how educational research has contributed to school change in the past and how it might be reorganized to increase its influence in the future. Research is a quest for new knowledge, and it can provide the foundation upon which vigorous and just school practices can be built. Research is not the antithesis of reform. Rather, its fruits offer some of the firmest rational and intellectual bases for dramatic and carefully developed changes in schooling.

Conceptions of educational research have often been meager and disjointed. The training of personnel to conduct educational research is among the least rigorous and extensive of any scholarly or scientific field. Researchers are typically caught between those who would have them deal with educational practice and those who stress the importance of pure research. The practical emphasis usually wins out. Consequently, a large majority of those who are trained to do educational research never follow their graduate school work with any additional inquiry. This trend is much more marked in education than in other disciplines.

Educational research is also characterized by work that is not programmatic. Programmatic research defines a problem or a set of issues in need of resolution for the improvement of or better understanding about the phenomena of learning, instruction, child development, the curriculum, etc. Since much educational research is "single shot" in nature, with a single investigator, it is more likely to be nonprogrammatic, noncumulative, and nonsystematic. Even though individual, isolated investigations may be well-conceptualized and executed, they add up to little, for seldom can the single study pose and answer questions of the breadth and depth required for important understanding of educational topics.

Recent trends in educational research indicate that studies may become more cumulative and systematic, provide for replicability of outcomes, and be tied more closely to the operations of schools. Inquiry should not necessarily center upon the conduct of schooling in traditional settings, such as the classroom, but it must deal with the variables, contents, and people who constitute those settings, however novel or unorthodox they may be.

Finally, many share the belief that reliable answers to fundamental educational questions will be neither easy to come by nor inexpensive to obtain. Most critically of all, however, there must be a dramatic reshaping of expectations about the time that will be required to complete meaningful and dependable research to support the reform of schooling. Approaches to basic as well as applied research that provide the latitude to think in terms of a decade or longer are likely to prove more productive than projects developed and completed within short time spans. The ultimate success of educational research, as measured by its contributions to school reform, may well be predetermined by society's willingness to afford such generous time arrangements.

Ordinarily the necessity for reform of a social institution emerges from social injustices, or from a failure to function in the ways the society expects it to function. Changes in the organization would be demanded even if it were functioning as designed if the population or segments of it receives fewer or lower-quality benefits than are desired. The first part of this book has examined the benefits of schooling and the ways in which some parts of the population, particularly that segment identified as "the poor," are not well served by the school. Hypotheses have been suggested to rectify malfunctions of the system. A pilot study has been proposed to test some of these hypotheses. The chapter on pilots described how such studies might function and the care and investment required to improve the chances that dependable knowledge will result—knowledge good enough to enable other educational institutions or agencies to determine if their purposes can be served by adoption of the pilot studies. There is integrity in what has been proposed. That is, the shortcomings of a social institution designed to serve the children of all the people, and therefore the whole society, have been analyzed; ways of bringing about desired and necessary reforms in the system have been proposed; and a procedure for introducing a reasonable degree of reflection upon and assessment of the efficacy of those reforms has been elaborated. Beyond this integrity, the question must be asked and answered: Is there a necessary, or even a viable relationship between school reform and the educational research community? The answer to both parts of this question is "yes," but this affirmation is made on the basis of new trends in educational research that have only recently appeared, in current self-criticism going on within the educational research community, and in further changes to be recommended. The balance of the paper is addressed to an examination of these issues.

The Researcher and the Practitioner

One of the difficulties in relationships between research and reform is antagonism between their respective advocates. This issue has frequently been glossed over in discussions of the contribution of research to the practice of education, but to do so is an error. Problems do not receive serious attention and solution when their existence tends to go unrecognized, or their impact minimized. Yates strikes at the heart of the conflict between researchers and reformers with the following brief description of the former.

> A researcher is required to be detached, dispassionate, objective, and even skeptical concerning the value and effectiveness of any form of educational organization or method of instruction. If he is not already endowed with these qualities he must seek them strenuously to cultivate them. His favorite prediction is couched in the form of the null hypothesis. He would be a most depressing and unwelcome person to have permanently around in the staff-

room of a go-ahead, progressive school. He could be counted on to question the wisdom of any proposed reform, to refuse to display even a modicum of enthusiasm for its adoption, and to be irritatingly prone to say "I told you so" when it met the unhappy fate of most of its predecessors.[1]

Although Yates' description is a bit of a caricature, the point he makes is valid. Often, by temperament and training, the research worker is a skeptic and a critic. His talent is to test, to weigh and measure, to assess programs and their participants until his analysis tells him all he wishes to know about the components, how they fit together, and what outcomes can be expected. The orientation is in many ways antithetical to that of the educational entrepreneur or the reformer anxious to induce change for the betterment of his fellow man.

A well-known research worker in education begins his course for teachers by reading them the table of contents of the current issue of the *Journal of Educational Psychology.* The implication is that articles with esoteric titles, which are unrelated to the problems and concerns of teachers who confront children and adolescents in a classroom every school day of the year, is what the teacher can expect from research workers in the field of educational psychology. It is easy to make the field appear ridiculous, but such denigrations of research miss a fundamental point that contributes heavily to the antagonism and misunderstanding between researchers and practitioners. This concerns the purposes of research and its contribution to the improvement of the school and the process of schooling. The illustration given above generates a certain sardonic mirth only if one assumes that each article published in a research journal has the primary purpose of directly contributing to the process of instruction. Such an objective is seldom the intention of those who publish the papers. Individual articles are usually reports of small-scale studies, parts of larger investigations, or tests of hypotheses that pertain indirectly to instruction but are part of more general theories being examined. It may be that antagonism between research and practice resides in a misunderstanding on the part of the practitioner about how research is produced, and what it contributes to the enterprise of schooling.

Unfortunately, the same misconceptions about research are held by many individuals who contribute to the literature of educational research. Educational research is sometimes characterized as being noncumulative, unsystematic, idiosyncratic, and inconclusive. Such a cluster of indictments is lethal. To the extent that they can be verified, the contribution of educational research to the schooling process is meager.

A critical study of educational research was reported several years ago by Barton and Wilder. Their study looked particularly at the training of researchers in the field of reading, a crucial area of educational research and a vital area in school reform.

They level three basic criticisms against the experts in the field of reading. 1) That the same research questions being asked today were being asked forty years ago; no resolution of them has been forthcoming, and little apparent progress has been made through systematic, cumulative research. 2) The basic research upon which basal reading series are developed was done in the 1930s, and changes in reading series since then amount mostly to tinkering, with few new concepts or data being built into later editions of readers. 3) Achievement in reading for children from the lower classes (especially inner cities) is below the average of middle-class children by the end of the first grade, and the discrepancy grows from one year of schooling to the next. Little research attention has been directed toward this problem by the reading experts.[2]

But Barton and Wilder did more than lay out what they regard as the deficiencies of research in reading. They also used questionnaires and interviews to analyze the educational and career patterns of the reading experts. These analyses are fascinating, and, although analogies are notoriously dangerous, much that is true of the training of the researcher in reading probably applies to research workers in many other areas of educational research. Compared to graduate students in other disciplines (such as the sciences and social sciences), individuals beginning graduate work in the field of reading are older, are already involved in careers (mostly teaching, supervision, or administration), and, by inference, have a lower commitment to conducting research. This latter point is evident from data showing that the reading experts, although their graduate studies contained less research training than their counterparts in other disciplines, regard their research training as more adequate than do other graduate students. In fact, many report that more attention was given to research than was necessary or advisable. Additional characteristics of their training and attitude add up to the same message: The training in research given to students in the field of reading is minimal; their models (their professors and thesis directors) often do not engage actively in research; their commitment to research is low; and when they do engage in research, it tends to be isolated and individual.

In another report of wider scope than that of Barton and Wilder, Yates concludes that professional preparation of potential educational researchers is similar to that provided for prospective teachers, and, in some cases, even coterminous with it.[3] The Yates statement was prepared for UNESCO and is the summarization of reports about the nature of educational research in countries around the world. To find that educational research training lacks the depth and rigor that workers in most other fields of inquiry routinely receive is unsettling. At the same time, it does call attention to what is one of the most desperately needed renovations of the research training process: intensive programs for educational researchers in one of the disciplines that underlies the study of education and that combines with work in the field of education a program that helps the budding research worker to identify problems of significance in education and to make those adaptations of his discipline that are required to work effectively within the school.

One indispensable way to increase the relevance of educational research to change in the schools is to improve the quality of research training. The assumption in this summary is that people who choose to be trained as educational researchers rather than experts in reading or methods of teaching (for whom some research training is a hurdle to overcome in the path of their professional goal), will select significant problems for inquiry, and that competent research does have a contribution to make to the conduct of the schools and to their reform.

The research training programs now offered by universities will not be altered easily or quickly. But the problem has been identified. For example, Cronbach and Suppes, writing for the National Academy of Education, have registered criticisms of the research training activity of the nation's universities in much the manner cited above.[4] Training programs are sensitive to such criticisms, and do change in response to them, according to Austin, who observes that proposals have been made to provide differentiation in the degree program.[5]

A separation of the degree program into programs for research workers, for practitioners, and for college instructors has been proposed. Many universities have required prospective researchers to take the same courses as other students enrolled in graduate education with only minor changes. Under the degree-separation plan, persons preparing for specialization in research would engage in formal study that emphasized research methodology, the scientific study of education, instruction in behavioral sciences, and the interaction of research and theory. A special residency in local school systems, encompassing classroom observations, presence at school board and administrative meetings to become acquainted with policy- and decision-making processes, and familiarity with the work of staff specialists, would provide current knowledge of public schools.[6]

Basic and Applied Research

The following quotation from Berlyne poses an apt analogy for educational research between "basic" and "applied" work. Although it is a common distinction, the two concepts lack

clarity. What one person identifies as basic may be applied
as far as others are concerned, and vice versa. The Berlyne
quotation illustrates how limited efforts may be to apply and
extend current concepts and practices, when one is concerned
with the ultimate improvement or revolution of a practical
concern.

If somebody had been asked to do research about the year
1800 into how transportation could be improved, what would
he have done? He might have looked for some improved diet
that would give horses greater stamina. He might have sought
some way of breeding faster horses. He might have wondered
whether coaching inns could be better spaced along the highways
or whether more pliable springs could be installed in stage coaches.
In those days, transportation was equine. Transportation was
what happened to people when they found themselves on horseback
or in a horse-drawn vehicle, just as today education means what
happens to children when they find themselves in those buildings
that dot the landscape and contain rooms with desks in them.
After all, if there is one statement that has stood the test of
time and has been borne out by thousands of years of experience,
it is that the horse has come to stay. Since the horse was first
ridden five thousand years ago, its usefulness has been appreciated
all over the world in many different climes and societies, in
many different periods of history. Men like Genghis Khan and
Buffalo Bill, Dick Turpin and William Cobbett, Julius Caesar
and Paul Revere, who would undoubtedly have disagreed on so
many other points, would have heartily concurred that there is
no better way of getting from one place to another than by horse.
So it is only reasonable that, as long as travel depended on the
horse, anybody concerned to improve transportation should have
sought ways of improving equitation.

But this was not the kind of research that led to such advances
as the steam locomotive, the internal combustion engine and
the airplane. While the horse was still without any serious
competition, some apparently unrelated things were going on.
A man called James Watt was trying to improve steam-driven
machinery for pumping water out of mines. Towards the end
of his life, Watt began to realize that the steam engine could
operate other machinery besides mine pumps, but he steadfastly

refused to believe that it had any future whatever for transportation. At about the same time, an eccentric Italian called Galvani was following up some strange discoveries that he had made about frog's legs. He had found that, if a frog's leg is severed and touched with metal rods in certain conditions, the leg will twitch. Nobody would have thought, least of all Galvani, that when the horse-drawn omnibus and the horse-drawn street-car disappeared from the city streets, they would be succeeded and replaced by an invention that can be traced back directly to these experiments of his on frog's legs. It is not difficult to imagine what would have happened if Galvani had come to some agency responsible for financing research on transportation and asked for help to study frog's legs. . . . Horses' legs might have been acceptable, but frog's legs . . . Watt, as already mentioned, believed that his own work had nothing whatever to do with transportation. Fortunately, these men did obtain whatever facilities they needed to complete their work. If however, some agency had supported them, and also supported 999 others whose research got nowhere, this might not have been a bad bargain. In fact, there may have been some bonuses on the side. The whole industrial revolution was, in part, a by-product of Watt's work, and out of Galvani's work came everything that we now know about the working of the brain and the rest of the nervous system, with all its medical and other implications.[7]

One would guess that any direct impact of research upon school reform would come about through applied research, or through the development of products based upon more fundamental research ideas. An examination of what direct influence past research has had upon changes in the process of schooling should prove instructive. Fortunately, Cronbach's and Suppes' work bears closely upon this issue. They trace a series of "chains of significant inquiry." These traditions of inquiry stem from different sources and disciplines. For instance, the mental testing movement had its inception with Darwin's early work on the differentiation of species through the process of evolution, the monumental but largely unsuccessful efforts of such men as Galton to produce valid tests of intelligence, and Binet's persistence with tests of reasoning and judgment, which finally unlocked the basic problem of conceptualizing and measuring human intelligence.

Of somewhat later origin than the testing movement is the impact upon the teaching of elementary school arithmetic fostered by the work of Edward L. Thorndike. Thorndike's training was in the experimental psychology of the 1890s, and his dissertation was the famous study of animal intelligence, as part of which he formulated the Law of Effect, one of the most renowned laws in the history of psychology, and the progenitor of today's sophisticated and systematic formulations of reinforcement. During the second decade of the twentieth century, Thorndike produced the massive three-volume series titled *Educational Psychology*. The second volume of the trilogy, *The Psychology of Learning,* provided the scientific basis for Thorndike's own application to the teaching of arithmetic. Not only did he teach courses to elementary school teachers about arithmetic and write a book on the topic of the teaching of elementary school arithmetic, he also published his own series of textbooks. To determine how his work effected change in the teaching of elementary arithmetic would be a difficult matter, but Cronbach and Suppes make an admirable case for the fact that his influence was strong. They selected several series of arithmetic textbooks, some of which preceded Thorndike's series, and some published shortly after it. There appears not only to be a shift in the selection of topics and the methods by which the topics are presented in the later series, but the shifts are also heavily in accord with Thorndike's recommendations for change. The two cases reviewed by reference to the work of Cronbach and Suppes have a common thread that is seen in other influential programs of research. The changes are incorporated into published materials that, in turn, are used in the schools. When the theories and research findings of the scientist find their way into the materials used directly and on a day-to-day basis by educational practitioners, there can be little doubt that research has had an effect upon the conduct of schooling.

Not all of the impact of research upon education is felt

through ideas that can be incorporated into materials. Cronbach and Suppes point out that most occupations and professions operate in the context of a series of "prevailing views." The prevailing view may be shaped or modified by numerous influences from the research community. For example, when Pavlov's conditioning studies of the salivation response in dogs became widely known, psychologists undertook investigations of learning that followed the paradigm of classical conditioning, but in which the stimuli and responses departed from the physiological variables of the original investigations. More importantly for the conduct of education, Pavlov's views led to a conception of man as a machine whose responses are conditioned to various stimuli. The importance of the prevailing view, of course, is that it provides a direction or a focus for thinking about the conduct of practical affairs, such as education. A social studies or science curriculum developed by people who hold a Pavlovian view of the child as learner could be expected to be quite different from one developed by a curriculum worker with a Piagetian or Freudian orientation.

Elements of Reform

Statements about educational research now in the literature indicate that attempts are now under way to make research more applicable to school reform. These changes are to be found in three elements that affect the nature and conduct of research. One concerns the amount and quality of training provided for research workers. A second concerns the organization of research and the emergence of new institutions such as educational research and development centers, and regional educational laboratories. These institutions have been created within the last decade. There is continuing ambiguity, discussion, and, in some cases, conflict over the mission of the centers and laboratories.

In any event, their direct contact with educational settings will be more encompassing than has been the case with university departments of education or bureaus of educational research. The third element concerns the characteristics of research activities. Demands are increasing for educational research to come to grips with the fundamental problems of teaching and learning, both as they now go on in classrooms, and as they might occur in reconstructed schooling settings. Obviously, these three elements are related to one another. If research is to be conducted in settings that include students and adult teachers, the research worker or the research team must have access to those teachers and pupils and control over what occurs there. Similarly, research personnel must be able to develop, or to respond sympathetically to the development of, instruction problems. Their training must be of appropriate depth and quality to permit them to work effectively on problems whose solutions contribute directly to improvement of schooling for the target population of the day. Today, notably, that population is children of the poor, whether they live in the heart of the cities, in rural mining and agricultural areas, or on the reservations of the Southwest.

Training of Personnel for Educational Research. The previous discussion of the criticisms of research in reading by Barton and Wilder opened the topic of the amount, type, and quality of research training that personnel in education receive. A fundamental part of this problem is that individuals with diverse goals enter the education profession and pursue higher degrees because they wish to improve their professional status and not because they wish to become research workers. Thus, the training is often partially research training, capped by a dissertation that represents to the student (and to his dissertation director) an artificial obstacle to the continued pursuit of his occupational goals. Little or no research worthy of the name comes from such projects, or in the future from such students. The concept of educational research suffers further damage because students who earn advanced degrees in this way neither understand nor respect research, and some faculty members come to develop skepticism or contempt for what they legitimately perceive to be the institutionally sanctioned products of a preparatory course in research.

This description, congruent with that by Barton and Wilder, has been ameliorated to some extent in recent years through the availability of research training fellowships, notably those granted to schools of education through Title IV of the Elementary and Secondary Education Act of 1965. These fellowships provided tuition and living stipends for qualified students to pursue training in educational research for periods of up to three years. Unfortunately, funds for these fellowships expired with the end of the 1972–73 academic year, and it is not clear that any other fellowships of similar caliber will be available for research training in education within the foreseeable future.

The expiration of that program, combined with the more general dearth of research funds and the associated training which such money makes possible, is a critical blow to the improvement of educational research. The obvious consequence is that the profession of educational research loses its attractiveness for talented people. There is, however, an equally serious problem that resides in the research training offered to those who seek it. The trainees of the 1960s and early 1970s were typically supported in one of two ways. Either they were recipients of fellowships that made concentrated full-time study possible, or they were employed by their professors on supported research projects. In many cases, trainees were subsidized by fellowships, but they also had the opportunity to obtain first-rate, on-the-job research training.

The severe reductions in funding that the educational research community has encountered in recent years means that trainees must often pursue their advanced education on a part-time basis. Thus, one remains a full-time teacher at the local school, and aspires to research training on nights and weekends. Full-time residence is reduced to six or eight weeks on the university campus during summers. Because faculty members have severe difficulty obtaining new money for research, much of the research training provided for novices is administered through courses in which research procedures are advanced, and sample studies are perused and analyzed in lieu of the more desirable firsthand training demanded when research departments bustle with ongoing projects. In short, research training is in danger of retreating to the part-time study *about* the research process that characterized it in many institutions before the affluent decade of the 1960s. The first and most important reform that research must undergo today is to find ways to bring the amount and quality of training available back to the levels which a few years ago appeared adequate as the place to begin careers in research, but which in retrospect seem to have been a halcyon era.

Cronbach and Suppes reviewed the basic findings of a major study of the productivity of recipients of doctoral degrees in education. Their principal conclusion was that very few of the recipients continue to produce research papers after the receipt of the advanced degree. Thirty-one individuals were identified as having produced outstanding educational research. Whereas the average productivity of all individuals receiving doctorates in education the same year (1954) was a meager single publication, these thirty-one outstanding graduates had a mean productivity of sixty articles and papers during the same ten-year period. It is instructive that of the thirty-one, seventeen had received their degrees from departments of psychology, eight others were distributed across a variety of academic fields, and only six were graduates of schools of education. Of these six, four were educational psychologists. "Hence, out of thousands of doctorates granted in such fields as educational administration, curriculum, instructional methods, and secondary education, only two persons reached this roster of significant contributions."[8]

Recommendations given by Cronbach and Suppes stress that research training should not be restricted to the offerings available through the schools of education. The best foundations for educational research are often found in the academic departments. Students should take significant portions of their course work in one or two of these departments, and arrangements might often be made for an individual professor from one of those departments to become actively involved in the training of research workers in educational psychology, educational sociology, educational policy studies, etc. At a somewhat broader level, Cronbach and Suppes give the following recommendations:

> Certain features are likely to characterize any superior program of training for research on education. These include: (1) full-time study for three consecutive years, preferably at an early age; (2) training as part of a student group individually and collectively dedicated to research careers; (3) participation in research, at a steadily advancing level of responsibility, starting in the first year of graduate school if not earlier; (4) a thorough grounding in at least one academic discipline, together with solid training in whatever technical skills that discipline employs; and (5) study of the educational process and educational institutions, bringing into a single perspective the social goals of education, the bases on which policy decisions are made, the historical development of the curriculum, the nature of the learner, and other factors.[9]

Limitations upon educational research training programs are universal. Yates, summarizing the sentiments of research statesmen from all over the world, voices similar laments.[10] The absence of an extensive array of course work and seminars devised specifically to provide the training in research needed by prospective laborers in the vineyards is a problem of widespread scope. Both Cronbach's and Suppes' observations and Yates' summarization, although they appropriately criticize a weakness in research training, fail to identify one of the issues that lies at the heart of the problem, namely the organization of educational research.

The Organization of Educational Research. Research goes on in a variety of institutional arrangements. Historically, most educational research has been conducted by people employed in departments or schools of education. Other institutional arrangements within the university have also generated research on educational topics, but inquiry conducted through the education departments deserves special analysis.

Individuals who work within a university setting are especially well placed to contribute to the store of fundamental knowledge about questions that underlie effective school reform. Rohwer's inquiry about "decisive research," reviewed later in this chapter, is an example of research that probably could be conducted only at a university. In one sense, this research does not answer any practical questions. Rather, its thrust is to identify bases for research that could lead to effective school reform. The program has developed over a period of years and has involved numerous scientific publications in esoteric journals. The schoolman who is in a hurry for answers to questions about altering curriculum and instruction in reading, for example, would find little reassurance in a review of the titles of these and similar articles.

Moreover, the scholar who holds a university appointment is in the best position to raise questions that are unpopular in the ethos of the day, to investigate them, and to furnish the profession with the best answers. This is no trivial point, even for those who are urgently concerned with changing the schools. The university professor, by virtue of tenure and academic freedom, is not only in a position to ask the difficult questions, but is also, in a sense, obligated to do so. His is one of the few roles in our society that affords the opportunity to pursue the paths of inquiry over long periods of time, with objectivity and dispassion, and with no economic, political, or even social obligation that the results of his scholarship lead to practical outcomes or the improvement of the human condition. None of this, of course, means that the scholar is freed from the consequences of faulty scholarship. The same freedom extended to him is extended to others as well. Thus, research and reports of scholarly work are frequently criticized, sometimes brutally.

Basic research, or research that tries to deal with long-range issues, as opposed to day-by-day problem solving, is necessary to the academic profession, and to the ways in which people view their institutions. Of the researchers Cronbach and Suppes included in their discussion of "significant chains of inquiry," most began from the basis of a discipline (psychology, philosophy, or political science) that permitted the researcher to use concepts, data, and tools of inquiry that would not have been available to him if his approach had been to confront an existing problem and to try to solve it. If it is true that the basic researcher often does not solve immediate problems, it is also true that the solutions to today's problems often start with scholarly inquiry that is well advanced by the time it confronts the urgent, contemporary problem.

From the tenor of the foregoing remarks, the reader might mistakenly conclude that the future of educational research lies largely outside the departments or schools of education. This is not the case. Individuals who are going to conduct educational research must be better trained in one or two disciplines than has been the case for most people in the past. This observation has been made repeatedly. (See, for example, the volume by Cronbach and Suppes.) Probably the finest basic educational research can be performed by individuals within schools of education working cooperatively in like-discipline or cross-discipline teams. Such teams should be close to the realities of school life and the lives of colleagues who are engaged in the difficult work of preparing educational personnel, so that their research is influenced by the concerns of those individuals and responsive to the continuing, persistent problems of schools, teachers, and teacher educators.

Implicit in these comments is the recommendation that instructional responsibilities of those charged with conducting educational research in university settings should include the training of future research workers, and not the training of practicing educational personnel (that is, teachers, principals, counselors, and like professional workers). Although the involvement of research workers in the training of professional practitioners is probably the more common pattern, it may well account for some of the worst characteristics of contemporary research. Despite disclaimers to the contrary, it seems obvious that the professor caught in this way probably cannot be very productive with regard to either of his central charges. Professional workers in training are notoriously skeptical of what they regard as esoteric, technical research, which is also considered to be peripheral to their concerns with the daily practice of their profession.* Such pressures cause the professor, as teacher educator, to cast about for concepts, readings, and activities that are more germane to the concerns of the teacher in training. The fact is that the preparation of professionals and educational research are two distinctively different kinds of fields, which, although they ought to have much in common, are often incompatible in practice. Thus the recommendation that the educational researcher's teaching and research should have consistency and singleness of purpose—no more than the conditions of work established for virtually all others in the academic world. Were such arrangements possible for those who wish to work as educational researchers, the quantity and quality of educational research would improve.

Two additional patterns for the conduct of educational research have been developed within the last decade. These are the research and development centers housed within a handful of major universities sponsored by the U.S. Office of Education, and the regional laboratories, originally twenty in number, and now reduced to eleven. Although their arrival on the scene was lauded widely at the time they were launched, the mission of these organizations has never been entirely clear. At the moment, even as this is being written, the centers and laboratories are undergoing a "transition phase" as their administrative center is shifted from the Office of Education to the National Institute of Education. How this transition will affect either individual centers and laboratories or the programs as a whole cannot now be seen clearly. There are some indications that the program may undergo further attrition as more centers or laboratories lose federal financing.

*This concern is not limited to prospective teachers, although it may be as clearly manifested by them as by any other group in training. See, for example, Becker's *Boys in White* for similar concerns expressed by physicians in medical school.

There is some reason to believe their programs will be more critically reviewed than in the past. One can only hope that programs with a history of productivity will be funded at a high level and for long periods of time.

Apart from the fact that the chief intellectual traditions that influence school reform will be found in basic research in universities, much of the impact of research upon school reform will stem from applied studies. The regional educational laboratories, in particular, seem especially well suited to conduct such investigations, and to exercise influence upon the reform of the public schools, since they have been engaged in precisely this kind of effort for some time.

Calls for Educational Research to be More Closely Tied to the Functioning of Schools. At least three writers within the space of a year have called for educational research to venture forth from the safe and sterile surrounding of the traditional laboratory and address itself to that most threatening of settings for the educational researcher, the classroom or its carefully created equivalent. "Instead of viewing experimental treatments in terms of single variables, such as 'phonetic' versus 'whole-word' or 'discovery' versus 'rote,' researchers must begin to contrast total educational approaches, e.g., curricula or their parts, whose components have been carefully selected and combined."[11]

Gage has called for the development of packaged materials and "tools of the trade," which will be useful both for teachers and for the trainers of teachers. He calls attention to the fact that the traditional role of the teacher in the classroom is changing in many particulars. However it changes, certain skills and activities will still be demanded of teachers. For example, they must be skillful at listening, at explaining subject matter, and at asking questions about it. His emphasis is upon research that will enable the "average teacher" to perform at a more expert level.[12]

> The new kind of experimental variable should also reduce the demands that teaching imposes upon practitioners of the art. Teaching is less effective than it ought to be because it requires

skills, abilities, habits, and powers possessed by only a small
proportion of the hundreds of thousands of adults needed as
teachers. Teaching now requires levels of sensitivity in listening
to students that only clinical psychologists and psychiatrists can
routinely supply. It now requires adaptability and intellectual
agility in discussions with students at levels that only professional
debaters, trial lawyers, and parliamentarians can regularly attain.
It requires the quick inventions of definitions, explanations, and
justifications in classroom discourse, according to rules that only
professors of logic can adhere to.

Other professions and crafts give their practitioners whole
arrays of techniques, instruments, tools, devices, formulas, strategies, tactics, algorithms, and tricks of the trade. Engineering,
medicine, law, and journalism, to name just a few, have all of
these kinds of aids that make the job possible for ordinary mortals.
The engineer has his slide rule, transit, and handbook of stress
tables; the physician, his plethysomograph, sphygmomanometer,
and pharmacopoeia; the lawyer, his codes, classified collections
of precedents, and interrogation skills; the journalist, his formulas
for writing leads and his standard rules of content and style.

But in teaching we find relatively few of these ways of making
complex tasks more manageable. Teachers are expected too often
to rediscover for themselves the formulas that experienced and
ingenious teachers have acquired over the years. Each generation
of teachers benefits too little from the inventions of its predecessors. The wisdom of the profession does not get saved and passed
along well enough for the benefit of the novice. What teaching
needs—if it is to be improved in the hands of ordinary persons,
who are not geniuses or inspired artists, and if it is to be improved
with resources at a level not inconceivably high—is much more
abundant and helpful "tools of the trade."

The term "tools of the trade" has appropriately unpretentious
connotations. It suggests not theoretical perspectives but quick
and easy guides for asking questions and answering them; not
conceptual frameworks, but easily applied rules of behavior and
performance; not an emphasis on the complexities, subtleties,
and profundities of the teacher's task in understanding and
helping his students, but ways of making the task manageable.
The tools must be usable by persons with the intellectual and
emotional makeup that we can expect to find in two million

teachers. What teachers need is a demand for arcane insight and creativity and a greater supply of mundane tools.[13]

Gage's position is arguable, and it would undoubtedly infuriate many teachers who do not regard themselves as lacking in either inspiration or creativity. The implications of the position for educational research, however, are clear enough. Concrete answers must be found to the persistent questions that plague instruction. These would probably include many others in addition to the specifics cited by Gage. His disposition is to translate answers to research questions into materials and ready references such as handbooks and guides for teachers by means of a development process.

Finally, Rosenshine argues that educational research must become more relevant to the practice of schooling. A principal and much neglected way of accomplishing this is to relate classroom procedures, methods, and styles of instruction to learning outcomes for pupils. Although it seems scarcely credible, Rosenshine offers documentation that only seventy studies that deal with the classroom have attempted to relate classroom behavior to some kind of pupil outcome. Most of these have been done within the last seven years, and to date, few of those outcomes have been incorporated into the "packed down" knowledge of textbooks or handbooks.[14]

Decisive Research

A provocative chain of reasoning and research is suggested in the recent work of Rohwer, who calls for "decisive research," that is, research on instruction in basic skills such as reading and arithmetic, with large samples of ongoing elementary school classes. When studies of that type are conducted, based upon what is known about interactions between children's cognitive development and instructional methods, the outcomes will represent a basis for policy decisions about what kind of instruction should be offered to what kind of children at what age, and under what instructional method. Experiments of that magnitude, however, cannot be conducted until assurances can be given that children will benefit rather than suffer from experimental treatment.

> At present, we not only lack answers to fundamental questions about instruction, we lack a workable mechanism for obtaining answers. Building such a mechanism requires a commitment to entertain hypotheses that challenge established assumptions about instruction . . . But this attitude, by itself, is not sufficient. We must also be able to verify the hypotheses by conducting research that tests them. A major obstacle to such research is that it entails experimental alterations in aspects of schooling that are regarded as vital by students, parents, educators, and legislators alike. That is, such research is seen as a threat to the academic survival of the children who might be involved. Thus, the problem is to open an avenue to the conduct of decisive research—research that can resolve the fundamental issues of instruction.[15]

What is needed as a preliminary to "decisive research" is evidence that furnishes a basis for the assurances cited above; that is, evidence that suggests variables and treatments likely to be fruitful for the conduct of "decisive research."

Rohwer submits a case study of experiments conducted over the past several years at Berkeley as an example of the research that must precede decisive studies.

The essence of the proposed strategy is that basic research can be used to generate instructional hypotheses that are believable enough to gain public support for decisive re-search—research involving direct experimentation with in-struction.

This case study has five significant characteristics.

1. The research is cumulative. The same tasks are used repeatedly in studies to ensure that the same underlying processes are being studied.

2. The research is developmental. Performance changes that signal important developmental shifts in the underlying process are examined.

3. The research is experimental. It is designed to test conditions that produce optimal outcomes or that initiate underlying processes.

4. The research is comparative. In the case study, comparative studies are made of high-SES pupils and low-SES pupils.
This is to generate data about the range of individual differences among different kinds of children, at different ages
and developmental stages.

5. The research is realistic. It is intended to match the
timing of instruction to evidence that the underlying process
requisite for learning has developed in a substantial proportion
of the population. As Rohwer puts it, the intention is not
to make children precocious but to assist them in becoming
optimally effective.

The task chosen for the experiments that constitute the
case study is paired associates, a task with a venerable history
in the experimental psychology of verbal learning. Specifically,
the tasks utilized are the learning of noun pairs. That is,
children are presented with lists of words such as "bat-cup,"
and when one member of the pair is presented later, the
response is to produce the other member of the pair. Educational psychologists have challenged the validity of tasks such
as paired associates for the study of classroom learning, but
Rohwer indicates that the task possesses merits of two kinds.
In the first place, it correlates with skills and abilities related
to some school tasks; secondly, the learning of paired associates
is not a task that most children are taught directly. These
points are critical to an understanding of Rohwer's position
about "decisive research." The case studies he reports are
not decisive research; rather, they suggest guidelines for such
research and define the problem with sufficient care that
effective research for purposes of instructional decision making can be conducted.

In the beginning of his experiments, Rohwer operated with
assumptions that were shown to be untenable by ensuing
events. For example, he assumed that underlying processes
were responsible for performance on the noun learning task,
that during the years between the ages of 4 and 7 children
shifted from inefficient learning processes to more efficient
ones, and during the same years of the preoperational stage,

the higher-SES children were more efficient in learning the task than low-SES children, and that special instruction would be helpful to the low-SES children.

However, as the basic program of research proceeded, it became increasingly clear that these assumptions were untenable. They were subsequently replaced by others.

1. There is *one* underlying process, identified as *elaboration*. How well the learner performs depends upon triggering this process.

2. Development involves shifts in the conditions required to trigger elaboration. Three such shifts in conditions occur; one between ages 4 and 7, another from 7 to 9, and the third from 12 to 16.

3. Individual differences exist in the conditions required to trigger elaboration, but through the years of childhood the conditions are not related either to SES or ethnicity of learners. At the time of adolescence, however, a relationship does appear between social class and the conditions that produce optimal performance. This shift in conditions that produce optimal outcomes appears earlier in high-SES than in low-SES students.

Rohwer's work has made use of four kinds of conditions for facilitating optimal performance with noun pairs. These conditions are variations in prompting procedures used. The prompting conditions are identified as maximal, substantial, moderate, and minimal. Figure 6, taken from Rohwer's manuscript, shows that with increasing age, prompts of diminishing degrees of explicitness are sufficient to produce optimal performance. Notice, also, that for every age level sampled from 3 through 12, the displays are identical for high-SES and for low-SES pupils. By age 15, performance of high-SES students with minimal prompts is improving substantially, while that for low-SES students is not, and by age 18, the high-SES students can master the task with minimal prompts. Some progress, but not much, is the rule for the low-SES students. Rohwer's interpretation of this finding is quoted directly to minimize the chances that it will be misunderstood.

Figure 6
Summary of prompt types required to achieve optimal performance as
a function of age. Schematic patterns for high-SES (upper panel) and
low-SES (lower panel) populations.[16]

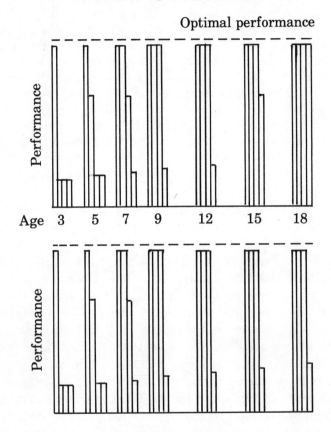

Prompt
type ⬚ Maximal ⬚ Substantial ⬚ Moderate ⬚ Minimal

    In the adolescent age range, a substantial between-groups
difference is evident in the effectiveness of minimal prompts.
The shift for the high-SES group contrasts sharply with the
continuing insufficiency of minimal prompts for the low-SES
group, even after age 12. The difference in the average develop-

mental pattern for the two populations appears to be quite reliable. However, the interpretation of the difference is disputable. I regard as insupportable the claim that differences in underlying capability are responsible for the discrepant effectiveness of minimal prompts for the two populations, since it is too difficult to square this interpretation with the fact that only a moderate prompt—the suggestion to the subject that he generate an event—is necessary to produce optimal performance. The equivalent effectiveness of such moderate prompts seems to me to demonstrate that the underlying capability is distributed equally in both populations. Thus, rather than stemming from a difference in underlying process, the source of the phenomenon appears to be that members of one group have acquired a propensity for autonomous activation of the elaboration process while members of the other group have not learned this skill.[17]

With reference to the same task, what guidance does research offer for the timing of instruction? An important question is the objective of instruction. Rohwer's answer to this, both for content of instruction and for skills (such as the skill of learning noun pairs), is that the ultimate aim of instruction is mastery. Timing of instruction, then, is dictated as that time when most children can master the skill or the content with relative ease and efficiency. The graphs shown in Figure 7 show that optimal performance with noun-pair learning under different conditions of prompting can be predicted from knowledge of the developmental curves represented in the figure. Rohwer reports that when he attempted to offer formal instruction to 7-year-olds in the use of minimal prompts, success was much less than optimal. Later, he developed a two-week unit of instruction for use with 4- and 5-year-olds, with disastrous results. The entire unit was ineffective. Presumably, it would have been highly effective with 13- or 14-year-olds. Rohwer's "rule of thumb" for the timing of instruction is to begin with the ultimate objective of instruction. The next step is to begin instruction only after the immediately prior skill has been mastered, and when the developmental curve for the skill is rising.

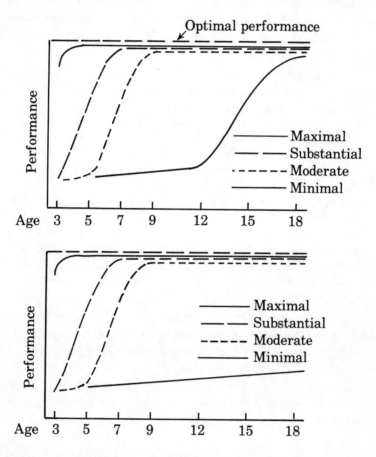

Figure 7

Hypothetical course of developmental changes in sensitivity to four kinds of elaborative prompts: upper panel—high-SES populations; lower panel—low-SES populations.[18]

Reference to Figure 7 again would suggest that while training in the use of moderate prompts would probably be productive for most children sometime during the 7- to 9-year range, instruction in utilizing minimal prompts would be relatively useless in that range, a finding that occurred, as previously seen, when such instruction is undertaken. The figure suggests also that such instruction should be productive for high-SES subjects in the 13- to 14-year range.

The payoff of this strategy is its productive use in "decisive research" about instruction in school subjects. Rohwer's program has not produced such research, but it begins to specify the conditions that must be met to generate useful research at the classroom level.

> Consider how the proposed rule of thumb can be applied to derive hypotheses about the timing and aims of instruction in school-subject skills. Use of the rule depends on knowing five things: (a) the conditions necessary for optimal performance on the task of interest; (b) the character of the underlying process responsible for performance on the task; (c) the extent to which a substantial majority of adults possess the skill of activating the process; (d) the major landmarks along the way to achieving the final form of the skill; and (e) knowing the form of the developmental function so as to identify the ages at which the achievement of each landmark can be accomplished with ease and efficiency. At present, however, these prerequisites to successful application of the rule are not available for school subjects.[19]

Rohwer's work fits the classical mold of scientific research in numerous ways. It is cumulative and leads to definitive results about the kind and timing of school instruction that will facilitate optimal performance among children of specified school populations. In addition, the ease and efficiency that accompanies such learning replaces the painful, half-hearted efforts that frequently occur in school, with resulting incomplete learning and attitudes of disinterest in or dislike of learning.

An outgrowth of Rohwer's work, and his synthesis of others', is the fundamental challenge to the foundations of early childhood education.

> However, until some fundamental assumptions of early childhood educators are seriously questioned, increased investment in current preschool and primary school programs may be unwise; in particular it has not been established that early childhood is the optimal age range for imposing the academic content

traditionally required. In addition, early childhood or early elementary school programs may have a slight, or even negative, affect on the attainment of educational goals. Thus, research and policy in early childhood education should be evaluated in light of two larger educational issues: (1) developmental changes in children's mental capacity and (2) the relationship of educational objectives to the demands of society.[19]

The broad point of Rohwer's argument is that changes in cognitive development may render the early content and skill learning of children relatively useless in its benefits to later learning. For example, it may be much easier for a child to learn to read when he is 9- or 10-years-old than when he is 6 or 7, and the effort expended in the earlier years may contribute little to his learning to read two or three years later.

Educational research needs to be conceived on broader and more wide-ranging bases than has usually been true, and the time needed for fruitful research must be longer than many would anticipate. It is evident that those bent upon the reform of the public school system are gripped by the urgency that goes with identifying critical and devastating social problems that have a day-by-day effect upon the lives of children. The desire to act now, to eradicate those social injustices is powerful.

For fundamental answers to questions about equal educational opportunity for all American children, continued research upon those questions, research that is cumulative, systematic, and programmatic in its conception, organization, and execution, is an indispensable element. Whether the society has the forbearance to allow this kind of research its day to demonstrate its ability to produce important answers to these questions will be one of the most significant decisions confronting the future of American public education.

APPENDIX A

[1] Alfred Yates (ed.), *The Role of Research in Educational Change,* paper sponsored by the UNESCO Institute for Education (Palo Alto: Hamburg, Pacific Book Publishers, 1971), p. 52.

[2] Allen H. Barton and David E. Wilder, "Research and Practice in the Teaching of Reading: A Progress Report," *Innovation in Education*, (ed.), Matthew B. Miles (New York: Columbia University, 1964).

[3] Yates, op. cit.

[4] Lee J. Cronbach and Patrick Suppes, *Research for Tomorrow's Schools: Disciplined Inquiry for Education* (London: The Macmillan Company, Collier-Macmillan Limited, 1969).

[5] Mary C. Austin, "Professional Training of Reading Personnel," *Innovation and Change in Reading Instruction, Sixty-seventh Yearbook of the National Society for the Study of Education*, Part II (Chicago, Ill.: University of Chicago Press, 1968).

[6] Ibid., pp. 388–89.

[7] Quoted in Yates, op. cit., pp. 32–33.

[8] Cronbach and Suppes, op. cit., p. 212.

[9] Ibid., pp. 212–13.

[10] Yates, op. cit.

[11] Barton and Wilder, op. cit., p. 383.

[12] N. L. Gage, "A Tool Development Strategy for Research on Teaching," *How Teachers Make a Difference*, Bureau of Educational Personnel Development, Office of Education (Washington, D.C.: U.S. Government Printing Office, 1971).

[13] Ibid., pp. 35–36.

[14] Barak Rosenshine, "New Directions for Research on Teaching," *How Teachers Make a Difference*, op. cit.

[15] W. D. Rohwer, Jr., "Decisive Research: A Means for Answering Fundamental Questions about Instruction," *Educational Researcher*, 1972, No. 7, pp. 5–11.

[16] Ibid.

[17] Ibid., p. 8.

[18] Ibid., p. 10.

[19] Ibid., p. 10.

[20] W. D. Rohwer, Jr., "Prime Time for Education: Early Childhood or Adolescence?" *Harvard Educational Review*, 1971, 41, p. 317.

APPENDIX B

Socialization and Minority Youth

Although reform in relation to ethnic minority pupils is not extensively discussed, reference is made in a number of ways to the relation of reform measures to them. This fact, as well as the crucial importance of the socialization and schooling of minority children and youth, has led us to ask a number of outstanding minority scholars to react to the manuscript in terms of the needs of ethnic minority children and youth. We believe that these criticisms will serve to focus attention on significant points we have either inadequately explored or ignored for lack of insight.

Teacher Education and Multi-Cultural Instruction
James A. Banks
University of Washington

Most of the attitudes, skills, and knowledge that the school teaches are components of the dominant ethnic culture within our society: the white, Anglo-Saxon, Protestant culture. The school has been highly successful in helping most American youths to master the basic skills that it teaches. The school has been successful with this group largely because its culture reinforces the values, behavior patterns, and norms that Anglo-Saxon students learn in their homes and family communities.

The school, however, has grossly failed to teach the basic skills to children who are socialized within social and cultural environments that differ, often substantially from the school's culture and community. These are primarily low-income, ethnic minority group students. Large segments of Afro-Americans, Mexican-Americans, Puerto Rican-Americans, and American Indians constitute majorities in many cities and urban communities. Groups such as Mexican-Americans and American Indians are majorities in some parts of the rural Southwest. Because the school has been so unsuccessful in helping these students to master basic skills and knowledge, their special problems must be given special and thoughtful attention in any effort to reform teacher education.

Most low-income minority students experience a "culture conflict" in the classroom because the school's language, norms, knowledge, and values are often quite different from those which the child must have to function effectively within his home and community. The language problems that Spanish-speaking students experience in the school cogently illustrate this point. Many Puerto Rican- and Mexican-American students are unable to speak English when they enter school. Most often they attend schools where the teachers do not speak Spanish, where all of the printed materials are in English, and where the speaking of Spanish is prohibited or discouraged or both. At home, these children must speak Spanish in order to communicate with their parents and relatives. Urban Black children often experience similar problems. Teachers often reject their dialect of English and prohibit its use in the classroom. These kinds of school practices retard the language and concept development of minority students.

These children also experience special problems within the school because it teaches them, either explicitly or implicitly, to reject and devalue their cultures. Most examples used to illustrate concepts in materials and instruction are taken from American cultures that are often foreign to minority students. This not only puts them at a cognitive disadvantage, but it teaches them, by commission, that their culture is unworthy of serious study. Because standardized tests and many other aspects of the school's instructional program are foreign to these children, they often perform poorly in school.

The school faces a double and tremendous responsibility: 1) to build upon and respect the diverse cultures that minority students bring to school, and 2) to help them acquire the skills, abilities, and knowledge they will need to attain occupational mobility and success in the wider society. The results of compensatory programs such as "Head Start" and

"Follow Through" teaches us that to attempt to eradicate and demean minority cultures will not solve these student achievement problems but will compound them. Novel instructional approaches must be based upon a concept of cultural diversity, in which all cultures within this society are respected and become part of the instructional program. To implement a multi-cultural instructional program, teachers must be trained so that they will have both a sophisticated knowledge of and a respect for America's minority cultures. They must also acquire the skills to effectively teach students who must learn to function successfully within and between two cultures.

Reaction to Preceding Discussion
Charles E. Scruggs
State University of New York
at Geneseo

Professor Banks makes two interesting points in the first paragraph; both of them, however, are subject to different interpretations, and both can lead to quite different suggestions as to what might be educationally desirable for the various ethnic groups.

> Point One: Schools emphasize attitudes, skills, and knowledge of the dominant culture.
>
> Point Two: Schools have been successful with this group (the white Anglo-Saxon, Protestant group) because it reinforces the values, behavior patterns, and norms that are learned in the home and in the community.

First, white, Anglo-Saxon Protestantism has become a coded expression. It is a battle cry both for those who wish to defend aspects of what it is and for those who wish to attack some of the specifics that it has come to represent. In that coded terms, in general, function as affective mobilizers rather than as elements of cognitive strategies, its present use of WASP leads to an emotional response rather than to cognitive applications in which it can be used as an analytic concept facilitating understanding of the functions and structures of contemporary American education.

Terms such as "busing," "law and order," "quotas," etc. are politicized terms that have come to communicate at the level of emotional appeals rather than conveying cognitive information. It is, in my opinion, precisely in this way that the expression "WASP" has been politicized. Further, its emotional appeal has little to do with either Anglo-Saxonism or Protestantism. From an analytic stance, I would argue that the significant and overriding import of the coding is its appeal to the white characteristic of the dominant culture. The Protestant political and economic domination of Puritan New England has long since eroded under gains made by non-Protestants and non-Anglo-Saxons. In my opinion, it has been supplanted as an independent mechanism of control by classism, racism, politicism, agism, elitism, etc. as the classifactory basis for establishing economic and political privilege involving the granting and withholding of wealth, status, prestige, and power. What remains politically useful in the expression is the criterion of whiteness, and it is this criterion that has been educationally politicized in Boston, Buffalo, New York City, Phoenix, southern California, etc.

With reference to the first point, there is the implication that the schools emphasize, for the most part, only the content—knowledge, norms, and values—of the dominant culture. To correct this, it is implied that the curriculum should be expanded to include multi-cultural instruction. Before a judgment can be made about this, the details of what content, to whom and by whom it is to be transmitted, by what methods, in which settings and under what conditions it is to be done have to be specified. Further, the questions of the immediate effects of such instruction as well as the long-range consequences of such instruction have to be asked and eventually answered. To call for multi-cultural instruction at this point in time is at best a first speculation and not a solution to the educational needs of minorities.

With reference to the dominant culture, the key question

is who or what represents the dominant culture. As has been indicated, it is not, in my opinion, white Anglo-Saxon Protestantism. Apparently, the current controlling element tying the dominant culture together is "whiteness" and, this, in and of itself, is an inadequate basis on which to build the processes of cultural transmission. In my opinion the dominant culture, then, is most accurately described as simply a dynamic, white culture. Such a description acknowledges the Anglo-Saxon origins of our basic institutions but recognizes the Americanization of those institutions in the East, the South, the Southwest, as well as the West. The dynamic aspect also recognizes the continuous influence of immigration waves from Western Europe.

The key point is that the dominant culture is and has been a changing culture but all groups have not been encouraged to participate fully and to contribute freely to the processes of change. For the most part, the racial minorities have been systematically excluded from the processes of full and free participation. Whereas, the European ethnic groups have participated in and contributed to the processes of modifying the basic Anglo-Saxon institutions. To be sure this participation has been done under varying conditions of acceptance and encouragement involving circumstances of time, place, national origin, religious conviction, etc.

With reference to the second point, I would not say that the school has been successful with respect to transmitting the attitudes, skills, and knowledge of the dominant culture, particularly if one defines the dominant culture as white, dynamic culture. In my opinion, if one speaks of success it can be done only in a normative sense. In this manner, the school needs the minority group failures to justify and buttress its claims of success with majority youngsters. My own interpretation is that the failure of the school to transmit the attitudes, skills, and knowledge of the dominant culture to the youth of the dominant culture lies behind the present reform efforts. What characterizes the present situation is not success but, more to the point, the failure to assimilate the youth of the dominant culture into the adult community.

With reference to both points one and two, an interesting interpretation of education and schooling is that the assimilation-accommodation relationships have functioned differently for the majority and minority cultures. Historically, the school has accommodated to a dynamic, dominant culture. As the values, skills, attitudes, interests, motivations, and needs of the dominant culture have changed (e.g. from cultural singularity to cultural pluralism), the school has altered its structure to adjust to these changes. This is not to say that the school has not made accommodations relative to the nonwhite minority cultures; it has. The difference has been in terms of orientation and motivation. The school has consistently oriented to the dominant culture. There is little question that the goal of the school, over time, has been assimilation for youth into the ways of the dominant culture—it could not be otherwise.

What has happened historically is that the characteristics of the dominant culture have changed, and, as a result, social needs and institutional structures have changed.

In short, as the needs associated with a dynamic, emergent, dominant culture have changed, the structures of the school have changed in an effort to meet those needs. Cultural pluralism is nothing new in our society, and our institutions have long since initiated the process of accommodating European ethnic minorities—and, indeed, assimilating them into the current dominant culture.

As an explanation, pluralism in our society has functioned as a mechanism that prevents one group from locking in on power. The overall equilibrium of the system is maintained if the various groups and factions are allowed periodic access to at least minimal, and at times, massive economic and political power. If this is done on some kind of fluid, rotating basis, it fosters dynamic competition and helps to legitimize a given group's exercise of power and privilege at a given point in time. The difficulty and the dilemma is that this system has not worked for the present minorities because

as nonwhite minorities, they have not been admitted into
the processes of the sharing of power. They have not gained
economic and political power and they have not been in a
position to use education as a legitimizing mechanism to justify
the exercise of the privileges that accompany power.

My own view is that accommodation as it relates to the
youth of the dominant culture is best understood in terms
of its psychological usage: New experiences modify prior
structures which then allow subsequent encounters to be more
easily assimilated. Accommodation with reference to racial
minority groups, on the other hand, is best understood in
sociological terms in which structural change occurs to reduce
or eliminate social conflict, through conciliation, compromise,
giving in, establishing parallel structures, etc. In short, the
school's accommodation to majority youth—in which the school
changes its structures—has the intent of easing future assimilation; for racial minorities, the intent of accommodation
is not future assimilation but minimizing social conflict.

Given this position, then, the comments that follow the
first paragraph in Professor Banks' paper can be viewed in
several different lights and can be agreed to or criticized
on several different levels.

1) School has not taught the children from subcultures the
   basic skills.   (Yes.)
2) The worst failures are primarily low-income, ethnic minority group students.   (Yes.)
3) Schools have been unsuccessful with minorities in both
   rural and urban settings.   (Yes.)
4) These pupils must be given thoughtful and special attention.   (Yes.)

Before I would agree to Professor Banks' multi-cultural instruction, however, I would have to know something of his
specific intentions with reference to economic, political, social,
and educational assimilation—accommodation structures and
strategies. Specifically, I would be concerned that multi-cul-

tural instruction would not facilitate physical exclusion, socio-logical accommodation, and political and economic isolation.

For example, with reference to economics, the authors' observation that youth has been alienated from work is comparable to the observation that nonwhite minorities have been alienated from mainstream involvement in our political and economic institutions. To integrate (assimilate) youth into the world of work is comparable, in my opinion, to integrating nonwhite minorities into the political and economic main-stream.

The fundamental educational problem and the overriding dilemma is that the two groups are different. For white youth, it is a problem of assimilation into the dominant culture, but for nonwhite minorities, it is a problem of acculturation and the conflict and consequences that arise out of contact between two cultural systems.

Points one and two assert:

> School emphasizes attitudes, skills, and knowledge of the domi-nant culture: white, Anglo-Saxon, Protestant culture.

> School has been successful with this group because it reinforces the values, behavior patterns, and norms the dominant group learns in home and the community.

First, if the minorities continue to perceive the problem as white, Anglo-Saxon Protestantism and act upon those percep-tions, one can expect little change as the result of minority efforts in the present economic, political, and social relation-ships between minorities and the dominant culture.

In that coded words function as affective mobilizers rather than cognitive tools, to use and to respond to politicized-coded expressions is likely to keep the problem out of focus, to dissipate energies, and to lead to unproductive and undesirable consequences. From my point of view, the danger is to fail to perceive the current mechanism of coding, co-optation, affective independence, cultural pluralism, ethnic integrity, etc. as potentially fragmentive, dissipative, and functionally nonintegrative. In my opinion, the current mechanisms, except for minimal residues, do not reflect the Puritan period as much as they reflect current manifestations of racism, classism, politicism, agism, and elitism.

From my point of view, the danger is in failing to identify, analyze, and judge the consequences of such current mechanisms. They may well be leading to structural accommodations that in the long run may prevent educational, economic, political, social, and cultural assimilation.

The problem then, as I see it, is a cultural dilemma between majority and minority cultures that is being played out in terms of assimilation and accommodation strategies.

Accommodation and separatism are clearly wrong for youth as well as for minority groups, if they lead to economic and political exclusion as they have done in the past. Similarly, assimilation and integration are clearly wrong for youth as well as for minority groups if they are at the cost of self- and group rejection.

I think we are presently in a period in which the old structures for the assimilation of youth into the dominant culture have broken down, and we are clearly searching for new structures to accommodate a changing society. To me, the times represent an opportunity to establish new structures. I hope the new school structures will, for the first time, begin to meet the needs of minorities, as they have consistently attempted to do for the youth of the dominant culture.

Further Reactions to Professor Banks' Comments
Richard O. Ulibarri
Weber State College

When your note arrived with Professor Banks' paper on multi-cultural instruction, I was in the midst of preparing a short statement on the same subject. I find no particular disagreement with what he has written. For that reason I will just make some comments in reference to that general area as follows:

People who believe that minority children can be taught in the same manner as other children simply do not take into consideration the great cultural difference that exists between minority and majority people in this country. Neither do they take into consideration the facts of mistrust, ignorance, apathy, racism, and general intolerance toward minority people and their reaction of distrust, fear, and relative impotence. Individuals who believe that there is no difference between the minority child and the majority child are simply ignoring the obvious magnitude of the issues of race in this country. These are issues that will not go away simply because they are ignored.

There was a time when the general belief was that the issue of minorities in this country would be solved if people could just come to believe that there was no difference in people. However, many minority people have now concluded that it is important to stress differences as well as similarities among people in the United States. Some of those differences are illustrated by the fact that the United States has erroneously been called a melting pot. The fact is that what is called the American melting pot has only been a European melting pot in America. The failure or inability of minorites to melt in this melting pot is due in part at least to the following reasons: 1) profound differences in physical characteristics between minority and majority people; 2) the non-European origin of minority people—that is, Blacks were from Africa, Indians were native to this country, Chicanos are a cosmic people who are the cultural children of the European Spaniards and the American Indians, and Orientals were, of course, from Asia; 3) the fact that minorities were either not immigrants or nontypical immigrants to this country—that is, Indians were native to this country, Blacks were brought against their will from Africa, the Indian ancestors of the Chicanos were already here, Spanish ancestors were here before Jamestown, and Asians came through the west coast and then only for a limited period; 4) Blacks and Indians suffered deculturation and Chicanos cultural isolation, as they were all conquered people in this country. The consequences of deculturation and cultural isolation should be well known by any teacher who aspires to relate to minority children. Without an appreciation of these differences, teachers would be dealing in ignorance as they attempt to teach minority youngsters.

Teachers who are ignorant of these differences, however good their skills in other areas of diagnostics and remediations, will not be able to teach the minority child adequately. Teachers of minority children must have training that relates to information concerning the cultural traits and values of minority people, and they must also have training in affective areas relating to issues such as myths and stereotypes, institutional racism, and the like so that they can realistically and comfortably deal with minority children.

The preceding is simply the rationale for the inclusion of culturally pluralistic teacher training in the chapter on preservice preparation and school reform. As I noted earlier, Professor Banks' statement relates to the heart of the matter.

Further Comments, by Charles E. Scruggs

On the surface, there seems to be one problem that requires solving—the assimilation of youth. The educational reform strategies that are presently being offered address themselves cogently, creatively, and realistically to this necessity. However, as I read the material and think about what is being proposed, it appears to me that the current educational problems that we face exist at two very distinct levels. At one level, there is the problem of educating the youth of the majority culture, and at a different level, there is the problem of educating the children of the various subcultures within our society.

I think the school has functioned differently toward these two groups, in the past as well as in the present, and I think the reform strategies continue to reflect these differences.

For children and youth who are members of the dominant culture, the school has functioned in an uneven but nevertheless assimilative way. As a socializing agency, it has facilitated the social induction of the young into the ways of the dominant group.

For children and youth who are members of the various subcultures in our larger society, the school has functioned in an accommodative way. This accomodation function has led to a long-standing structural separateness in education as well as other areas of the society.

In my opinion, the current educational reforms involving youth and work are not motivated by moral convictions to alter long-standing accommodating structures and practices that relate to minority youth. They are the result of a breakdown in the socialization process as it relates to large numbers of youth from the dominant culture. The reforms are attempts to cope with problems that result from the growing phenomenon of horizontal socialization and the decreasing effectiveness of the more traditional processes of vertical socialization. What we have today is the growing development of value mixing of majority and minority youth at the peer level, constituting a growing counterculture that is socializing youth. This horizontal socialization is taking the place of the traditional vertical socialization that leads to the more standard and stable transmission of the traditional culture. It is interesting to note that an apparent function of the peer group is assimilative and integrative, and the social structures associated with the youth peer group—music identification, style of dress, language usage, value systems—facilitate assimilation. The adult world with reference to majority and minority groups (racial, social, economic, class, ethnic) is structurally separate and is accommodative in orientation. In this respect, the reform manuscript is traditional and counter-reform in spirit.

The current emphasis on the needs of youth (as is evidenced by the Panel on Youth Reports, the various strategies relating to the assimilation of youth into the adult community, and career education programs) is a continuation of the historical practice of identifying and solving problems in terms of the needs of the dominant culture. The reform manuscript, as I read it, simply continues this practice. From my point of view, the youth of the dominant culture and the youth of the various subcultures have to be analytically separated.

The function of education with reference to minority youth has never been to assimilate them into the adult world of the dominant culture. Education for minority youth has always served an accomodating function that has been separatist in character rather than assimilative and integrative.

The functions of education defined in the general literature have always stressed the problems and needs of the dominant culture. As a result, the structures that have evolved around these functions have led to an advantage for the youth of the dominant culture and a continuing disadvantage for minority youth. The manuscript, as I read it, is a continuation of precisely these kinds of tensions. In reading the chapters, I was left with the feeling that although the emphasis with reference to function was assimilation—the induction of youth into the social ways of the group—the problems and needs addressed were the problems and needs of the dominant culture. Reference to youth from the minority cultures was not in terms of functions, but in terms of accommodating structural mechanisms (such as achievement floors) that by the wildest leaps of imaginative optimism would never lead to the consequence of assimilation (integrative equality) within the dominant culture.

My own view is that equality of knowledge (knowledge according to rule; knowledge that is rationally and empirically based; knowledge that is modified as a result of judging its consequences and use) is the only basis for equality in our society. Protocols, rules for inference, rules of evidence, and strategies for judging use and the consequences of use were, in my opinion, steps in the right direction. They were steps intended to lead to an equality of knowledge that involved understanding, action, and the judgment of consequences. In this respect, no matter how disparate groups were in other ways, they shared a common knowledge base. This would allow them—if not as individuals, then certainly from a group point of view, as in the case of a culturally plural society—to judge the consequences of action rationally and empirically.

In reading the reform manuscript, I had the feeling that this goal was being abandoned. Needless to say, I hope that I have misinterpreted the document.

Critical Observations: Another Look at Socialization in Public Schools
Frederick A. Rodgers
University of Illinois

Last night I carefully reread Chapters II and III and concluded that your statement is a tight and thought-provoking argument that covers most of the concerns I would raise. Your proposal for mobilizing the community for socialization of youth is insightful and revealing. However, I do not believe that this proposal takes advantage of the power the school exerts over the socialization of youth from the standpoint of appropriate practice of rules and procedures by individuals and groups in relation to improving the general welfare and extending individual freedom. Since I do not have the time to support my assertions with reasoned argument, I will run the risk of overstatement beyond data in order to make my point.

In general, I agree with your notion that the community should be expected to exert more leadership in providing experiences that educate youth with regard to the functions of society, but I don't think it is possible to achieve your objective given the way the society is organized and staffed to conduct its functions. Likewise, the reward system governing one's action in functional societal areas is not geared to support the education of youth as an outcome. Further, it is a costly and disrupting activity for functional units in a society to work with youth who have only a nominal interest in the activities being performed. There is also some doubt (as you pointed out in the chapter) as to whether experience in an institutional setting will enable youth to acquire a mental picture of the social functions being performed. This is a formidable challenge to overcome if youth are to acquire an education from participating in societal functions rather than supplying low-level labor skills needed by the institutions serving as the practice arena in question.

It is my contention that the school must take a greater responsibility for and play a larger role in the socialization of youth. This conclusion is supported in part by the fact that schools touch a larger proportion and number of all kinds of youth than any other institution. In short, the school has a broad-based captive audience of all youth in every community. It also has a mandate to influence youth's behavior consistent with the ideals and values of a democratic society that promotes the greatest social good for the greatest number while preserving individual choice. No other institution has such a pervasive and continuous influence over the majority of all youth in our society. It is my belief that institutions and agencies engaged in the remaining functions required to maintain the society are too specialized and fragmented in their efforts to provide meaningful socialization experiences for the number of youth needing such experience. Individual activity in such institutions and agencies is so highly rationalized that youth would have a difficult time learning more than the shape of a specific vocational activity within a total system. It should also be noted that a great deal of activity characterizing social functions is situation-specific (environmentally and in relation to problems encountered) geared to cater to special interests of those who maintain these social functions. In such an instance youth would be educated in the ways of one type of social function and how it operated to achieve objectives in its setting. I personally have a problem with relying on such a system to carry the bulk of the socialization experienced outside the home.

One of the critical problems facing youth today is related to how to make "good" decisions (democratically oriented) about and participate effectively in collective action. Many of the problems facing our society require collective thinking and actions to find solutions that have the power to limit the number and complexity of problems created by those who did not take part in or know about the actions being undertaken. Socialization experiences that deal with individual development apart from group skills, attitudes, and understandings are not consistent with the needs of citizens to make collective decisions about problems that affect all people. It seems to me that any socialization experience today that omits practice with an exposure to collective experiences affecting a broad cross-section of people fails to provide youth with an educational experience that will better prepare them to deal with the types of problems they are likely to face in society. Because the school is pervasive in its influence on youth, a large part of the consciously planned socialization experiences should take place as an integral part of the total school program. Social functions in society become partly the product of informal interactions of people who staff and come in direct contact with the institutions and agencies in question. People performing social functions have special interests related to those activities and as such, react to the body politic and individuals performing different social functions within the context of those special interests. At this point, individuals act to enhance their position in the society by advocating an advantage for the social functions they perform. Youth who are exposed to people who perform selected social functions are influenced to view society from their perspective. That in itself is not necessarily without virtue, but it is a worry that should not be taken lightly in a planned socialization experience.

One solution to the dilemma is to plan a socialization experience that is an integral part of the total curriculum program. The primary focus of such a socialization experience should be the correct statement, elucidation, and employment of rules and procedures that should govern some social functions in a democratic society. For example, youth might study political science as an academic course yet have little experience with its practical application in the form of politics. Youth who only witness politics in a natural state in or out of school have not been afforded the opportunity to see the political process operate as it should according to a formal rule structure. The political process in schools should not reflect the special interest group patterns that characterize politics in the real world because it is critical that youth have an opportunity to experience political action resulting from the correct and fair deployment of appropriate rules and procedures. School is the only institution that can legitimately design extracurricular experiences that allow youth to practice certain social functions according to rules and procedures that define the correct operationalization of the activity in question. It is the only institution where youth can practice a real social function as a controlled and rational experiment in social interaction between and among youth whose differences reflect the composition of the society as a whole. Other institutions in the society are not in the business of *practicing* social functions; they are *playing the game* for keeps and to achieve specified and unspecified goals. The activities or people in these institutions must necessarily differ because the game they participate in affects the people in ways that count. Essentially, that is the difference between socialization in a school setting and other institutional settings. For many youth, the school serves (and probably will continue to serve) to provide the single most important group socialization experience available in a given community. The school is also the only institution where the practice of social functions legitimately proceeds according to accepted public rules and procedures and youth are afforded the opportunity to see the consequences of actions so governed. Youth who are not afforded an opportunity to practice rules and procedures governing a given social function receive a socialization experience that is not bound by specific requirements of democratic processes that maximize equality of opportunity.

It is doubtful that an adequate number of meaningful placements for youth are available in institutions and agencies performing social functions in the society. There is also some question about the relative worth of such a placement experience when compared to real and simulated experiences in school. My acquaintance with the social functions performed by many institutions and agencies suggests that the needed slots required to serve the number of youth who might profit from such socialization experience are not available and are unlikely to be. That is a formidable challenge to any advocate of systematic community involvement in the socialization experience of youth utilizing time allocated for school activity. The stakes are sufficiently large to consider alternate arrangements for educational socialization experiences that are an integral part of the total school program.

In a democratic society, every individual is assumed to have an equal opportunity to participate in society's functions. Since to participate in those functions is to be involved in the process of education, an individual's personal experience determines the quality, extent, and value of the education he receives. Early in the history of America, individuals were required and encouraged to learn to execute many functions crucial to the operation of the society as a whole. This situation enabled individuals to learn about and participate in many functions that served to broaden their educational experience. As the population increased and demands for goods and services expanded, specialization was required to keep the society functioning to provide the greatest good for the greatest number. Specialization of functions in a society shapes the nature and availability of the educational experience in that society. The extent of openness and equality of opportunity available can mitigate against some of the negative effects of socialization on education possibilities. However, the type of education a person can acquire in a society is tied to the functions available to him for personal practice and pursuit.

One of the persistent problems in a democracy is to ensure an equal opportunity for all individuals to exercise choice over the functions of society to which they can be exposed and permanently attached. Specialization of a function limits the availability of knowledge about that function and reduces its power to serve as an educative experience for a broad cross-section of youth. Evidence suggests that this trend is likely to accelerate at a faster pace than is now the case.

Before the functions that characterize our society became highly specialized, compartmentalized, complex, and increasingly interrelated in new and different ways, schools furnished knowledge that could be employed directly to conduct a useful function in society. For example, banking during the early days of the development of America required skills that could be largely acquired in school. Students could learn enough about math to keep records, count money, compute simple interest, compute payment schedules, appraise the value of goods or real property, and demonstrate how one earned a profit in business. Today a Ph.D. graduate without experience cannot be proficient in any one of these areas for many reasons. The knowledge in each area of concern is too vast, too complicated, too fluid, too situationally specific, and too new for any one person to be able to become proficient by studying in school. Also, much of the current knowledge of practice is not available to the school and can only be obtained from those who are members of the in-group (specialists/professionals). Oftentimes this knowledge is not written or cannot be written because it is the result of practice in a particular place at a given time. By the time knowledge is organized, packaged, and generalized for consumption in school, the practice specialty to which it refers has changed to such an extent that the information in question only approximates the reality being described. In addition, each specialty produces knowledge as a by-product of practice, and sometimes this knowledge is utilized, revised, or discarded without ever being made available to schools. In this situation youth can only become operationally acquainted with specialized functions by being allowed to practice these functions.

At first glance, the solution to this problem is readily apparent. Youth can be given the opportunity to work with specialists so that they can learn the functions of society. This is basically the apprenticeship pattern of educating youth about the functions of society. A close examination of the functions performed by specialists, however, reveals that this may not be a practical course to follow. For the most part specialists' functions are not organized for teaching novices who are not serious about an activity as a vocational choice.

Index